Contents

- **3** Editorial: The Same Better Hope for an Anxious World
- **7** *Bruce Henning*, Hekate in Matthew's Gospel?: Greco-Roman Mythology in Matt. 16:19
- **19** *Peter G. Bolt*, How Mark Moved/s the World
- **33** *Ali Robinson*, Is Mary blessed?: Reconsidering Luke 11:27–28 and Mary's embodied discipleship
- **51** *Paul N. Anderson*, Authentic worship in John and in Luke-Acts: Influence, interfluence, and resonance
- **85** *Alan H. Cadwallader*, Bad smells at a religious gathering
- **101** *James R. Harrison*, 'Signs on the earth' below (Acts 2:19b): Luke-Acts and the Miraculous in the Graeco-Roman World

Book Reviews

- **135** Elekosi F. Lafitaga, *Apocalyptic Sheep and Goats in Matthew and 1 Enoch.*
- **137** M. John-Patrick O'Connor, *The Last Will Be First: Divine Judgment in the Gospel of Mark.*
- **140** Jens-Arne Edelmann., *Das Römische Imperium im Lukanischen Doppelwerk.*
- **142** Joshua Paul Smith, *Luke Was Not a Christian: Reading the Third Gospel and Acts within Judaism.*
- **144** James W. Barker., *Writing and Rewriting the Gospels: John and the Synoptics*
- **147** Wil Rogan, *Purity in the Gospel of John: Early Jewish Tradition, Christology, and Ethics.*
- **149** Simon Gathercole, *The Gospel and the Gospels: Christian Proclamation and Early Jesus Books.*

The Same Better Hope for an Anxious World

EDITORIAL

As the ninth issue of the *Journal of Gospels and Acts Research* hits the news-stands, it joins other heralds forced to continue their accounts of an anxious world in disarray, sorely needing healing but uncertain about from whence it might come. There are certainly some promising signs of a greater willingness to listen to the 'old, old story' of Jesus of Nazareth, such as the 'resurgence' led by Generation Z (Google it!). But, nevertheless, the struggle against the powers of cancellation and threat continues—even (or especially?) in nations who have received such great benefit from their Christian heritage.

With politicians and power-brokers, educationalists and ethicists (?), big business and big tech apparently hell-bent upon engaging in ideological warfare, rather than sticking to the 'core business' that ought to be the proper subject of their various domains, the trail of damage is also evident in economic pressures on ordinary households, declining standards and outcomes in schools and educational institutions, and the apparent disregard for ethics and humanity in the technological charge to make more money as what is now possible takes us further into realms unknown. More cause for anxiety. World anxiety. Anxiety for us poor mortals already struggling to live with the deep-seated anxiety of having to live in the valley of the shadow of death.

Yet again, to Gospels and Acts scholars living in and writing into this present context a clarion call must be issued to keep working hard at their proper task. Each essay from the cluster in *JGAR 9* speaks in its own way to the message of Jesus that still needs to be announced and heard well.

Exploring Jesus' reference to 'the keys to the kingdom of heaven' (Matt 16:19), **Bruce Henning** argues that Matthew and his readers would be well aware that deities such as Hekate bore the keys to the underworld. Similarly to the writer of Revelation 1:8, Matthew is proclaiming Jesus as the one who holds the power over Hades and Death, just as he holds the key to the eschatological future.

Presenting a model for reading the narrative about Jesus that we know as Mark's Gospel, **Peter G. Bolt** shows the account moving its readers towards a greater engagement in the gospel mission. Coming into Galilee, Jesus announced the kingdom of God had drawn very near. With the empty tomb signalling that the one who was crucified is now risen, the subsequent period is a time for speech, not silence. Mark's strange ending presents a challenge to readers not to be silent, but to speak. And as the gospel of Jesus Christ, the Son of God, continues to be spoken, that is how the world will continue to be changed. Other graves will also be overcome.

Challenging the negative portrayal of the woman in the crowd in Luke 11:27–28 and the post-reformation reduction of 'the maternal significance of Mary's role', **Ali Robinson** argues that Jesus affirms both women. Just as—to continue the theme of this editorial—, we must continue to participate in this world of anxiety in the tenuous form of our embodiment, Robinson argues here that Luke portrays 'Mary as blessed precisely because of her physical and bodily participation in the gospel'.

In order to continue to participate in the proclamation of this gospel, the fundamental sources that bring us into connection with Jesus and the earliest gospel mission require further and continual scrutiny, with old questions revisited and, where necessary, revised. In a detailed and fascinating account, **Paul N. Anderson** brings the Acts of the Apostles into the dialogue about the relationship between the Gospels of John and Luke, noting several similar theological themes and images. In particular, the book of Acts and John seem to coalesce around the lines of 'authentic worship', with themes including 'challenges to religious elites, the workings of the Holy Spirit, presentations of Samaritans and their worship, the place of women in religious leadership, and the character of authentic worship'. Such explorations assist a better understanding of the origins and development of the Jesus movement with its message to a wayward world.

In a playful and reflective meditation on the sense of smell, prompted by a manuscript illumination of a slave covering his nose as he leads Lazarus from the grave, **Alan H. Cadwallader** explores the meaning and control of odour, with special attention to death and curses. Bringing the odour of both life and death to a dying world, the Jesus movement operates on the fundamental premise 'that death for all its stink is forever changed'.

As a counter-part to his essay in JGAR 8, 'Wonders in the heaven above', in this issue **James R. Harrison** turns to the 'signs on the earth below', once again reading the miraculous phenomena reported in Luke-Acts against their intersections within those known to the wider Graeco-Roman context. While being well-aware of the similarities of his miraculous phenomena to those of the world of his day, Luke also shows the distinctiveness of the approach of Jesus and the first Christian missionaries. This not only reveals the emerging conflict between the new Christian movement and the old religious traditions, but that, even within that conflict, there is the promise of a new way forward. Legitimated by the prophecy-fulfilment framework that was so attractive to both Jew and Graeco-Roman, 'Jesus of Nazareth will always remain a man attested by God with mighty works and wonders and signs'. With rival claims that exceed those of both religion and magic, the word of the risen Jesus went out into the ancient world which was full of the need for healing, and, as it did so, 'anxiety was replaced by hope'.

Not only is it a privilege for those engaged in Gospels and Acts Research to continue 'to hold forth the word of life' (Phil 2:16), it is an imperative.

Peter G. Bolt
Executive Editor
October 2025

Hekate in Matthew's Gospel?
Greco-Roman Mythology in Matt. 16:19

BRUCE HENNING

Abstract

Though the majority of current Matthean scholarship seeks to understand Jesus' reference to the 'keys to the kingdom of heaven' in Matt 16:19 from a Jewish context, this article argues that the Greco-Roman background is significant as well. Matthew and his audience would have been familiar with Greco-Roman depictions of deities such as Hekate as bearing keys to the underworld. Many scholars combine a Jewish context and Greco-Roman mythology in the interpretation of the keys of Hades and Death in Rev 1:18. This article argues that Matthew 16 makes similar connections to both worlds. Incorporating Greco-Roman mythology into the interpretation of Matt 16:19 elevates the description of Peter, forges a connection with Satan in 16:23, and emphasizes the eschatological role of the keys.

Much of Matthean scholarship favors Second Temple Literature as well as later Jewish literature as the primary, if not exclusive, comparanda for the first gospel. As a result, the keys of the kingdom in Matt 16:19 are now predominately understood in light of later Rabbinic debates of *halakha*. For example, Luz refers to this as 'the usual interpretation,' explaining that:

> 'The primary meaning is 'forbidding' and 'permitting' with a halakic decision of the rabbis, that is, the interpretation of the law ... it is the rabbinic conviction that God or the heavenly court recognizes the halakic decisions and the judgments of rabbinical courts. Thus not only the concepts 'binding/loosing' but the entire saying is rooted in Jewish thought.'[1]

However, while the Jewishness of Matthew's gospel is well established and incontrovertible, this does not disallow interaction with Greco-Roman sources which might add other layers of significance and impact the way we understand the metaphor of the keys. Kinney's monograph,

---

1 Luz, *Matthew*, 365. Other Matthean commentators who take this view include Davies and Allison, *Matthew*, 2:635–639; Culpepper, *Matthew*, 315; Runneson, *Divine Salvation*, 50 n26, 267, 269; Quarles, *Matthew*, 417; Konradt, *Das Evangelium nach Matthäus*, 254; France, *Matthew*, 625; Nolland, *Matthew*, 681; Kampen, *Matthew*, 152, 198; Overman, *Matthew's Gospel*, 20–21. Turner, *Matthew*, 408, Blomberg, *Matthew*, 254 and Carson, 'Matthew', 1:372 are in the minority in denying a connection. For a helpful overview of major interpretations, see Korting, 'Binden oder lösen', 39–91 (he takes 'binding' as 'hardening'). The widespread shift to this interpretation seems to come from John Lightfoot, *Hebraicae et Talmudicae*, 236–241, who says 'One might produce thousands of examples out of their [Jewish schools] writings' (236).

Hellenistic Dimensions of the Gospel of Matthew rightly begins,

> 'Recent trends in Matthean scholarship focus on the relationship of Matthew's gospel to contemporary Judaism, but they do so to the exclusion of Matthew's place in a broader Hellenism…an important voice in understanding the background of the Gospel of Matthew has been dampened. Scholarship has largely neglected to pursue the broader literary and cultural dimensions of the Gospel beyond a narrowly defined interest in its Judaism.'[2]

This article explores the impact of incorporating both Jewish and Greco-Roman backgrounds for an interpretation of Matt 16:19. We will begin by considering Revelation 1:18 as a comparable text that should be understood against both a Jewish and a Greco-Roman backdrop, then see indications within Matthew 16 that such a comparison is at work there, and conclude with a proposal for how Jewish and Roman backgrounds come together to inform our understanding of the keys of the kingdom.

Revelation and Hekate

In Revelation 1:18, Jesus says 'I am he that lives and became dead, and behold, I am alive forever and I have the keys of Death and Hades' (ἔχω τὰς κλεῖς τοῦ θανάτου καὶ τοῦ ᾅδου) and 3:7 further describes him as ὁ ἔχων τὴν κλεῖν Δαυίδ, ὁ ἀνοίγων καὶ οὐδεὶς κλείσει καὶ κλείων καὶ οὐδεὶς ἀνοίγει.[3] There is certainly a Scriptural background to consider. Rev 1:18 and 3:7 are mutually interpretive[4] and the latter clearly echoes Eliakim in Isa 22:22.[5] Yet, the former does not so easily evoke an OT image. Assuming Δαυίδ in τὴν κλεῖν Δαυίδ is a genitive, the parallel structure τὰς κλεῖς τοῦ θανάτου καὶ τοῦ ᾅδου suggests some kind of personification. Moreover, the pair θάνατος and ᾅδης are portrayed as persons elsewhere in Revelation (6:8; 20:13).

Though scholars give ample attention to Revelation's frequent allusions to the Scriptures, this does not preclude them seeing statements like 1:18 as being against a Greco-Roman background. Aune argues that this text is a polemic particularly against Hekate.[6] Indeed, he has had many takers.[7] Hekate (identified as Selene) is addressed in the magical papyri thus, 'Mother of all things, for you frequent Olympos, and the broad and boundless chasm you traverse. Beginning and end are you, and you alone rule all. For all things are from you, and in you do all things, Eternal one, come to their end…you hold in Your hands a golden scepter.'[8] This, of course, has several parallels to the description of Jesus in Revelation. Less similarly, Lucian describes Hekate as 'three hundred feet tall, carr[ying] a torch in her left hand and a sword in her right, she has snakes in place of hair and is an anguipede (serpents for legs); she could stamp her foot on the

---

2 Kinney, *Hellenistic Dimensions*, 2.
3 Translations are mine unless noted otherwise.
4 As witnessed by early manuscripts that replace Δαυιδ with αδου, e.g. 104* 218 459 620 2050 2067.
5 Rucker, *Temple Keys*; Beale, *Revelation*, 283–84; Chilton, 'Shebna, Eliakim, and the Promise to Peter', 311–26. There is some variation in the manuscripts, but the uncorrected Sinaiticus of Isa 22:22 reads δωσω και αυτω την κλιδαν οικου δ‾α‾δ‾ επι τω ωμω αυτου και ανοιξει · και ουκ εστε ο αποκλινων και κλισει και ουκ εσται ο αντιλεγω(ν). (International Greek New Testament Project, Codex Sinaiticus, Is 22:22).
6 Aune, 'The Apocalypse of John', 481–501.
7 E.g. Witherington, *Revelation*, 82; Koester, *Revelation*, 247; Charlesworth, 'Exploring the Origins', 375; Trebilco, *The Early Christians in Ephesus*, 396; Bass, *Battle for the Keys*, 32–34; Thomas, *Magical Motifs*, 89.
8 PGM 4.2836-37. Betz, *Greek Magical Papyri*, 91; Cf. Bass, *Battle for the Keys*, 32–34.

ground and break open a chasm to Hades' (*Philospeudes* 23).⁹ Moreover, the Orphic Hymns (ca. 200 CE) describe her as πάντος κόσμου κληδοῦχον ἄνασσαν, 'master key holder of all the cosmos' (1:7) and one of her symbols is the keys to the gates of Hades. Eight times in curse tablets from Cyprus she is referred to as 'you who possess the keys of Hades, who breaks open the earth'[10] and she is connected to the title κλειδοφόρος, ‹key-bearer,' found on many inscriptions.[11] A reference to Hekate is all the more likely for Revelation since worship of this deity was especially prominent in Turkey.[12] Lawrence convincingly argues, 'It is upon the basis of her [Hekate's] popularity in Asia Minor, in particular, that consideration must be given…that it would seem unimaginable that his audience would not have conceived of the phrase κλεῖς τοῦ θανάτου καί τοῦ ᾅδου as some form of reference to this goddess.'[13]

Certainly there are others who have access to the underworld in Greco-Roman mythology, and Beale suggests that John's polemic should be understood more broadly against all alleged 'key-bearers.'[14] This broader approach would also allow room for sources which depict angels such as Metatron (3 *En* 48C.3), Iaoel (*Apoc. Abr.* 10.11), Eremiel (*4 Ezra* 4:36) and Michael (3 Bar. 11.1–2) as possessing keys, whether to the underworld or the kingdom.[15] But though Jewish literature may be in the periphery in Rev 1:18, Hekate, *the* predominate key bearer to the underworld, has the most parallels and is likely the foregrounded comparison. Jesus, not Hekate controls the powers of Death and Hades, and any operation of those forces only happens by Jesus' allowance. Though reference to the keys of Death and Hades is understandable without Greco-Roman mythology, an exegesis which ignores it misses John's intention. Again, we should connect Revelation 1:18 to 3:7 and link the keys of death and Hades to the key of David, which in turn points toward Davidic Messianism and an allusion to Eliakim in Isaiah, but those Jewish elements should not crowd out the Greco-Roman resonances.

Matthew and the Gates of Hades

Should Matthean exegetes take a similar approach to Matt 16:19?[16] The fact that another first-century Christ-follower linked Jesus' keys to both Jewish and Greco-Roman matrices at least suggests that Matthew might have done something similar. Granted, Matthew does not seem to have been written in Asia Minor, where Hekate was especially popular, but this should not distract us from Roman mythology being well known throughout the empire. While a specific reference to Hekate goes beyond the evidence, what she represents—a Greco-Roman deity possessing keys to Hades – is in view. There are two features in Matt[16] that suggest this text should be understood

---

9   As cited in Aune, 'The Apocalypse,' 488.
10 Aune, 'The Apocalypse,' 486 cites Audollent, *Defixionum tabellae*, 22.53 f.; 23. 12 ff.; 26. 39; 29. 36; 31. 36; 32. 39; 35. 36; 37. 36.
11 For more on the role of κλειδοῦχος and κλειδοφόρος, see Johnston, *Hekate Soteira*, 41–42.
12 Aune, 'Apocalypse of John,' 486; Kraus, *Hekate*, 24–56, 166–68; Thomas, *Magical Motifs*, 89.
13 Lawrence, *Magical Motifs*, 90.
14 Beale, *Revelation*, 215.
15 Bass, *Battle for the Keys*, 34. Rev 9:1 references ἡ κλεὶς τοῦ φρέατος τῆς ἀβύσσου, 'the key of the shaft of the abyss,' which is used to release locusts that torment the earth. This is given (by Jesus?) to an angel, who is likely the same figure as in v 11, βασιλέα τὸν ἄγγελον τῆς ἀβύσσου, ὄνομα αὐτῷ Ἑβραϊστὶ Ἀβαδδών, καὶ ἐν τῇ Ἑλληνικῇ ὄνομα ἔχει Ἀπολλύων. The narrative progression suggests Apollyon/Abaddon is not in view in 1:18.
16 The similarities between Matt 16:19 and Rev 1:18 are frequently noted (e.g. Hagner, *Matthew*, 2:473) but not the Hekate or Greco-Roman mythology polemic.

within Greco-Roman mythology of the underworld. First, 16:18 has an expression that resonates with the material we just considered. There, Jesus says to Peter that πύλαι ᾅδου οὐ κατισχύσουσιν αὐτῆς, 'the gates of Hades will not overpower it/her,' with the antecedent either being the feminine ταύτῃ τῇ πέτρᾳ or, more likely, τὴν ἐκκλησίαν. The use of πύλαι ᾅδου, 'gates of Hades,' instead of the simpler ᾅδης leaves room for a connection to κλεῖς in the next verse. Some have seen a break in the symbolism here since the keys most likely bind and loose, as opposed open and shut/lock.[17] However, Korting argues that doors were often tied, so that loosening essentially means open.[18] The presence of πύλαι ᾅδου instead of ᾅδης would be most easily explained by Roman mythology, which frequently depicts the underworld as being guarded with gates whose access required keys. Jewish literature also refers to 'gates,'[19] so this alone is not determinative – but these references are far outnumbered by those in non-Jewish literature which has a close connection between gates, Hades, and keys.

Moreover, the use of ᾅδης instead of γέεννα suggests Matthew does point to Roman mythology. Matthew's preferred term for 'Hell' is γέεννα, which he uses seven times – 5:22, 29, 30, 10:28, 18:9, 23:15, 33. His only other reference to Hell is ᾅδης in 11:23 'But you, Capernaum, are you exalted to heaven? You will be brought down to Hades' (ἕως ᾅδου καταβήσῃ) is due to being a quotation from Isaiah 14:15 (LXX: νῦν δὲ εἰς ᾅδου καταβήσῃ; MT: אַךְ אֶל־שְׁאוֹל תּוּרָד). But Matt 16:19 is not such a quotation. There, it seems Matthew goes out of his way, not using his preferred term γέεννα, but uses ᾅδης. The result is a collocation of terms κλεῖς, πύλαι, and ᾅδης that together point to a Greco-Roman background more easily than a Jewish background. Again, each one of these words does occur in Jewish texts, but looking exclusively there does not do justice to the frequency with which the three of them occur together in Roman mythology.[20]

Second, Matthew has retained Mark's location of the event, Caesarea Philippi (Matt 16:13; cf. Mark 8:27), famous for its Grotto of Pan. Some allege that this is associated directly with the underworld. Witherington states, 'at Caesarea Philippi an underground stream surfaced and can still be seen today. There were traditions that this was one of the gates to the underworld and the river Styx. Both the saying of Peter and the saying of Jesus take on especial relevance and poignancy if they were given in the locale of all these shrines to other sons of the gods and next to the river thought to go into the underworld.'[21] This connection is often made (more in popular literature than academic)[22] and Witherington does not identity these traditions. If the connection is valid, this would strongly imply Matthew at least has one foot in Roman mythology as being at a place known as the 'gates of Hades,' understood in a Roman matrix must have bearing on how Jesus uses the expression.

However, there does not seem to be any literary or archeological evidence in support of identifying the Grotto of Pan at Caesarea Philippi as 'the Gates of Hades.' There is evidence that some places were thought of this way, such as the Ploutonion at Hierapolis (cf. Strabo, *Geography*, 13.4.14), which had a statue of Hades and Cerberus. This was a temple built over a cave and underground water source. We do have literary sources about descending to Hades by river or lake (e.g., the Stygian Lake; cf. Virgil, *Aen.* 98–155) and caves were seen as entryways. Ustinova writes

---

17 E.g. Nolland, *Matthew*, 679.
18 Korting, 'Binden oder lösen,' 84 ('Bis zur Kaiserzeit, in der das sog. römische Schloß aufkam, scheinen überall die Riemen zum Verschließen in Gebrauch gewesen zu sein').
19 E.g. Mangan, *Targum of Job*, 83 and Chilton et al, *Comparative Handbook*, 510 compare the text to TgJob 37:20 and 38:17, in which 'gates of death' are in contrast to 'flesh and blood' to show humanity's inability to control death.
20 See R. Bauckham, 'Descent,' 2:145–159.
21 Witherington, *Matthew*, 318.
22 See also Heiser, *The Unseen Realm*, 32 and Wilson, *Caesarea Philippi*, 206 n61.

Caves, dark and menacing, seemed bottomless to people who did not dare to penetrate their damp depths. Unsurprisingly, they invited the image of the netherworld, were often considered entrances to Hades, and called Charonia or Plutonia after Charon the ferryman of the dead and Pluto the lord of the netherworld. The idea that caves served as passages to the netherworld was so common that even relatively unimposing grottoes could be given the title of Plutonium.[23]

Thus, we could hypothesise that such a connection was made at Caesarea Philippi since it has all the makings of the gates to Hades, but no evidence that the first century actually made such a connection.

But though we should not go so far as connecting Caesarea Philippi explicitly with the gates of Hades, the fact remains that the Grotto of Pan was well known for its temples and cultic practices, all of which would have been understood within a Greco-Roman matrix. Granted, evidence that this site was understood as 'the Gates of Hades' would be more definitive. But even without such an explicit reference, the location nonetheless activates the field of Greco-Roman mythology. We have abundant numismatic and inscriptional evidence that Pan was worshipped there, and this expanded to include Zeus, Hermes, and Nemesis.

Impact on Exegesis

If Matthew's keys of the kingdom of heaven is to be understood similarly to John's keys of death and Hades in contrasting Greco-Roman mythology, what difference would this make to our interpretation? Three impacts seem likely. First, it would underscore the high role given to Peter. Whereas Revelation 1:18 says that Jesus, not Hekate, has the keys, Matthew 16 says that Jesus, not Hekate or any other figure, has the keys *and that he has given them to Peter*, so that Peter becomes the 'key bearer,' the commissioned κλειδοφόρος.[24] A convincing case can be made for seeing Peter as the foundation of the temple in 16:18,[25] and identifying him as the 'key bearer,' in terms of Greco-Roman mythology, would continue the elevation of Peter in our passage (though still leaving open the question of whether Peter functions as a representative of others).

Second, a Greco-Roman comparison would signal deities associated with Hades, so that, with Jeremias, we should see them as 'the ungodly powers of the underworld which assail the rock.'[26] This would forge a stronger link between 16:18–19 and the later references to Σατανᾶ (v 23). Again, this interpretation is possible without recourse to Greco-Roman Mythology. Jewish sources alone show that 'the gates of Hades' can refer not only to physical death,[27] but by synecdoche to the evil powers

---

23 Ustinova, *Caves*, 68.
24 See Silver, *Taking Ancient Mythology Economically*, 208–210 for a discussion of priestesses as 'key-bearers.' Ancient inscriptions (3rd century BCE to 1st century CE) depict a procession called κλειδος πομπη or κλειδος αγωγη in Turkey in which a priestess Κλειδοφορος walked in a procession for Hekate (Johnston, *Hekate Soteira*, 41). The idea of a deity entrusting keys to a priestly figure was not uncommon.
25 B. Henning, *Matthew's Non-Messianic Mapping*, 165–172 argues this is messianic imagery applied to Peter. For Peter as the temple foundation, see also Barber, 'Jesus as the Davidic Temple Builder', 935–53; Beale, *The Temple*, 187; Meyer, *The Aims of Jesus*, 185–202; Wright, 'Jerusalem', 57; Shäfer, 'Tempel', 126; Schreiner, 'Peter', 99–117. See also Hillyer, 'Rock-Stone Imagery', 58–81.
26 Jeremias, 'Πύλη, Πυλῶν', 927. Cf. Betz, 'Felsenmann und Felsengemeinde'.
27 Luz, *Matthew 8–20*, 363.

attached to it (e.g. Rev 20:1–3; T. Levi 18:10–12; Gospel of Nicodemus 16).[28] While there are a variety of opinions about how to understand καισχύσουσιν in v 18 (either 'prevail' or 'withstand'),[29] the verb has something to do with having superior power, introducing some kind of conflict. But if we are to connect the gates of Hades with Σατανᾶ, the conflict in v 18 likely prepares us for the interaction in v 22–23. In this text, Peter's attempt to stop Jesus from dying is seen as Satanic. The claim, 'this will not happen to you' (v 22) is an 'offense,' a σκάνδαλον. If, in v 18, Jesus says that Satan will fight against the mission of the new ἐκκλησία but lose, the interaction in vv 22–23 is an instance of this 'battle.' Moreover, this would connect well with the future tense of the verbs. Peter will someday have authority over the powers of Hades, but as the following interaction demonstrates, he is not there yet. Eventually, the process of syncing his thoughts with the Father in Heaven (see v 17) will be sufficiently complete so that he will have the authority to deliver the saving message, involving the concept of a dying-rising messiah. But at this point in the narrative, he does not have the keys. Satan is at work in him.[30] He does not think the things of God, but the things of humans (v 23).

Third, a Greco-Roman background would reinforce the interpretation that the function of these keys relates to entrance into the kingdom. Although many commentators see these keys as interpretational authority (Rabbinic halakha) as we saw earlier, a Greco-Roman background would emphasize their eschatological role. Seeing the keys as forgiveness is a major strand of interpretation found through history, with an impressive pedigree.[31]

This interpretation does not *require* a Greco-Roman background, but since there are other textual indicators that point in this direction, Roman mythology would play a supporting role. Though there are convincing reasons to see the keys referring to interpretational authority, the older view that they regard entrance into the kingdom still has merit. We can consider four observations, independent of a reference to Greco-Roman mythology, that favor this interpretation. First, the expression, 'whatever you bind on earth will be bound in earth, and whatever you loosen on earth will be loosed in heaven' matches Matthew 18:18 almost verbatim and there the context concerns expulsion from the ἐκκλησία. Since Jesus comes to 'save his people from their sins' (Matt 1:21), not being a part of Jesus' community clearly has eschatological significance.

Second, this imagery fits well with Matthew, since he elsewhere pictures the kingdom as a place one finally enters. 7:13–14 describes ultimate salvation as going through a narrow gate and 23:13 indicts the Pharisees, 'you shut the kingdom of heaven in people's faces. For you neither enter yourselves nor allow those who would enter to go in.'

Thirdly, Matthew elsewhere depicts the disciples as having authority to pronounce forgiveness and judgment. 9:8 concludes the story of the healing of the paralytic, 'they glorified God who had given such authority to people' (ἐδόξασαν τὸν θεὸν τὸν δόντα ἐξουσίαν τοιαύτην τοῖς ἀνθρώποις). This use of the plural, ἀνθρώποις must relate to its previous use in ὁ υἱὸς τοῦ ἀνθρώπου, who has ἐξουσίαν (9:6). Matthew's choice to add to Mark's account such a conclusion with the plural 'humans'

---

28 Recently discussed by Dalton, *Fulfilled Israel*, 94–95, who shows that the likelihood that keys to the kingdom would function as keys to Hades. Davies and Allison, *Matthew*, 2:632–33 call this the view of 'most exegetes.' Cf. Carter, *Matthew*, 335; Gibbs, *Matthew 11:2–20:34*, 321–22; Garland, *Reading Matthew*, 174; Marcus, 'The Gates of Hades', 445; Hiers, 'Binding and Loosing', 245.
29 See discussion in Nolland, *Matthew*, 675 and Marcus, 'The Gates of Hades,' 444.
30 Other texts show a belief that Satan can be simply resisted (James 4:7; Apoc. Ps. 5:4–8; TJob 27:1–6; History of Rechabites 19:1–2). Matthew likely concurs, but the narrative shows how far Peter is from being able to bind Satan.
31 See Luz, *Matthew 8–20*, 375 for a list of the most relevant past literature.

is best understood in light of the later commission given to other human beings.³² The pair of proclaiming forgiveness vs. condemnation is quite explicit in the Mission Discourse (esp. 10:13-15). Again, we are not too far from Johannine literature, in which Jesus breathes on the disciples and says 'If you forgive the sins of any people, they are forgiven them; if you hold of any, they are held' (John 20:23). The disciples in Matthew already having *this* kind of authority supports understanding kingdom entrance in 16:19.

Fourthly, ultimate salvation is a topic in the immediate context. 16:24–28 refers to saving one's soul (ψυχή) and repayment when the Son of Man comes in his kingdom. Thus, seeing the keys as concerning kingdom entrance has support from the context and fits well with Matthean theology. This interpretation is reinforced by a reference to Greco-Roman mythology, though it by no means requires it. In fact, there are other possible allusions. Jewish sources do reference the gates of Hades (cf. 3 Macc 5:51; Odes 11:10; Job 38:17, Wisdom of Solomon 16:13, Psalms of Solomon 16:2, and Isa 38:10) and so Matt 16:19 is intelligible without a reference to Greco-Roman mythology. The argument for the keys as allowing kingdom entrance does not require seeing a Greco-Roman background.³³ As with Rev 1:18, having a foot in the world of Jewish literature should still allow for Matthew to have a foot in other worlds too.

However, there are also convincing reasons to understand the imagery as mentioned earlier, in which this is seen against a Rabbinic background so that Peter is given authority to make halakhic decisions about the meaning of the law. There are *several* parallels in Rabbinic literature.³⁴ For example, m. Git. 9:1a–c states 'With regard to one who divorces his wife and said to her while handing her the bill of divorce: You are hereby permitted to marry any man except for so-and-so, Rabbi Eliezer permits (מתיר, "loosens") her to remarry based on this divorce. And the Rabbis prohibit (אוסרין, "bind") her from remarrying.' Some view this explanation with suspicion because of the difficulty in dating Rabbinic tradition,³⁵ but there is evidence for this view within Matthew itself. Since others have established this and it is the majority view, a brief summary of some supporting points will suffice.

First, the very similar expression in 18:18 may be an instance of saying when the broader command to forgive (i.e. Matt 6:12, 14–15) is binding or not. The command is 'always forgive,' but Matt 18 fleshes out the particulars of what happens in the particular situation of an unrepentance person, much like Rabbinic discussion explores what is and is not required in the particulars of resting on the Sabbath.³⁶

Second, the larger context of Matthew contains several examples of Jesus 'binding/loosing' such as in the Sermon on the Mount with its antithesis of current explanation 'you have heard' vs.

---

32 So Culpepper, *Matthew*, Jipp, *Messianic Theology*, 54; Luz, *Matthew*, 2:28; Dupont, 'Le Paralytique Pardonné', 940–58; Beare, *Matthew*, 223-224; Bruner, *Matthew*, 416; Gundry, *Matthew*, 165, Davies and Allison, *Matthew*, 2:96; Konradt, *Matthew*, 144. Henning, 'Who Forgives Sins', 26 n14 argues, 'While the case would be stronger had Matthew specifically recorded the disciples forgiving sins...absence of evidence is not evidence of absence. In fact, in Matthew and Mark, Jesus only forgives someone once – in this pericope. Inasmuch as the disciples' actions receive far less attention that Jesus', we should avoid drawing conclusions from what the Gospel authors do not record them saying. In Luke, the bestowal of forgiveness only occurs here, 7:36-50, and perhaps also 23:34. In John, the only time forgiveness language explicitly occurs is at 20:23, where the disciples are the subject' (26 n14).

33 After referencing Jeremias' view Culpepper, *Matthew*, 314 rightly states that 'The meaning of Jesus' assurance is clear enough, however, without adducing a mythological background.' However, the pursuit of relevant comparative texts need not stop when meaning is 'clear enough.'

34 Strack and Billerbeck's treatment goes from pp 839–850! Keener, *Matthew*, 455 n.25 lists the following: m. Gi. 9:1; t. Sanh. 7:2; b. Abod. Zar. 7a, bar.; Erub. 17a; ul. 39b, bar.; Pesa. 42a; p. Ter. 11:7; Besa 3:6, §5; 55:2, §13; Gen. Rab. 7:2; 80:9; 85:5; Num. Rab. 20:24; Deut. Rab. 2:19.

35 E.g. Turner, *Matthew*, 408.

36 Powell, 'Binding and Loosing', esp. 443–444.

how Jesus interprets the law 'I say to you.' In fact, this language does occur in 5:19 – 'Therefore, whoever loosens (λύσῃ) one of the least of these commands and teaches men thus.' Being Jesus' disciple-apprentice involves not only hearing his binding and loosing, but also replicating his example as they teach people. However, the language is not exactly the same as in later Rabbinic discussion since here Jesus forbids all loosing – but there is still proximity in that the word λυώ occurs in the context of proclaiming what obedience to the law looks like. Also, δεσμεύω, a similar word to δέω, ("bind" in 16:19) occurs in 23:4 – the Pharisees "tie heavy burdens and put them on the shoulders of men.'

Third, the previous pericope does address teaching, as Jesus warns his disciples about the leaven of the Pharisees and Sadducees, which 16:12 says is the 'teaching of the Pharisees and Sadducees' (in contrast to Luke 12:1 which equates it to hypocrisy). Teaching and proclaiming fit the immediate context as well since Peter has just announced what heaven revealed to him, that Jesus is the Messiah.

Fourth, there is likely an allusion to Eliakim in Isa 22:22 in Matt 16:19 (as well as in Rev 3:7), which Sifre Debarim 321 sees as teaching: 'One (of these scholars) speaks and the rest remain silent. 'and "the *masger*"' (lit., the 'closer') All sit before him and learn from him. After he 'closes,' no one 'opens,' and after he 'opens,' no one 'closes,' in fulfilment of (Isaiah 22:22) 'And he (David) will open, and none will close; and he will close, and none will open.'

Evidence pointing in both directions hardly means we are at an impasse. Kingdom entrance and interpretation go hand in hand. For example, consider the reference to Matt 16:19 in Pseudo-Clement of Rome regarding Peter,

> Wherefore do you indeed preside over them without occupation, so as to send forth seasonably the words that are able to save them; and so let them listen to you, knowing that whatever the ambassador of the truth shall bind upon earth is bound also in heaven, and what he shall loose is loosed. But you shall bind what ought to be bound, and loose what ought to be loosed. And these, and such like, are the things that relate to you as president.

This quotation is often brought up as support for the 'halakha-interpretation,'[37] but note that, though it does support that take, this ability results in Peter 'send[ing] seasonably the words that are able to save them.' Both interpretation and salvation are in view. Perhaps the best example is the Sermon on the Mount since it clearly concerns both about the right interpretation of the law and entering the kingdom of heaven. Similarly, Jesus invests Peter with authority to continue doing what Jesus started – expounding the correct meaning of the law in light of the kingdom so that people are able to enter. Seeing Matt 16:19 against the background of Greco-Roman mythology would emphasize the eschatological import of Peter's authority, but this in no way excludes a role in determining halakha which is evidenced clearly in later Rabbinic literature and is an important element to Matthean theology.

Both people (Josephus, *Wars*, 1:110[38]) and laws (Rabbinic literature cited above) can be bound and loosed. I have tried to emphasize that both are at play in Matt 16:19. Some have opposed seeing people being loosed on grammatical grounds, no less than Nolland[39] and France.[40] The neuter (ὅ) is used, so the reference is to 'whatever you bind' instead of 'whomever you bind.' We might

---

37 E.g. Quarles, *Matthew*, 417, n. 471.
38 Whiston, *Works of Josephus*, 551–552, comments 'Here we have the oldest and most authentic Jewish exposition of binding and loosing, for punishing or absolving men; not for declaring actions lawful or unlawful, as some more modern Jews and Christians vainly pretend'.
39 *Matthew*, 681.
40 *Matthew*, 626.

expect that if people are being bound or loosed, then we would have the masculine pronoun (ὅς) instead of the neuter (ὅ). However, at least three observations lessen the impact of this objection. First, if the idea is that 'wrongdoing' is bound or loosed, then the neuter is unproblematic. There is little conceptual difference between saying a person is forgiven and a person's sins are forgiven. Second, the neuter is often used for classes of people.[41] Third, the realm of metaphor means we should not demand too much precision. If keys lock or unlock 'things,' the word 'things' can be grammatically neuter but symbolize masculine or feminine referents.[42] From neither the Greek grammar nor the context is it clear if the keys bind/loose people or commands. I suggest that the imagery is imprecise and that both are intended.

Thus, the arguments in favor of the halakha interpretation are not in competition with the idea of kingdom entrance. This Jewish background does not count against a Greco-Roman background. With Greco-Roman mythology in view, Peter is the κλειδοφόρος, who has authority over the powers of Hades. However, the text emphasizes that this will come later – once Peter has fully learned the role that Jesus' death must play in the plan of salvation, then the keys will be given, then he will grant people entrance into the kingdom by sufficiently revealing the will of God.

Bruce Henning
Assistant Professor of New Testament
Cornerstone Theological Seminary

---

41 Granted by Nolland, *Matthew*, 681.
42 The antecedent needs to agree with the pronoun, but not the referent (or to use the language of Cognitive Linguistics, the target). For example, John 1:4–5 reads καὶ ἡ ζωὴ ἦν τὸ φῶς τῶν ἀνθρώπων τὸ φῶς ἐν τῇ σκοτίᾳ φαίνει, καὶ ἡ σκοτία αὐτὸ οὐ κατέλαβεν. That last αὐτό is neuter to match the neuter τὸ φῶς. However, this does not rule out the interpretation that the darkness does not grasp/overpower the life, ἡ ζωή. We are dealing with a metaphor with the key ἡ ζωὴ ἦν τὸ φῶς. The antecedent of αὐτό is neuter, φῶς, but its referent is the feminine 'life,' ζωή. Similarly, Peter uses keys to unlock things, and to expect that he would say he would people is to abandon the sphere of the metaphor.

Bibliography

Aune, D.	'The Apocalypse of John and Graeco-Roman Revelatory Magic', *NTS* 33 (1987), 481–501.
Barber, M. P.	'Jesus as the Davidic Temple Builder and Peter's Priestly Role in Matthew 16:16–19', *JBL* 132.4 (2013), 935–53.
Bass, J. W.	*The Battle for the Keys: Revelation 1:18 and Christ's Descent into the Underworld* (Paternoster Biblical Monographs; Eugene, OR: Wipf & Stock 2014).
Bauckham, R.	'Descent to the Underworld', *The Anchor Yale Bible Dictionary* (New York, NY: Doubleday, 1992).
Beale, G. K.	*The Book of Revelation: A Commentary on the Greek Text* (Grand Rapids, MI: Eerdmans, 1999).
Beale, G. K.	*The Temple and the Church's Mission: A Biblical Theology of the Dwelling Place of God* (Downers Grove, IL: IVP Academic, 2004).
Beare, F. W.	*The Gospel according to Matthew: Translation, Introduction and Commentary* (San Francisco, CA: Harper & Row, 1981).
Betz, H. D. (ed.)	The Greek Magical Papyri in Translation (London: University of Chicago Press, 1986).
Betz, O.	'Felsenmann und Felsengemeinde', *ZNW* 48 (1957) 49–77.
Blomberg, C.	*Matthew* (Nashville, TN: Broadman & Holman, 1992).
Bruner, F. D.	*The Christbook, Matthew: A Commentary, Revised and* Expanded (Grand Rapids, MI: Eerdmans, 2007).
Carson, D. A.	'Matthew' in *The Expositor's Bible Commentary* (ed. Frank Gaebelein; Grand Rapids, MI: Zondervan, 1984).
Carter, W.	*Matthew and the Margins: A Socio-Political and Religious* Reading (Sheffield: Sheffield Academic, 2000).
Charlesworth, J. H.	'Exploring the Origins of the Descensus ad Inferos', in A. J. Avery-Peck, C. A. Evans, and J. Neusner (eds.), *Earliest Christianity within the Boundaries of Judaism: Essays in Honor of Bruce Chilton* (Leiden: Brill).
Chilton, B.	'Shebna, Eliakim, and the Promise to Peter', in J. Neusner et al. (eds.), *The Social World of Formative Christianity and Judaism: Essays in Tribute to Howard Clark Key* (Philadelphia, PA: Fortress, 1989), 311–26.
Chilton, B., et al. (eds.)	*A Comparative Handbook to the Gospels of Matthew and Luke: Comparisons with Pseudepigrapha, the Qumran Scrolls, and Rabbinic Literature* (Leiden: Brill, 2021).
Culpepper, R. A.	*Matthew: A Commentary* (Louisville, KY: Westminster John Knox, 2021).
Dalton, A.	*Fulfilled Israel According to Matthew's Plerosis Paradigm* (Tübingen: Mohr Siebeck, 2024).

Davies, W. D., and D. C. Allison Jr.   *A Critical and Exegetical Commentary on the Gospel according to Saint Matthew* (London: T&T Clark, 2004).

Dupont, J.   'Le Paralytique Pardonné (Matthieu 9, 1–18)', *Nouvelle Revue Théologique* 82.9 (1960), 940–58.

France, R. T.   *The Gospel of Matthew* (Grand Rapids, MI: Eerdmans, 2007).

Garland, D. E.   *Reading Matthew: A Literary and Theological Commentary* (Macon, GA: Smyth & Helwys, 2012).

Gibbs, J. A.   *Matthew 11:2—20:34* (Saint Louis, MO: Concordia, 2010).

Heiser, M.   *The Unseen Realm* (Bellingham, WA: Lexham, 2015).

Henning, B.   *Matthew's Non-Messianic Mapping of Messianic Texts: Evidences of a Broadly Eschatological Hermeneutics* (Leiden: Brill, 2021).

Henning, B.   'Who Forgives Sins but God? None, One, or Many? How Luke's Intratextual Contributions Nuance His Answer', *NovTest* 67 (2025), 21–38.

Hiers, R.   '"Binding and Loosing": The Matthean Authorizations' *JBL* 104.2 (1985), 233–50.

Hillyer, C. N.   '"Rock-Stone" Imagery in I Peter', *TynBul* 22 (1971), 58–81.

Jeremias, J.   'Πύλη, Πυλῶν', in Gerhard Kittel, Geoffrey W. Bromiley, and Gerhard Friedrich (eds.), *Theological Dictionary of the New Testament* (Grand Rapids, MI: Eerdmans, 1964–).

Jipp, J.   *The Messianic Theology of the New Testament* (Grand Rapids, MI; Eerdmans, 2020).

Johnston, S. I.   *Hekate Soteira: A Study of Hekate's Roles in the Chaldean Oracles and Related Literature* (Atlanta, GA: Scholars, 1990).

Josephus, Flavius, and William Whiston   *The Works of Josephus: Complete and Unabridged* (Peabody, MA: Hendrickson, 1987).

Kampen, J.   *Matthew within Sectarian Judaism* (New Haven, CT: Yale, 2019).

Keener, C.   *The Gospel of Matthew: A Social-Rhetorical Commentary* (Grand Rapids, MI: Eerdmans, 2009).

Kinney, R. S.   *Hellenistic Dimensions of the Gospel of Matthew: Background and Rhetoric* (Tübingen: Mohr Siebeck, 2016).

Koester, C. R.   *Revelation: A New Translation with Introduction and* Commentary (New Haven, CT: Yale University, 2014).

Konradt, M.   *Das Evangelium nach Matthäus* (Göttingen: Vandenhock & Ruprecht, 2015).

Korting, G.   'Binden oder lösen: Zu Verstockungs-und Befreiungstheologie in Mt 16, 19; 18, 18.21–35 und Joh 15, 1–17; 20, 23', *SNTU* 14 (1989), 39–91.

Kraus, T.	*Hekate: Studien zu Wesen und Bild der Göttin in Kleinasien und Griechenland* (Heidelberg: Carl Winter Universitätsverlage, 1960).
Lightfoot, J.	*Horae Hebraicae et Talmudicae in quattuor Evangelistas* (Leipzig, 1675).
Luz, U.	*Matthew: A Commentary*, ed. Helmut Koester (Minneapolis, MN: Augsburg, 2001).
Mangan, C.	*The Targum of Job* (Collegeville, MN: Liturgical Press, 1991).
Marcus, J.	'The Gates of Hades and the Keys of the Kingdom (Matt. 16:18–19)', *CBQ* 50.3 (1988), 443–55.
Meyer, B.	*The Aims of Jesus* (London: SCM, 1979).
Nolland, J.	*Matthew* (Grand Rapids, MI: Eerdmans, 2005).
Overman, J. A.	*Matthew's Gospel and Formative Judaism: The Social World of the Matthean Community* (Minneapolis, MN: Fortress, 1990).
Powell, M. A.	'Binding and Loosing: A Paradigm for Ethical Discernment in the Gospel of Matthew', *Currents in Theology and Mission* 30.6 (Dec 2003), 438–45.
Quarles, C.	*Matthew* (Bellingham, WA: Lexham, 2022).
Rucker, T. M.	*The Temple Keys of Isaiah 22:22, Revelation 3:7, and Matthew 16:19: The Isaianic Temple Background and Its Spatial Significance for the Mission of Early Christ Followers* (Tübingen: Mohr Siebeck, 2021).
Runneson, A.	*Divine Salvation and Wrath in Matthew: The Narrative World of the First Gospel* (Minneapolis, MN: Fortress, 2016).
Schreiner, P.	'Peter, the Rock: Matthew 16 in light of Daniel 2', *CTR* 13.2 (2016), 99–117.
Shäfer, P.	'Tempel und Schopfung: Zur Interpretation einiger Heiligtumstraditionen in der rabbischen Literatur', in P. Shäfer, *Studien zur geschichte und Theologie des rabbinischen Judentums* (Leiden: Brill, 1978).
Silver, M.	*Taking Ancient Mythology Economically* (Leiden: Brill, 2023).
Thomas, R. L.	*Magical Motifs in the Book of Revelation* (London: Bloomsbury, 2010).
Trebilco, P.	*The Early Christians in Ephesus from Paul to Ignatius* (Tübingen: Mohr Siebeck, 2004).
Turner, D.	*Matthew* (Grand Rapids, MI: Baker, 2006).
Ustinova, Y.	*Caves and the Ancient Greek Mind: Descending Underground for the Search of Ultimate Truth* (Oxford: Oxford University, 2009).
Wilson, J. F.	*Caesarea Philippi: In Search for the Lost City of Pan* (London: I. B. Taurus, 2004).
Witherington, B. III	*Revelation* (Cambridge: Cambridge University, 2003).
Wright, N. T.	'Jerusalem in the New Testament', in P. W. L. Walker (ed.), *Jerusalem, Past and Present in the Purposes of God* (Grand Rapids, MI: Baker, 1994).

How Mark Moved/s the World

PETER G. BOLT

Abstract
This essay presents a model for reading the narrative about Jesus that we know as Mark's Gospel.

∙ ∙ ∙

Mark's story of Jesus once moved the world and continues to do so every time it is carefully read.[1] Great rewards come not only from trying to understand Mark's message as well as we can, but also from trying to understand how Mark's message moves its readers/hearers towards faith in Jesus, and hope for the coming kingdom of God.

What is a Gospel? In the history of their interpretation the Gospels have been read as *history*, or *theology*, or *story*. Rather than drawing false dichotomies, we should recognise the element of truth in all three categories, and add a fourth. Because the Gospels reveal the truth about God that has arrived in the world in Jesus Christ and his work that brings about the coming kingdom of God, the Gospels are inescapably *apocalyptic*. So, the Gospel of Mark (as with the other three Gospels) is an *apocalyptic narrative of theologically significant historical events*; and, more particularly, the theologically significant historical events associated with the life, death, and resurrection of Jesus of Nazareth who brought us into the last days.

But how does the Gospel of Mark work? When the reader begins reading at 1:1 and reads through to 16:8 (the original and intended ending), how does the Gospel of Mark make its impact on the reader, and change the world one reader at a time?

Part of the secret of its power is its narrative flow.

1. A Narrative Flow
1.1 Beginning and Ending with Gospel Mission

Mark's narrative opens dramatically with a statement which immediately directs the reader to its content: 'The beginning of the gospel of Jesus Christ, the Son of God' (1:1). This should be taken, not as an introduction to the next paragraph, but as a title for the whole narrative to follow.[2] The

---

1   An earlier form of this essay was published in two parts on https://christoverall.com, 25 and 26 August 2025. Given its aim to present a model for reading Mark developed over some years, I have drawn upon my own published work and interacted minimally with the work of others.
2   Bolt, *Jesus' Defeat of Death*, 44–45.

word 'gospel' refers to a spoken message of great victory, so good news, and Mark is particularly concerned with the good news of the victory of Jesus Christ, the Son of God. This gospel message would already be known to Mark's readers, for they had heard it—or at least heard of it—from others already, but now, through the reading of Mark, they have the opportunity to hear *the beginning* of this gospel message. Mark is about to tell them how the good news of Jesus Christ, the Son of God, came about. His book tells its readers where it all began.

Mark's narrative ends just as dramatically with the enigmatic report of the women's response to finding Jesus' tomb empty: 'So they went out and started running from the tomb, because trembling and astonishment overwhelmed them. And they said nothing to anyone, since they were afraid' (16:8). In its own strange way, this enigmatic ending uses the women's fearful silence to implicitly call for the reader to repent from their own fearful silence because after the resurrection of Jesus it is not the time for silence anymore. Now it is time for speech (9:9).[3]

The four Gospels arose from the context of the early Christian mission and were written to serve that Christian mission.[4] As they are read, the Gospels move those who haven't previously responded to Christ towards faith in Christ; and they move those who have already put their faith in Christ to continue to do so as they engage in his mission to a lost world. The first and last verses of the Gospel of Mark help us to see the same thing: the title promises that the book will anchor the gospel message in its proper origins (the life, death, and resurrection of Jesus Christ, the Son of God—all at 'the end of the ages' 1 Cor. 10:11), and after that story is told, the reader is sent back into an often intimidating mission-field with a better grounding and a new resolve not to be afraid and silent, but to speak for Jesus, who has risen from the dead.

But how does Mark work this miraculous transformation from fear (and silence) to faith (and proclamation)?

1.2 Dramatic Narrative Movement and Flow

In large part, this comes from a well-told narrative that is fast-paced and well structured. Anyone who dabbles with biblical commentaries knows that it is usual to propose a 'structure' of the biblical book under the commentator's gaze. The language of 'structure', however, conveys a static picture, as if the text just sits there on someone's desk, ready and waiting for them to carve it up into its constituent parts. But for the Gospel narrative it is better to talk of its narrative *flow*, because there is a relentless movement forwards: there are dramatic characters; there is a plot; there are counter-plots; and through the network of interacting characters, the drama of the narrative intensifies as one scene builds upon another towards a great moment of climax near the end, when all threads come together.

After the title and prologue (1:1–13), the ministry of Jesus begins with the dramatic announcement that is an introduction to, and a summary of, his abiding message first to Israel and then to the world (cf. 14:9): 'The time is fulfilled; the kingdom of God has come near. Repent and believe in the good news!' (1:14–15). Without going into detail, from that point, the flow of Mark's narrative can be described in five movements, and each of those movements has clear narrative markers and each can be given a content-led description:[5]

---

3   Following Boomershine and Bartholomew, 'Narrative Technique'.
4   See further, Bolt, 'Following Jesus'.
5   This narrative flow forms the organising principle for the chapters in *Jesus' Defeat of Death*, see, e.g., 48, 131, 217, 244, 254; and for Bolt, *The Cross from a Distance*, see, e.g., 18–19, and then its further development in the rest of that work.

Movement	Narrative Markers	Content-led description
1:16–4:34	Four Calls:	The Kingdom is Near: Expecting the End
4:35–8:26	Three Sea Crossings:	Jesus and the Perishing
8:27–10:52	Three Predictions of Jesus' Passion and Resurrection:	Entering the Coming Kingdom
11–13	Three Days and Three Journeys:	The Clash of Kingdoms: Preparing for the End
14–16:8	Four 'Watches':[6]	The Coming of the Kingdom: the Arrival of the End

2. Six Interlocking Stories

But Mark's genius is more than simply a flow that can be discerned within the narrative. This narrative flow is such that it engages and moves the readers. In critical terms, it is not enough to practise *narrative* criticism alone. Since Mark's narrative constantly has the reader in view, we must engage in *narrative–reader* criticism—that is, we need to ask two questions, not just one. As well as asking *What* does the narrative say?, we also need to ask *How* does it say it? *How* does Mark use *what* he says to make an impact on his world by moving his readers?

In order to begin to explore how Mark communicates his message to his readers, the narrative can be discussed in terms of a model based on six interrelated stories.[7]

2.1 The Main Story: Jesus

From the opening verse (1:1), it is clear that Mark's main story concerns Jesus. The opening prologue (1:2–13) informs the reader of his true identity. He is immediately linked with OT promises which give him a most exalted status, since, according to those promises, the one who would come after the messenger (John the Baptist) was the Lord himself. After his baptism the Spirit comes upon him, designating him the long-awaited Servant-Messiah (1:11, cf. Isa. 42:1; Ps. 2:7).[8] He clashes with Satan (1:13) before launching out on his mission (1:14–15). His authority is immediately apparent (1:21–28), and eventually explained as the authority of the Son of Man who is able to forgive sins (2:10). John the Baptist had promised the people of Israel that the stronger one was coming, bringing the forgiveness they were after. Jesus now reveals that he is authorised to do so as the Son of Man. They need to recognise his authority, or they will miss out on forgiveness altogether, and be liable for eternal sin (3:22–30). Thus, the opening chapters of Mark take up where the OT left off: Israel is already under judgement and awaiting forgiveness (cf. Isa. 40:1ff.). The new thing that is disclosed is that Jesus as Son of Man (cf. Dan. 7:13–14) is authorised to bring that forgiveness to the land of Israel.[9] Through a series of parables (4:1–34) Jesus calls upon 'anyone with ears to hear' within Israel to recognise that Jesus is a lamp on the lampstand, and to listen to the word, in the light of the coming kingdom.

---

6   I.e. the 'watch' of a sentry or a soldier, see Mark 13:32–37.
7   See Bolt, 'What is the Gospel?'. A similar model can be derived from Rhoads and Michie, *Mark as Story*.
8   For an exposition of the significance of Jesus as the Isaianic Servant in the Synoptic Gospels, see Bolt, 'The Spirit in the Synoptic Gospels'.
9   See further Bolt, '"With a View to the Forgiveness of Sins"'.

The next section (4:35—8:26) is structured around three sea crossings. The opening scene, 'the storm at sea' (4:35–41), raises three significant questions that the subsequent narrative will guide Mark's readers to answer properly: 1. Don't you care that we are perishing? (v.38); 2. Why are you afraid? Do you still have no faith? (v.40); 3. Who then is this, that even the wind and the waves obey him? (v.41). To put these questions together: if the disciples (and Mark's readers) understand who Jesus is properly, and put their faith in him, then they won't be afraid, even in the face of death. This is the position towards which Jesus is moving his disciples, and it is the position towards which Mark is moving his readers.

The rest of this section (5:1—8:26) shows Jesus demonstrating that he has come to restore those suffering under the shadow of death and to bring in the kingdom, as he continues to urge Israel to respond to him. Nevertheless, on the whole, Israel is hard-hearted to what is going on in their midst. Even the disciples do not understand who Jesus is, despite being present at several miracles which display Jesus' servanthood, messiahship and even divinity. If they are to be changed, Jesus will have to open their blind eyes.

The middle chapters (8:27—10:52) open with a glimmer of recognition from the disciples, and further teaching from Jesus regarding his future suffering. The suffering of the Son of Man is the only thing that must still occur before the imminent arrival of the kingdom (9:1, 9–13). He stresses not only that the need to enter the kingdom is urgent, and necessary for salvation, but that entry is a difficult thing that only God can make possible (10:27). He also promises that God will do the impossible for all those who have radically committed themselves to following him. The climax of this section comes when he reveals that the suffering of the Son of Man must happen (8:31; 9:31; 10:32–33), because this is how God will do the impossible. Entry to the kingdom will come about through the Son of Man dying as the Servant of the Lord, a ransom for many (10:45).

In the next section of Mark (11—13), Jesus arrives in Jerusalem and clashes with the religious leaders. As he prepares for his own end on the cross, he prepares his disciples for *the* end, the arrival of the kingdom of God.[10]

In the passion narrative, Jesus once again explains his death theologically, this time as the Passover sacrifice that brings in the new covenant, the last Passover before the kingdom of God arrives (14:12–25). He is arrested in a great time of distress for himself and his disciples. At his trial, he reveals that he is Israel's Messiah, and that he will soon be installed as the Lord of Psalm 110, and the Son of Man of Daniel 7:13 (14:61–62). In the midst of great tragedy, he dies, ironically recognised as king, and even by a Gentile as 'the Son of God' (15:39). In his death, the structures of national Israel are judged and theologically come to an end. Jesus is buried, but three days later, in fulfilment of his own predictions, his grave is found empty, because he has risen from the dead (16:1–8), which appears to be the moment he receives the kingdom of God in power, before launching the mission to the nations.

In a nutshell, the main story is about Jesus. He was the Messiah of Israel, the Servant of the Lord, the Son of Man, who did things only God could do. It is about how he achieved what is impossible for any human being, through his own sacrificial death. For it is the story about how Jesus not only inaugurated the kingdom of God through his resurrection, but through his death enabled people to enter it. Such a story asks for repentance and faith, and radical loyalty to this Jesus and his cause.

---

10 See further Bolt, 'Mark 13: An Apocalyptic Precursor'; *The Cross from a Distance*, ch. 3; and, completed in 1991 but now recently published, *The Narrative Integrity of Mark 13:24–27*.

2.2 The Big Story: the Kingdom of God

Mark's Gospel sets Jesus' story against an even bigger story. Since his story cannot be understood without the OT, it is rooted into the real events of Israel's history, into their pains and turmoils, into the judgement of God they had experienced since the exile, and into their hopes and expectations for forgiveness and salvation in the future. When he announces that 'the times are fulfilled' (1:15) he announces that world history has come to a decisive turning point. Since Jesus brings the kingdom of God near, urges people to enter it to avoid destruction and to find life and salvation, dies to make entry possible and then inaugurates that kingdom in his resurrection, it is clear that Jesus' story is set within a bigger story about ultimate issues in human life which concern people's future and the future of the world. In other words, Jesus' story says something real about the real world, and it says that this real world of human history has changed as a result of his arrival, and changed in a way that has implications for everyone. His cause is a big cause—it concerns the kingdom of God. This phrase sums up the expectations of the OT for not only the end of all ungodly human power and sinfulness, but also, through such a judgement process, the subsequent removal of God's judgement. Jesus equated it with ultimate salvation, and eternal life in the age to come.

In other words, the coming of the kingdom of God which Jesus provokes speaks of the renovation of the world on the grandest scale, the restoration of all things.

2.3 The Counter Story: the Opponents

Not everyone recognises Jesus' significance. From the beginning he meets with opposition from the Jewish religious and political leaders of the day. Mark's story also sets this human opposition on a cosmic stage, by clearly linking it with that of the demonic forces. Their opposition comes from a hard-hearted refusal to listen to the word, and it results in the horrifying spectacle of the killing of the Son of God.

2.4 The Vacillating Story: the Disciples

Another story that is played out alongside Jesus' story is that of his disciples. It appears that the disciples vacillate between two leaders. They are firmly on Jesus' side, and yet they fail to understand what he is on about. Most of the time they appear to share in the hard-heartedness of Jesus' opponents (cf. 7:18, 'are you *also* so dull?'). They ultimately desert Jesus, but even as they do so, there is the hope that he would restore them after all (14:28; 16:7), according to the promise that he gave them at the beginning that he would turn them into 'fishers of people' (1:16–20).

2.5 The Episodic Stories: the 'Minor Characters', and the 'Suppliants'

The main story is made up of many other stories that are episodic. Whereas the major characters (Jesus; his disciples; his opponents) are present from the beginning to the end of the narrative, providing the continuity, there are also a number of 'minor characters' who appear once, only to disappear almost immediately, never to return.

Some minor characters receive very little attention in the narrative, but there are thirteen characters, who are each involved in an extended scene, and who, as a group, play a significant role in the communication of Mark's message. These thirteen characters can be called 'the suppliants', because they all enter the narrative in some desperate situation of human need, and come to Jesus wanting something from him. He deals graciously with them all, and so they have their life turned right-side up, before they then disappear just as suddenly as they appeared.

Table 2. Mark's Thirteen Suppliants

1:21–28	The man with an unclean spirit
1:29–31	Simon's mother-in-law with fever
1:40–45	The leper
2:1–12	The paralytic
3:1–6	The man with a withered hand
5:1–20	The man amongst the tombs
5:21–24, 35–43	Jairus' daughter
5:25–34	The woman with the flow of blood
7:24–30	The Syro-Phoenecian girl
7:31–37	The deaf and mute man
8:22–26	The blind man at Bethsaida
9:14–29	The boy with the killing spirit
10:46–52	Blind Bartimaeus at Jericho

These suppliants are sometimes named, and Mark portrays all of them complete with the emotions and explanations of their behaviour and circumstances that make them very sympathetic characters. They often show more insight into Jesus than the disciples and the opponents, and they can even show characteristics of true discipleship, while the Twelve have no idea at all. If the Twelve provide continuity for the story of Jesus from beginning to end, the suppliants are the means by which the reader is drawn in to that story. By arousing the sympathy of the readers, the suppliants draw the readers into the story, so that they have their own encounter with Jesus and his grace.[11]

2.6 The Reader's Story?

Through these multi-faceted dynamics, the flow of Mark's Gospel moves towards making an impact upon the story of the reader. Of course this occurs in a far more profound manner than can be described in the space of this essay, but nevertheless I can make a few general comments about how the intra-narrative dynamics seem to be working.

Mark creates a close relationship between the reader and Jesus. From the beginning we are told who Jesus really is, and from that moment we share a privileged relationship with him, one that even the characters within the story do not share. He is always attractive, always appealing, and, although there are times when he is at some distance from the reader, even at those times we would prefer to be close![12] Such dynamics draw the reader towards Jesus.

On the other hand, the opponents are made repugnant to the reader in many ways. They are characterised negatively, they are stubborn, politically conniving, self-motivated, they have so little concern for justice that they will kill an innocent man, and even gloat over his death. What makes it

---

11   For my close analysis of the suppliants and their role in Mark's narrative dynamics, see Bolt, *Jesus' Defeat of Death*.
12   For a description of the particularly poignant readerly dynamics in the passion narrative, see Bolt, 'Feeling the Cross'.

all the more horrendous is that they are prepared to kill their own king who came to provide them with the way into the kingdom of God! In the reader's mind, they deserve to be set on the side of Satan himself! The opponents drive the reader away from such hard-hearted rejection of Jesus.

The relationship between the disciples and the reader is fairly complex and changes as the story proceeds. In the early sections there is a distance between them, and the reader sees them as fairly dull and stupid for missing what is plainly before their eyes. However, later on, the reader is drawn towards them more positively, and even begins to understand them and feel for them. In this way Mark's story subtly draws the reader into the experience of the disciples and makes the reader see that their vacillation can be found in the experience of us all. Through this strange love-hate relationship, Mark shows his reader that they too need to learn their lessons: to hear the call to follow, to recognise the hard heart within, to feel the impossibility of entry to the kingdom, to turn to Jesus as the only way into the kingdom, to keep on giving him that radical loyalty that he requires, even beyond our own failures.

The minor characters as a whole usually act as a foil in this enterprise, and the suppliants especially so. The reader quickly relates to these people, for the reader is drawn towards them with their very human needs, distresses and feelings. Providing a slice-of-life through the real world, they also provide concrete life illustrations of what Jesus is willing and able to do. In this way they are like entry points into the story of the disciples, and then into the story of Jesus, and then into the big kingdom story.

This appears to be the rhetorical intent of Mark's Gospel. The flesh-and-blood reader comes to the text very much a part of this real world that is filled with human misery, and which lies firmly under God's judgement and so under the shadow of death. By entering the narrative through the eyes of its implied reader, we are drawn towards these confused, suffering characters, and so to the one they found, who met them in all their need and was willing and able to do something for that need. Through being drawn towards this great one, we find that he is offering ultimate solutions, for through dying and leaving his tomb empty, he is able to take us into the kingdom of God, the ultimate renovation of all things. So, through being aligned with the suppliants, the reader is drawn to Jesus, and, through seeing who Jesus really was, and what he really did, the reader is confronted with the only one who can bring them from the midst of all their human need, into the kingdom of God.

This persuasive task is helped by Mark's strange, and in many ways unsatisfying, ending (16:8), which throws the story over for the reader to finish off in their own experience. In this way he cleverly challenges his readers to repent of previous failures and to become involved in the cause of the risen Christ, while they await their own arrival in the future kingdom.

3. The Intersection of Two Worlds—An Example from Mark 1:29–31

Having looked at the overall flow of the narrative, and introduced the 'six stories' model, I would like to now look at one of the suppliant stories in detail to illustrate how Mark communicates. When someone reads Mark, the reading experience can be described as the intersection of two worlds.

Mark describes the world of Jesus amongst first-century Israel, set within the first-century Graeco-Roman world. In many ways it is a very different world from ours, and there are things that any reader of Mark's Gospel throughout the ages would find strange and different from their own life-situation. However, at the level of what is truly significant, all human beings share exactly the same problem: we are living in a world that is under the shadow of death, because human beings have rebelled against our Creator. And because we live in this world, we are held in slavery all of our lives to the fear of death (see Heb. 2:14–15). We are estranged from our God, our world, each other, and even ourselves, because of our sin and God's answering judgement. The various cultures that our contemporary world wishes to make so primary are therefore relativised by common human experience. There is a profound commonality between human beings of all cultures and times. This is the world displayed by the suppliants in their various struggles under the shadow of death; and this is the world into which Jesus came, in order to bring people into the kingdom of God through dying as a ransom for many.

But as a person reads the Gospel, they bring their own world to the reading experience as well. In order to get the most out of the story, they need to enter the story-world and see things through the eyes of those within it. Several minor characters within Mark's Gospel (the suppliants) play a key role in bringing us from our own world into the world of the story, so that, in turn, our own world might be transformed by encountering Jesus in his world.

This process can be illustrated by examining one of the suppliant stories, the cure of Simon Peter's mother-in-law from a fever (Mark 1:29–31).[13] The reading experience can be described as two journeys. Because the text is written in such a way that it will make an impact upon the readers, the reading experience begins with a journey outwards, 'from the text to the (implied) reader'. However, because real flesh-and-blood readers bring their own 'repertoire' to the reading experience that is also brought to bear upon the reading experience, there is also a journey inwards, 'the (flesh-and-blood) reader to the text'.

3.1 Text to Reader

3.1.1 From the Synagogue to the House

Jesus immediately moves from the synagogue to Simon and Andrew's house (εὐθύς, 1:29), with James and John. The naming of the four recalls their enlistment (1:16–20), and Jesus' promise to make them 'fishers of men'. Their absence from the previous scene (1:21–28) suggests to the readers that Jesus is only now rejoining them after they were called and entered Capernaum with him (v.21). Although there is some ambiguity, there is nothing to suggest that they knew of the events in the synagogue, which therefore becomes shared knowledge between readers and Jesus only.

The narrator tells the readers the necessary background data that Simon's mother-in-law was lying ill with fever (v.30a, κατέκειτο πυρέσσουσα), before the disciples tell Jesus (v.30b), which gives them a position of privilege over all the characters. This is Mark's first mention of sickness. In terms of extraordinary abilities, the readers know only of Jesus' confrontation with the spirits of the dead (1:21–28). Although there was no hint of any spirits being involved in the narrator's description of the woman's condition, which is described simply as a fever, this information raises the question: if Jesus can deal with the unclean spirits, what can he do with a fever? What will he do now, when he learns of this woman already on her bed from a fever?

The second 'immediately' (εὐθύς) continues the frantic pace of events; as soon as he arrived in the house, they told him of the woman's situation (v.30b). This seems to be a case of simply mentioning a matter of concern for the household, for there is no indication that they expected that he would (or could) do anything for her. This adds to the readers' pleasant sense of privilege: the disciples may end up surprised, but the readers certainly won't be!

---

13   Bolt, *Jesus' Defeat of Death*, 74–89.

3.1.2 From Bed to Service

Alerted to her problem, without a word Jesus 'raised' the woman (v. 31a): 'and going to her, he raised her, after seizing her hand' (καὶ προσελθὼν ἤγειρεν αὐτὴν κρατήσας τῆς χειρός). The consequences of his action are narrated just as starkly, conveying the sense that it was achieved with simplicity and ease (v. 31b): καὶ ἀφῆκεν αὐτὴν ὁ πυρετός. As confirmation that the cure was instantaneous and complete, the story ends with the woman, who had begun on her bed (v. 30a), serving them (v. 31b, καὶ διηκόνει αὐτοῖς).

3.1.3 The Woman and the Implied Reader

How does this suppliant connect with the implied reader? A common problem in Gospels interpretation would be to 1) Assume that the Gospels are primarily about us (the readers) and then 2) immediately identify ourselves with the disciples. In search of nurture for their spiritual life, Christian readers across the centuries have tended to read the Gospels in a 'moralistic' way; that is, where we search for models we can 'identify' with, and often the model they find is Jesus, and/or the disciples. J. F. Williams provides an example of this common error when, instead of explaining the main point of the story in terms of the encounter between Jesus and the woman, he somewhat surprisingly states that its purpose is 'to reveal the trust of Jesus' four followers'.[14] But this kind of moralistic reading actually misses the way the Gospels work on the reader, and so destroys the reading experience proper to Mark's narrative. Although the disciples play an important role in Mark's communicative dynamics, they are not there simply to provide a model to imitate. Even more importantly, it must be said that the Gospel of Mark *never* encourages its readers to imitate Jesus. Mark does not call his readers to *imitate* Jesus, but to *see* what he said and did. He never calls upon his readers to *be like* Jesus, but to *like* Jesus, so that we can understand what Jesus has done *for* us and be drawn towards putting faith in him.

This scene provides a good example of how Mark's narrative works, and it shows that it does *not* intend readers to identify with the disciples. Although the four men provide continuity with the preceding scenes, they function here merely as the means by which Jesus is brought to this needy woman. The readers enter the scene with the group from the synagogue (v. 29), but are then provided with a narrative comment that directs their attention to the woman on her bed (v. 30a). Because it is Mark who informs the reader of the woman's situation prior to then telling the reader that the disciples told Jesus about her, the readers are not closely aligned with the disciples, but they are observers of them, not even hearing their actual words. The readers do not see things through their eyes.

This distance between readers and characters more closely aligns the readers with the Implied Author (the author who is sensed by the reader during the experience of reading the text) through the supply of privileged information. By making the Implied Readers (the reader the text aims to persuade—again, sensed during the reading of the text) privy to the woman's condition, the Implied Author has focalised the scene for them through the fevered woman. By knowing the secret of the fevered woman on her bed, the Implied Readers have been led to view the action from her perspective.

Having provided the proper perspective from which to view the scene, the distance between the Implied Reader and the main characters is quickly closed. The four disciples reveal they know about the woman; they tell Jesus of her situation (v. 30b), and the close relationship between the readers and Jesus is restored. The readers then travel with him to the bedside to observe what

---

14 Williams, *Other Followers of Jesus*, 94; cf. p.182 n.1.

happens (v. 31). The lack of mention of the four creates the sense that it is only the readers and Jesus who now stand at the bedside of the woman, encouraging an intimacy between these three parties. The finite verb which supplies his action does not focus upon her healing *per se* (contrast, e.g., θεραπεύω, cf. 1:34; 3:2,10; 6:5,13; ἰάομαι, cf. 5:29), but on the fact that 'he raised' (ἔγειρεν) her.

Thus, the focus of the scene is not upon the four disciples, but upon the encounter between Mark's main character and a woman with a fever. Viewing the scene from the woman's perspective, the reader learns that, despite her fever-stricken condition, Jesus raised her.

3.2 Reader to Text

As the first healing miracle in Mark, the raising of Simon's mother-in-law has a position of some significance. However, of all the miracles, this one is probably one of the least impressive for modern readers who know the benefits of antibiotics and paracetamol! In the interests of understanding the impact of this story upon Mark's early readers, it is therefore necessary to attempt to recover the ancient perspective on fever and so on its cure. From this perspective, Jesus' cure of Simon's mother-in-law is no minor matter; instead, it would be regarded as Jesus casting back the shadow of death itself.[15]

For the people of the First Century, fever was not a symptom, it was a disease. It was extremely common, and greatly feared. Without the benefit of post-WWII medicine, fever was very severe and was a known killer. If a fever came into your family home, you had seven days to know if you would live or die. Fever was such a painful malady, that magical curses regularly called upon the underworld gods to inflict fever on enemies. Because fever was a killer, occasionally these curses called for a fever that would kill the enemy. Because magic used the powers of the dead, these curses were a way of using the powers of the dead, to inflict deadly suffering upon the living. So when a fever came into your house, it was a cause of great fear, and this fear was the fear of death itself.

The ancient case studies also show that the doctors looked for signs that indicated how severe the fever was, which then indicated the prognosis for the afflicted person. One of the signs that receives regular comment is here in Mark's account. If a fever has already forced a person to lie upon their bed (as in v. 30), then this is a very severe fever and the future does not look good.

So with this social background, the first-century person hearing Mark's account of Jesus' first healing would be alarmed by the condition which Simon's mother-in-law is suffering. Not only is fever the biggest killer in the ancient world, but this poor woman has been cast upon her bed by fever, which means that her days are numbered.

3.3 Two Worlds Changed by Jesus

What is the effect of bringing the world of the text and the world of the reader together?

The early readers of Mark would realise that Simon's mother-in-law was at death's door. As a woman she was automatically in a high-risk category for illnesses the physicians found difficult, and, by the time the readers hear of her, she had already succumbed to her bed with fever (v. 30a, κατέκειτο πυρέσσουσα), which raises the prognostic question, will she ever arise again? In the Capernaum synagogue (1:21–28), Jesus had already demonstrated his ability to deal with the spirits of death, who in this magic-ridden world may well be behind any case of fever, and so to call him now makes complete sense. Jesus managed to so deal with her fever that she began to serve them; she was no longer in bed, under the shadow of death, but she had been thrust back into ordinary

---

15   This is the argument mounted in my *Jesus' Defeat of Death*, which provides copious ancient sources.

life. The way that Mark described the action he took seems peculiarly appropriate in this setting: 'he raised her'. For the early reader would recognise that here was a woman who had been brought back from the brink of death.

Mark had already presented Jesus as one who could deal with the spirits of the dead (1:21–28). In Mark's first healing miracle, Jesus comes face to face with a condition which, in a number of ways, the early readers would associate with death. The story makes its impact, by enabling the reader to view Jesus' action from the woman's perspective, for it draws them sympathetically towards her. They knew about fever, and they knew that a fever brought the shadow of death. Mark's account shows Jesus as someone powerful enough and compassionate enough to raise a person up; to bring them out from under the shadow of death, and cause them to live again. And since the reader has been sympathetically engaged with the woman, seeing the story through her eyes, the story also offers a promise to the reader that Jesus might also bring them out from under the shadow of death, if only they trust him. And this promise then provokes them to read further into the Gospel, to see how this might come about; how Jesus might change *their* world.

4. A Cross-Shaped Message

As they read on, it becomes clear that Mark's message is all about the cross.[16] The cross is the clear climax of the narrative, and it is the point where all the threads of the narrative come together as the Gentile centurion recognises Jesus for who he truly is: 'surely, this man was the Son of God' (15:39). The fact that Jesus is recognised as the Son of God, at the very moment he was crucified, demonstrates the point of Mark's narrative. Jesus, the Son of God, was crucified for sinners. This is the climax and point of Mark's message.

But even before it reaches the cross, Mark's narrative carefully prepares for the moment that Jesus will die, and carefully explains his death as part of God's plan, so that when it comes, the reader already knows why it happened. In three passion predictions, Jesus declares that his death is an absolute necessity in bringing God's plans for the world to their proper conclusion (8:31; 9:31; 10:33). When Jesus takes some of his disciples up on the Mount of Transfiguration, he reveals the nature of this necessity. His death is the final great event that must occur before the kingdom of God can come (9:9–13). Later on, the bickering between his disciples about which of them was the greatest became the occasion for him to reveal the final, climactic piece of the puzzle. It is impossible for anyone to be saved and to enter eternal life in the coming kingdom unless God makes it possible (10:27). And he has made it possible through sending his Son into this world, who would give his life as a ransom for many (10:45). That is why he must die: so that his life can be given in exchange, so that we might be forgiven and receive the gift of eternal life.

So when Mark 15 at last recounts the events of the crucifixion, this is the climax and maximal point of engagement between Mark's text and Mark's reader. But even here we are not simply being given information about Jesus, but we are also being tangled up those events for ourselves. Mark not only *informs* his readers that Jesus died 'as a ransom for many' (10:45), but his story also *transforms* the reader to actually feel that Jesus died as *their ransom*.[17] As the narrative moves towards the cross, it opens up an increasing distance between Jesus and the reader. Although the reader wants to be with Jesus, they feel that they are pushed away. Just like he tells his disciples,

---

16   See Bolt, *The Cross from a Distance*.
17   See Bolt, 'Feeling the Cross'.

the readers also cannot go through what he has to go through. One man must die for the many. And the crucifixion scene shows this with great poignancy. The reader is forced to gaze upon the cross, not participate in it. And there, as they gaze upon the cross, the theological point of Mark's narrative comes home: through the death of the Son of God for us, on our behalf, we can now receive forgiveness and securely enter the coming kingdom.

Following this moment of great climax, on the third day, the grave is found to be empty and the angel informs the women: 'he is not here. He is risen' (16:6). At that point the world changed forever. And because the world had changed forever, it was now the time for the world to hear the good news of the victory of Jesus Christ. Now that Jesus had risen, it was time for the proclamation of the gospel. The women were told to tell his disciples, so that they can get going.

But they were silent, because they were afraid (16:8).

And, says Mark, by ending his account on such a strange note,[18] what are you going to do, dear reader? You can see that they should have said something (cf. 9:9). But you can understand why they didn't. Tell me, you also know that Jesus has risen from the dead. You know that this is where the gospel of Jesus Christ the Son of God began (1:1). You know that Jesus once changed the world forever and the kingdom of God is so very near (1:15). So, next time you are afraid in this intimidating and fearful world, what are you going to do? Will you be silent? Or will you speak? For as the gospel of Jesus Christ, the Son of God, continues to be spoken, that is how the world will continue to be changed.

Peter G. Bolt
Australian University College of Divinity

---

[18] Following Boomershine and Bartholomew, 'Narrative Technique'.

Bibliography

Bolt, Peter G. *The Narrative Integrity of Mark 13:24–27* (ACT Monograph Series; Eugene, OR: Wipf & Stock, 2021). MTh thesis, completed in 1991, but published in 2021.

Bolt, Peter G. *The Cross from a Distance. Atonement in Mark's Gospel* (NSBT 18; Leicester: IVP, 2004).

Bolt, Peter G. *Jesus' Defeat of Death. Persuading Mark's Early Readers* (SNTSMS 125; Cambridge: Cambridge University Press, 2003 [Paperback: 2008]).

Bolt, Peter G. 'Feeling the Cross: Mark's Message of Atonement', *RTR* 60.1 (2001), 1–17.

Bolt, Peter G. '"With a View to the Forgiveness of Sins": Jesus and Forgiveness in Mark's Gospel', *RTR* 57.2 (1998), 53–69.

Bolt, Peter G. 'Mark 13: An Apocalyptic Precursor to the Passion Narrative', *RTR* 54.1 (1995), 10–32.

Bolt, Peter G. 'What is the Gospel for Today's Church?', in B. G. Webb (ed.), *Explorations 7: Exploring the Missionary Church* (Homebush West, NSW: Lancer, 1993), 27–61.

Bolt, Peter G. 'The Spirit in the Synoptic Gospels: The Equipment of the Servant', in B. G. Webb (ed.), *Explorations 5: Spirit of the Living God (Part 1)*, (Homebush West, NSW: Lancer, 1991), 45–75.

Bolt, Peter G. 'Following Jesus and Fishing for People. Evangelistic Mission in the Third Millennium', in R. J. Gibson (ed.), *Ripe for Harvest. Christian Mission in the New Testament and in our World* (Explorations 12; Carlisle & Adelaide: Paternoster & Open Book, 1998), 1–35.

Boomershine, Thomas E., and Gilbert L. Bartholomew 'The Narrative Technique of Mark 16:8', *JBL* 100.2 (1981), 213–23. Now republished in Thomas E. Boomershine, *First-Century Gospel Storytellers and Audiences. The Gospels as Performance Literature* (Biblical Performance Criticism, 17; Eugene, OR: Cascade, 2022), 71–82.

Rhoads, David, and Donald Michie *Mark as Story. An Introduction to the Narrative of a Gospel* (Philadelphia, PA: Fortress, 1982). Now updated as David Rhoads, Joanna Dewey, and Donald Michie *Mark as Story. An Introduction to the Narrative of a Gospel.* (3rd edn.; Minneapolis, MN: Fortress, 2012).

Williams, Joel F. *Other Followers of Jesus: Minor Characters as Major Figures in Mark's Gospel* (JSNTSup 102; Sheffield: JSOT Press, 1994).

Is Mary blessed?
Reconsidering Luke 11:27–28 and Mary's embodied discipleship

ALI ROBINSON

Abstract

Noting the controversial place that Mary, the mother of Jesus, has held throughout church history, this paper joins the growing body of scholarship that seeks to lift her from doctrinal battles. This study challenges the traditional reading of Luke 11:27–28 where a woman in the crowd raises her voice and says to Jesus, "Blessed is the womb that bore you and the breasts that nursed you!" To which Jesus replies, "Blessed rather (μενοῦν) are those who hear the word of God and obey it!" Since the Reformation, these verses have been predominantly interpreted as negative discourse, with Jesus' words functioning as a corrective or rebuke of the woman in the crowd. In turn, this verse is often seen as Jesus scorning the woman and reducing the maternal significance of Mary's role. However, using a linguistic, contextual, and theological argument, this paper seeks to challenge the dominant position, demonstrating, first, that Jesus is not correcting the woman from the crowd, and second, that Jesus affirms both his mother and the woman in the crowd (Luke 11:28). It will be suggested that in these verses we hear echoes of Luke's unique portrait of Mary as blessed precisely because of her physical and bodily participation in the gospel.

Key words: Mary; Embodied discipleship; Blessedness; Luke–Acts; μενοῦν or μὲν οὖν

1. Introduction

For centuries, Mary, the mother of Jesus, has occupied a contested space within Christian theology. Many Protestant traditions have limited their focus on Mary to the nativity narratives, approaching her cautiously to avoid crossing into what might be seen as needless devotion. As Beverley Gaventa helpfully states, "So fearful have we been of what seems to us excessive attention to Mary in Roman Catholic and Orthodox traditions that Mary is virtually absent among us".[1] Consequently, in certain traditions, Mary has been a marginal figure in New Testament scholarship. However, in recent years, a growing number of Protestant theologians and biblical scholars have called for a renewed engagement with the biblical witness of Mary.[2] This essay contributes to that effort

---

1   Gaventa and Rigby, *Blessed One*, 1.
2   Examples include Braaten and Jenson, *Mary Mother of God*; Kateusz, *Mary and Early Christian Women*; Gaventa, *Mary*; Bauckham, *Gospel Women*; Ralston, 'The Virgin Mary', 187–200. For an ecumenical discussion on Mary, see Brown, Donfried, Fitzmyer, and Reumann, *Mary in the New Testament*.

by re-examining a passage in the Gospel of Luke (Luke 11:27–28) that is frequently interpreted as minimising Mary's role and significance in the life of Jesus. In contrast, it will argue that the passage in question *affirms* Mary's distinctive and pivotal role within the Gospel narrative.

1.1. The Central Passage: Luke 11:27–28

In Luke 11:14–26, Jesus is teaching a crowd about his authority to cast out demons. Amid this teaching, an unnamed woman from the crowd raises her voice and declares, "Blessed is the womb that bore you and the breasts that nursed you!" (Luke 11:27)—to which Jesus makes the now famous reply (as rendered in most English Bibles), "Blessed rather are those who hear the word of God and obey it!" (Luke 11:28).[3] It has been argued by many scholars that Jesus in his reply is refuting this woman's comment with the use of the word "rather", either because the woman's words are mere flattery, because her statement is inadequate, or simply because it is inaccurate.[4] An inference, then, would be that Jesus' mother (the one whose womb bore him and whose breasts nursed him) does not have special status and is not to be considered especially noteworthy due to her maternal connection to Jesus.[5] Instead, the blessed one is the *theoretical* believer who hears and obeys God's word. And thus, Jesus rejects this woman's public assertion.

This paper will challenge the traditional interpretation of Luke 11:27–28, arguing that: (1) linguistically, this passage can be understood as an affirmation of Mary's role rather than a dismissal; (2) contextually, a positive reading of this passage fits with how Mary is portrayed throughout Luke's Gospel; (3) theologically, a positive reading highlights the importance of Mary's physical and spiritual participation in God's plan.

2. A Linguistic Argument for a Positive Reading of Luke 11:27–28

As mentioned, English Bibles predominantly employ negative language and phrasing to represent the words found in Luke 11:27–28 with Jesus' response being viewed as a corrective: "Blessed *rather* are those who hear the word of God and obey it!" The term on which these translations rest is the Greek particle μενοῦν, often taken to mean "rather" or "nay". This understanding first arose in Luther's 1522 commentary on the New Testament, where he asserted that Jesus rejected the woman's words in Luke 11:27 in the following verse (v.28) because they were nothing but "womanish shameful thoughts".[6] Luther's interpretation was a direct response to Erasmus' translation, penned a decade prior, which took Luke 11:28 (αὐτὸς δὲ εἶπεν μενοῦν μακάριοι) positively, "and he said, indeed blessed". Erasmus viewed the woman in the crowd as a symbol of the church rising against the slanderous voices of the crowd and marvelling at Jesus' wise and powerful words.[7] For Erasmus, Jesus' reply is not a rejection of this woman's words but an affirmation of them. This reading echoes that of Margery Kempe, a fifteenth-century English mystic who viewed this as a story about

---

3   For example, NRSV ("Blessed rather", NET ("Blessed rather"), NASB ("On the contrary"), ESV ("Blessed rather", and NIV ("Blessed rather"). For a helpful treatment of this, see MacCulloch, *The Later Reformation in England*, 4–5.
4   These various positions will be discussed in §2.1.
5   Pitre notes that many Christians are quick to assert the "ordinariness of Mary" despite the respect and reverence she received among ancient believers. See Pitre, *Jesus and the Jewish Roots of Mary*, 33.
6   Kreitzer, Manetsch, and George, *Luke*, 8272. See also Luther, *D. Martin Luthers Werke*, 281.
7   Erasmus, *Collected Works of Erasmus*, 15. Erasmus states, "Jesus did not reject her declaration but perfected it, in saying, [Yes] '*Truly* blessed are those who hear the word of God and keep'". Erasmus, *Collected Works of Erasmus*, 16, 48.

a woman who is praised by Jesus for recognising his healing.[8] Interestingly, Tyndale, working from both Erasmus' translation and an acquired copy of Luther's German translation of the New Testament (prior to its publication), stayed in line with the positive reading of this verse, "But he sayde: Ye happy are they that heare the worde of God and kepe it".[9] However, despite these early positive translations, the negative reading became dominant and then solidified in the Sixteenth Century when Calvin stressed in his commentary that while it cannot be denied that "God conferred the highest honour on Mary, by choosing and appointing her to be the mother of his Son [...] Christ's reply is so far from assenting to this female voice, that it contains an indirect reproof. *Nay, rather*".[10]

Most major modern translations of Luke 11:27–28 are still coloured by this hermeneutical lens, and many commentators hold similar positions. For instance, Marshall comments that the saying by this woman "has little positive importance in the present context (although Catholic scholars assess it more positively)".[11] Morris claims the particle "rather" points to a deeper and more profound truth, as it is "not a physical relationship to Jesus that is supremely important, but hearing and keeping the word of God".[12] Carroll supports a similar line of thinking, commenting, "Enthusiastic acclamation by an admirer receives gentle rebuke, for what matters, what conveys real blessing, is the reordered life made possible by Jesus' benefaction which requires enduring commitment".[13] In a slightly different argument, Parsons suggests that Jesus' response is an attempt to dispel cultural traditions of "flattery often bestowed on the women who bore great men (cf. Petronius, *Sat.* 94.1), so as not to be seduced by false praise".[14] While some scholars, such as John Nolland, do not accept that Jesus *rejects* the woman's words in Luke 11:27, they still hold the view that the particle functions either as a corrective or a modification of the previous statement.[15] Even Luke Timothy Johnson, a scholar in the Catholic tradition, concludes that Jesus redirects the woman's statement toward obedience, arguing that the woman's admiration is insufficient; thus Jesus seeks to direct our attention to those who hear and keep God's word instead.[16] This suggests that exegetical stances on this passage cut across confessional boundaries.[17]

---

8 See Kempe, *The Book of Margery Kempe*, 93. Interestingly, Margery Kempe used this passage in her argument to the archbishop to support her efforts to preach the good news.
9 For a survey of these translations, see Partridge, *English Biblical Translation*, 38–39.
10 Calvin, *Commentarii in harmoniam Evangelicorum*, 348. While Calvin recognises that Mary received the favour of God, he remained hostile to those who would elevate her beyond what he deemed to be acceptable, writing, "The Papists discover amazing stupidity by singing, in honour of Mary, those very words by which their superstition is expressly condemned, and who, in giving thanks, detach the woman's saying, and leave out the correction. But it was proper that such a universal stupefaction should come upon those who intentionally profane, at their pleasure, the sacred word of God". See Calvin, *Commentary on a Harmony of the Evangelists*, "Luke XI. 2".
11 Marshall, *The Gospel of Luke*, 481.
12 See Morris, *Luke*, 218. Even as far back as Plummer's 1896 critical commentary on Luke, we have this same assertion that "Jesus does not deny the woman's statement, but He points out how inadequate it is. She has missed the main point, to be the Mother of Jesus implies no more than a share in His humanity. To hear and keep the word of God implies communion with what is Divine". Plummer, *A Critical and Exegetical Commentary on the Gospel According to Saint Luke*, 348.
13 Carroll, *Luke*, 256.
14 See Parsons, *Luke*, 192. Here Parsons notes that "praising an offspring by extolling the parents and caregivers were common in the ancient world" (cf. Prov. 23:24–25). I concur with Parson's observation here, but do not see this as permission to read this verse in a negative light. This data could also support the view that the woman in the crowd is following a culturally appropriate practise which Jesus affirms. This will be discussed further in §3.2.
15 Nolland, *Luke 9:21–18:34*, 648–649. See also Thrall, *Greek Particles in the New Testament*, 34–35.
16 Johnson, *The Gospel of Luke*, 186.
17 Alternatively, Anthony Maas interprets these words as Jesus praising his mother "in a most emphatic way; for she excelled the rest of men in holiness not less than in dignity". See Maas, "The Blessed Virgin Mary". This sits in line with the Second Vatican Council: "In the course of her Son's preaching she [Mary] received the words whereby in extolling a kingdom beyond the calculations and bonds of flesh and blood, He declared blessed those who heard and kept the word of God, as she was faithfully doing". Vatican Council II, *Lumen Gentium*, 21 November 1964, sec. 58 lines 291–292.

There are scholars, of course, who recognise the flexibility of the particle. Fitzmyer comments that μενοῦν may be taken negatively or affirmatively depending on context, noting that in Luke 11:28 the latter is plausible given Luke's broader portrayal of Mary.[18] Likewise, Bock acknowledges that the particle allows for an inclusive affirmation in this setting.[19] Stein also notes the flexibility of this particle, offering an expanded translation: "What you have said is true as far as it goes. But Mary's blessedness does not consist simply in her relationship with me, but in the fact that she heard the word of God and kept it, which is where true blessedness lies".[20] On this Thompson agrees, noting that the particle is not necessarily a correction but might merely be used to emphasise Jesus' point that "a positive response to him must be accompanied with genuine adherence to his word".[21] This aligns with the view of Alicia D. Myers, who writes:

> [F]or Luke, Mary is indeed blessed, but not because she fulfilled her obligation as a woman to become a mother. Instead, she is rightly called blessed because of her willingness to hear and obey the "word" (*logos*) spoken to her—and thus implanted within her—as a part of God's plan rather than the cultural narrative of a maternal telos for all women.[22]

This paper will build on the work of Fitzmyer, Bock, Stein, Thompson, and Myers, arguing for a positive reading of Jesus' words. To demonstrate the validity of this positive reading, first the Greek particle, μενοῦν,[23] traditionally taken to mean "rather" or "nay", needs to be reconsidered. As mentioned, this word does not have an exclusively negative meaning. Importantly, the particle can also be used in an *affirmative* sense to agree with or emphasise a previous statement (that is, to mean "Yes", "Indeed", or "Yes and").[24] And there are linguistic grounds for this claim.

i) Though the particle μενοῦν as a single word does not appear anywhere else in the New Testament, it does appear as two words μὲν οὖν. Given that Greek manuscripts had no spaces between words, it is not clear if μενοῦν was intended to be read as one compound word or two separate words. Thus, it is reasonable to look at instances of μὲν οὖν in this study.

In other parts of Luke–Acts, μὲν οὖν is used to denote a continuation of thought, similar to the phrase "so then" (e.g. Luke 3:18, "so then [μὲν οὖν] with many other exhortations he proclaimed the good news" and Acts 1:6, "so then [μὲν οὖν] they welcomed his message").[25] There are also examples where μὲν οὖν is used in an emphatic sense to mean "indeed" (see Acts 5:41; 8:4,25; 9:31; 11:19; 14:3; 15:3; 16:5; 17:12; 23:18). Although these instances appear in the context of narrative, as opposed to dialogue, they nonetheless demonstrate the flexibility of this term.

ii) μενοῦν has connections to the term μενοῦνγε, which appears in Romans 9:20 and 10:18 and can be taken to mean either "indeed" or "rather", and in Philippians 3:8, where it is taken to mean

---

18   Fitzmyer, *The Gospel According to Luke X–XXIV*, 927–29.
19   Bock, *Luke 9:51–24:53*, 1095. Bock notes, "The connective μενοῦν (menoun) has three possible senses (Fitzmyer 1985: 928): (1) an adversative meaning 'on the contrary', thus rejecting the previous remark (Manson 1949: 88; Marshall 1978: 482); (2) an affirmation meaning 'indeed' (as in Phil. 3:8); or (3) a correction meaning 'yes, but rather' (Luce 1933: 216; Arndt 1956: 302; Plummer 1896: 306; Danker 1988: 235; Schneider 1977a: 269). The first meaning is not likely, since Luke has already affirmed such a blessing (Luke 1:42, 48) and elsewhere uses οὐχί, λέγω ὑμῖν (ouchi, legō hymin, no, I say to you) to express rejection of an idea (12:51; 13:3, 5; Fitzmyer 1985: 928). The sense is not complete affirmation either. Rather, the woman's remark is correct, but not exhaustive". Bock, *Luke 9:51–24:53*, 1094–95. See Bovon, *Luke 2*, 131–32.
20   Stein, *Luke*, 333.
21   Thompson, *Luke*, 190.
22   Myers, *Blessed among Women?*, 66.
23   BDAG, s.v., μενοῦν, 630. See also BDF §450. μὲν οὖν denotes continuation (BI-D. §451).
24   See Moule, *An Idiom Book of New Testament Greek*, 163–4; Nolland, *Luke*, 648–649.
25   See also Acts 1:6; 5:41; 8:25; 9:31; 11:19; 13:4; 14:3; 15:3,30; 16:5; 17:12; 19:32; 23:18,22,31; 25:4; 26:4,9. It should be noted that these examples are of μὲν οὖν being used in a narrative context as opposed to dialogue.

"indeed" or "more than that". Thus, just as μεν and οὖν independently can be progressive, adversative, affirmative, or emphatic, the combination μενοῦνγε, or μενοῦν in the case of Luke 11:28, presents the same "considerable diversity of usage".[26] It means that the particle does not have one single way of being translated.

iii) Additionally, when surveying texts outside the New Testament and LXX, Denniston's extensive study of Greek particles has developed a theory based on the emerging patterns found in contemporaneous texts of the New Testament. In narrowing down the most reliable options, Denniston suggests that when μενοῦν (or μεν οὖν) is used: (1) in *dialogue,* and (2) in *response to a non-question (i.e. a statement)*, the particle most often carries the meaning *"certainly"* or *"indeed"*, stating that, in these instances, the term is an *affirmation* and not a corrective (See Plato, *Theaet.* 158d, 159e, 189e; Plato, *Phaedrus,* 262a).[27] (3) If the replying speaker *repeats a word used by the first speaker,* μενοῦν can carry an emphatic sense, making the positive response slightly stronger (Plat. *Prot.* 309c–309d).[28]

Building on this, similar examples of the emphatic usage can be found in the New Testament. In Acts 25:11 Paul says, "if indeed I do wrong" (εἰ μὲν οὖν ἀδικῶ), and in Acts 26:4, "indeed my manner of life is from youth" (τὴν μὲν οὖν βίωσίν μου τὴν ἐκ νεότητος). (See also Acts 17:30; 19:38; 26:9).

Therefore, using Denniston's observations and the textual evidence, a case can be made linguistically that μενοῦν in Luke 11:28 should be read in the affirmative. First, there is *dialogue* between Jesus and the woman. Second, the first speaker [the woman] makes a statement *[non-question]*. Third, the second speaker [Jesus] *repeats a key word from the first speaker's phrase,* namely, the term "blessed". Therefore, based on the contemporaneous sources and the flexibility of this particle, it is at least possible that the particle μενοῦν in Luke 11:28 *affirms* the previous statement or offers something slightly stronger in the response (i.e. "yes and" or "indeed"). In this case, then, Luke 11:28 should be read as Jesus saying to the woman in the crowd, "*Yes indeed,* blessed are the ones who hear and obey the word of God" [with Mary being one of those who hear and obey, not apart from her maternal role but through it].

3. A Contextual Argument for a Positive Reading of Luke 11:27–28

This section seeks to demonstrate that there are contextual grounds for reading Luke 11:27–28 as a positive exchange. This will be demonstrated by examining how Luke categorises blessedness, assessing how Luke's Gospel portrays Mary, and considering the immediate context of Luke 11.

3.1. Blessedness According to Luke's Gospel

Before looking at Luke's portrayal of Mary, we must first ask who Luke deems as blessed. In Luke's Gospel, much like other parts of the New Testament, a person is blessed (μακάριος)[29] because they share in the salvation of the kingdom of God (see Luke 1:48, 11:27). Blessed are those who "see" and

---

26 For an extensive study of the use of μὲν οὖν see Denniston, *The Greek Particles,* 470–481.
27 Denniston, *The Greek Particles,* 476.
28 Denniston, *The Greek Particles,* 476–477.
29 BDAG, s.v. μακάριος, 611. According to Josephus, to say someone is blessed is to say they are the "privileged recipient of divine favour" (Jos., *Ant.* 9, 264; cf. Rom. 4:6; Isa. 30:18).

"hear" what the kings and prophets have longed to see (Luke 10:23–24; cf. Luke 4:21) and blessed are those who "keep" or "put into practice" the words of God (Luke 6:47; 11:28).[30] Luke says blessed are the steadfast (Luke 12:37), the ones devoted to God (Luke 12:43),[31] and those who fulfil God's moral requirements (Luke 14:14). Blessed are the poor, hungry, weeping, and hated (Luke 6:20–22). Jesus utters twelve *makarisms* (Luke 6:20–23; 7:23; 10:23; 12:37,38,43; 14:14,15; 23:29; see also Acts 20:35) in Luke–Acts. These are all viewed as statements of affirmation. Likewise, exclamations of blessedness by other characters throughout the Gospel are also seen as positive affirmations (See Luke 1:42,45,48). Thus, not only is blessedness exclusively spoken of in favourable terms in Luke's writings, but as will be seen in the next section, Mary, the mother of Jesus, is also portrayed as one who is blessed.[32]

3.2. The Blessedness of Mary in Luke

Several times throughout Luke's Gospel, Mary is either directly called blessed or is seen to display the aspects of blessedness which Luke describes (see §3.1).[33] In Luke 1:27–28, the angel Gabriel exclaims: "Greetings, favoured one! The Lord is with you" (χαῖρε, κεχαριτωμένη, ὁ κύριος μετὰ σοῦ, Luke 1:28).[34] "O graced one", "favoured one", or "the one blessed by God",[35] is the way in which Mary is addressed by God's messenger, and throughout Luke's opening chapter these sentiments are affirmed several times. For example, Mary is said to have "found favour with God" (Luke 1:30) and she is specifically called "blessed" by her cousin Elizabeth (Luke 1:42). Joel Green, noting the connection between Luke 1:42 and Luke 11:27, comments that while it is grammatically possible to read Jesus' words in Luke 11:28 as a contradiction of the woman's pronouncement in Luke 11:27, "the fact that Elizabeth had spoken similar words, and done so under the inspiration of the Holy Spirit (1:41–42), makes this option doubtful".[36] Likewise, according to Schreiner, within the context of Luke's Gospel, being filled with the Holy Spirit is usually related to prophetic activity. Therefore, Elizabeth is bringing forth prophetic speech, which is later echoed by the woman in Luke 11:27.[37] Moreover, Mary herself says that her soul magnifies God because "he has looked with favour on the lowliness of his servant",[38] and that now "all generations" will bless her

---

30 The term "keeping" comes from φυλάσσω (cf. Deut. 4:6; 28:13, 15 LXX), traditionally meaning "watch", "guard", or "protect" (BDAG, s.v. φυλάσσω, 1068) but can also express the idea of keeping a law or command (see Exod. 31:16; Rom. 2:26; John 12:47). Keeping God's word in Luke 11:28 is most likely linked to obeying and keeping the commands of God.
31 In Wittman's study he explores the blessedness of God, examining how Jesus' disciples are blessed as God works through them, and as they abide in God's love. See Wittman, "The Logic of Divine Blessedness", 151.
32 Green, *The Gospel of Luke*, 461.
33 See Brown, Donfried, Fitzmyer, and Reumann, *Mary in the New Testament*, 125–135.
34 Spencer, *The Gospel of Luke and Acts of the Apostles*, 104. For a detailed study on the birth narrative see Coleridge, *The Birth of the Lukan Narrative*; Brown, *The Birth of the Messiah*.
35 Brown, *The Birth of the Messiah*, 288, 325–326.
36 Green, "Blessed Is She Who Believed", 12. Interestingly, Green still sees the particle as a corrective, writing "the sense that best fits this narrative context is that the words of this woman are not altogether wrong but are in need of substantive modification". Here I part from Green. As I have argued, I do not see Jesus' words as a corrective but as an affirmation with the offering of additional information in support of Mary's blessedness.
37 See Schreiner, *Commentary on Luke*, "Luke 1:39–56", Kindle edition.
38 There are similarities here between Mary's song and that of Hannah. Mary proclaims that God "has looked on the lowliness of his servant" (Luke 1:48) and Hannah prays, "if you will look on the lowliness of your servant" (1 Sam. 1:11). These songs, as Bauckham suggests, highlight "God's gracious action for the singer herself" and through humility, those who are part of God's faithful community. See Bauckham, *Gospel Women*, 61. There are also connections between Mary's song and that of Moses (Exod. 15:1–18), Miriam (Exod. 15:21), Deborah and Barak (Judg. 6), Hannah (1 Sam. 2), David (2 Sam. 22), Hezekiah (Isa. 38:9–20), Judith (Jdt. 16), Tobit (Tob. 13), and Israel at the exodus (Isa. 12).

(Luke 1:49).[39] The lowliness spoken of here may not necessarily denote low social status,[40] but (as Bauckham suggests) indicates an *attitude* "of humility before God and trust in God", another mark of blessedness according to Luke.[41]

Not only is Mary's blessedness directly affirmed at multiple points,[42] but like so many of God's servants who hear the words "I am with you" at the commencement of a formidable and challenging ministry (e.g. Isaac in Gen. 26: 24; Jacob in Gen. 28:15; Moses in Exod. 3:12; Joshua in Josh. 1:5; Gideon in Judg. 6:16; and Jeremiah in Jer. 1:8), Mary responds with trust.[43] When receiving the news that she will bear a son, Mary responds, "Here am I, the servant of the Lord; let it be with me according to your word" (Luke 1:38). The title "servant of the Lord" also indicates this readiness to serve God, linking her to other great leaders who played an integral role in God's salvation story, such as Abraham (Ps. 105:42), Moses (Neh. 9:14), Joshua (Josh. 24:29), David (Ps. 89:3), and Daniel (Dan. 6:20), who are likewise identified as servants of God.[44] In her acceptance of the task ("you will conceive and give birth to a son"), Mary shows herself to be a model of faith and an example of obedient discipleship. Her "exemplary qualities" become evident as she ponders the incredibly demanding words spoken by the angel and yet responds in obedience and faith, calling herself a willing servant of the Lord.[45] This stands in sharp contrast to Zechariah's story, which is designed by Luke to be read in parallel to this account.[46] Prior to Mary's announcement, a priest from the order of Abijah (Luke 1:5) also receives a visit from Gabriel.[47] The angel meets Zechariah while he is offering incense in the sanctuary of the Lord (Luke 1:9).[48] Zechariah is "troubled" ($\tau\alpha\rho\acute{\alpha}\sigma\sigma\omega$), Mary is "deeply troubled" ($\delta\iota\alpha\tau\alpha\rho\acute{\alpha}\sigma\sigma\omega$) and both are told not to be afraid for God will give them a son. However, only Zechariah is told this in response to his prayers: "Your prayers have been heard. Your wife Elizabeth will bear a son" (Luke 1:13). Mary, by contrast, did not pray for this and therefore had no reason to expect the angel's visit or anticipate that this would be her calling. But still, when she hears the word of God, she responds with ready

---

39 Others who are called most blessed among women include Jael (Judg. 5:24; cf. *Bib. Ant.* 32.12) and Judith (Jdt. 13:19–20). On the Magnificat, Brown makes an interesting argument that Luke may have received this canticle from a group of Jewish Christians and that it, along with the other canticles, may have been originally written to praise the salvific action of God more generally. He writes, "In my hypothesis Luke took these general expressions of joy manifested by the Jewish Christian *Anawim* over the salvation accomplished in Jesus and applied them with a specificity that was not in their original purview". See Brown, *The Birth of the Messiah*, 353.
40 Especially given that Mary is a relative of Elizabeth (a woman of priestly descent, cf. Luke 1:5, 36) and that Joseph was of Davidic descent (Luke 1:27).
41 Bauckham, *Gospel Women*, 71.
42 Green, "The Social Status of Mary in Luke 1:5–2:52", 468.
43 Luke 1:28 may be calling to mind the prophecy of Zephaniah, "Sing aloud, O daughter Zion; shout, O Israel! Rejoice and exult with all your heart, O daughter Jerusalem [...] the Lord, is in your midst [...] Do not fear, O Zion; do not let your hands grow weak. The Lord, your God, is in your midst!" (Zeph. 3:14–17). As Sri suggests, the implication is that Mary is the one through whom the awaited salvation is brought. Sri, *Rethinking Mary in the New Testament*, 11. Bovon, however, rejects this connection, seeing it as a "far-fetched" claim made primarily by Catholic theologians. See Bovon, *Luke 1*, 50. Alternatively, Brown sees a connection between Luke 1:28 and Judges 6:12, stating that these two verses are closer in context and wording than the Zephaniah passage. Brown, *The Birth of the Messiah*, 324–325.
44 Bauckham, *Gospel Women*, 66.
45 See Ralston, "The Virgin Mary", 111.
46 Spencer, *The Gospel of Luke and Acts of the Apostles*, 101.
47 It is widely agreed by scholars that we are meant to read these stories together and in parallel. See Green, *The Gospel of Luke*, 82.
48 One can assume by his position that he was already held in high honour among his people, yet Zechariah does not receive the same honoured greeting that Mary does. Notably, he is not called "favoured" or "blessed".

acceptance: "Here, I am".[49] Zechariah, in stark contrast, even while serving the Lord in the sanctuary, questions the reliability of the angel's words and is rendered mute as a result (Luke 1:59–64).[50] When Mary journeys to Zechariah's house to share her news with Elizabeth, Zechariah remains mute while Mary is singing and prophesying.[51] Mary not only hears the news about her role in bringing in the kingdom of God, but she also believes it. This is why she is "blessed" (Luke 1:45–55).[52] It is emphasised in Luke's Gospel that Mary listens and acts on the word of God. This, according to Brittany E. Wilson, is "an essential aspect of discipleship in Luke. This dual response to the word [listening and acting on] is mentioned a total of three times, two of which have direct bearing on Mary".[53] Forbes and Harrower add that not only does Mary demonstrate great faith, but she is "the first person to link Israel's salvation history with God's actions in her own time".[54] Mary is, therefore, discussed by scholars as the "first believer" of the good news about Jesus.[55]

Mary, according to Ralston, is consistently portrayed in Luke's Gospel as "deliberate and thoughtful, a determined and persistent woman possessing deep spirituality tempered with a rich biblical understanding".[56] For instance, Mary is said to treasure (διατηρέω and συντηρέω) God's words and ponder them in her heart (Luke 2:19,51). The words used here for "treasure" (διατηρέω and συντηρέω) mean to watch closely, keep safe, preserve, or observe strictly.[57] "Treasuring" and "pondering" are symbols of Mary's growth and learning which go beyond the temple scene. She keeps the words and prophecies *of* Jesus and *about* Jesus in her heart.[58] While she may not have immediately understood all that she heard, she faithfully obeys the instructions of God and keeps these things in her mind in order to better understand them.[59] After Jesus' birth, Mary's devotion to God's word, laws, and commands "comes into sharper focus" when both she and Joseph do all things according to the law, including the required offerings and the presentation of Jesus for his circumcision (Luke 2:21–41).[60] This is in keeping with the larger image of Mary and Joseph as faithful and Torah-observant Jews (Luke 1:6,59; 2:21–27,36–38).[61] Helen Bond also notes that the offering of two small doves in the temple (Luke 2:24) may reflect Mary and Joseph's low economic status, which aligns with Luke's concern for the marginalised, drawing a further

---

49 In the context of ancient Judaism, both Mary and Elizabeth receive the blessing of a child. It is clear throughout the Hebrew Bible that children are viewed as a blessing from God (e.g. Ps. 127:3; Deut. 7:14; cf. Gen. 1:28). It is God who opens or closes a woman's womb (cf. Gen. 20:18). Myers notes that the pregnant Elizabeth ("filled with a holy Spirit" when seeing Mary) loudly shouts and "proclaims both the greatness of Mary's child and her own blessed status (1:41-45)". Myers, *Blessed among Women?*, 63–64.
50 Coleridge, *The Birth of the Lukan Narrative*, 70.
51 Spencer states: "In the absence of patriarchal priestly proclamation, the two spirit-filled women take the lead in sharing and declaring the good news". Spencer, *The Gospel of Luke and Acts of the Apostles*, 106. Mary hears and reflects on the divine word and responds positively, even proclaiming it in a prophetic fashion (Luke 1:26-38,46-55; 2:19,51). See also Green, *The Gospel of Luke*, 461; Witherington, *Women in the Ministry of Jesus*, 127.
52 McGrath adds that he sees an echo here of Jesus' own prayer in the Garden of Gethsemane. Where Jesus prays, "Your will be done", Mary utters, "Let it be unto me". McGrath, *What Jesus Learned from Women*, 33.
53 Wilson, "Pugnacious Precursors and the Bearer of Peace", 450.
54 Forbes and Harrower, *Raised from Obscurity*, 59.
55 See Fitzmyer, "Mary in Lukan Salvation History", 69. See also Brown, Donfried, Fitzmyer, and Reumann, *Mary in the New Testament*, 114-115.
56 Ralston, "The Virgin Mary", 109.
57 LSJ s.v., διατηρέω and συντηρέω. See also Webb, "Overcoming fear with Mary of Nazareth", 97.
58 Stein, *Luke*, 24, 110.
59 Bovon, *Luke 1*, 115. Compare also Dan. 4:28 LXX and Gen. 37:11 where a similar phrase is used to describe a person puzzled by what they have heard.
60 Ralston, "The Virgin Mary", 111.
61 Parsons, *Luke*, 58.

connection between those who are poor and those who are blessed (cf. Luke 6:20).[62]

Even though Mary's story is not front and centre throughout the remainder of Luke's Gospel,[63] we are assured of her continued faithfulness given that she is named explicitly by Luke among the first community of disciples at the ascension of Jesus (Acts 1:14). By being present among this community and specifically named as one of those "constantly devoting themselves to prayer" (Acts 1:14), Mary is seen to be a faithful and long-standing disciple.[64] As Brown notes, she not only appears "as a representative of the ideals of true discipleship" but she "endures till Pentecost to become a Christian and a member of the church".[65] The image, then, that Luke gives of Mary, the mother Jesus, is a woman who is favoured, called by God to a salvific role, faithful, humble, obedient, who treasures and keeps God's word in her heart, and, as Pablo Gadenz states, "sets an example for other disciples to follow on the way to beatitude: hear the word and act on it".[66] Within the context of Luke's Gospel, she is blessed.

There is, of course, a passage which can be used in opposition to this theory, namely Luke 8:19–21. It reads, "Then his mother and his brothers came to him, but they could not reach him because of the crowd. And he was told, 'Your mother and your brothers are standing outside, wanting to see you'. But he said to them, 'My mother and my brothers are those who hear the word of God and do it'". Mary Marshall helpfully unpacks this verse showing that Luke's account differs from that of Matthew (12:46–50) and Mark (3:31–35), with Luke notably "omitting elements that would evoke a negative understanding of the [Jesus'] family".[67] Luke's account omits the question, "Who are my mother and my brothers?" (Mark 3:33), along with the image of Jesus "looking at those who sat around him" and saying, "Here are my mother and my brothers" (Mark 3:33). Amy Peeler also challenges a negative reading of Luke 8:21, rejecting the view that this verse demonstrates Mary's lack of trust in her son, but rather suggests that Luke includes this story here to highlight that Mary's vocation is not limited to her biological role as mother but includes other forms of discipleship, too.[68] For Peeler, Luke's Jesus does not reject his earthly mother and brothers but expands his understanding of family by including those who are faithful to his word. To this, John Painter adds the observation that Luke reworks Mark 3:31–35, placing this story about his family directly after the Parable of the Sower, suggesting that his mother and brothers *are* the good soil (Luke 8:15).[69] Together these arguments demonstrate the way in which readers of Luke 8:19–21 often import the hostility witnessed in Mark 3:31–35 and have it colour Luke's relaying of the event.[70]

---

62 Bond and Taylor, *Women Remembered*, 124. The usual offering was a year-old lamb for a burnt offering and a young pigeon or a dove for a sin offering (Lev. 12:6), but Leviticus 12:8 allowed a woman after childbirth who could not afford a lamb to offer "two turtledoves or two young pigeons".

63 There is the inclusion of a Special Lucan account in Jesus' childhood when he is temporarily lost but later found by his parents in the temple (Luke 2:41–49). After this, Luke narrates that Jesus returns to Nazareth with his parents and "was obedient to them" (Luke 2:50), he increases "in wisdom and in years, and in divine and human favor" while "His mother treasured all these things in her heart" (Luke 2:50–52; cf. 2:19). See Green, *The Gospel of Luke*, 157.

64 Seim, *The Double Message*, 10–11.

65 Brown, *The Birth of the Messiah*, 499.

66 According to Gadenz, Mary is a model disciple. Referring to Luke 11:28, he writes, "Jesus replies to the woman with a beatitude that echoes Elizabeth's, specifying this more basic reason for blessedness: Blessed are those who hear the word of God and observe it. Indeed, Mary has a model response to God's word (1:38), and thus she is the *blessed* Virgin Mary". Gadenz, *The Gospel of Luke*, 228.

67 Marshall, "The Rise of James the Just in Luke–Acts", 96. These views build on the Markan priority theory. See Goodacre, *The Synoptic* Problem, 84–105.

68 Peeler, *Women and the Gender of God*, 194.

69 Painter, *Just James*, 41.

70 See also Maunder, *Mary*, 90–91. Maunder speaks here of both Luke 8:19–21 and Luke 11:27–28 noting that while it might initially appear as though these are instances of Jesus "distancing himself from his mother" the contexts suggest otherwise.

3.3. The Immediate Context of Luke 11

If we think about Luke's broader literary or narrative style, Luke tends to pair stories or characters together for emphasis, as we previously saw with Zechariah (1:5–25) and Mary (1:26–38). There are many other examples, including Simeon (2:25–35) and Anna (2:36–38); the searching shepherd (15:3–7) and the searching woman (15:8–10); male disciples who betray Jesus (22:54–62) and female disciples who remain faithful (23:49; 24:1–10).[71] With this literary and rhetorical preference in mind, if we examine the verses immediately surrounding Luke 11:27–28, it can be argued that there are two responses to Jesus' healing and subsequent teaching that are designed to be read side-by-side.

Prior to the verses in focus (Luke 11:27–28), Jesus casts out a demon and heals a mute man (Luke 11:14–26). Some in the crowd are stunned (Luke 11:14), others accused Jesus of casting out demons by the power of Beelzebul (Luke 11:15), and others test his power (Luke 11:16). Knowing this, Jesus uses the illustration of a divided kingdom to demonstrate that a kingdom cannot stand if it is turned against itself, professing, "whoever is not with me is against me" (Luke 11:23). After this teaching a woman from the masses raises her voice and—in contrast to the crowd who fail to recognise Jesus' authority (Luke 11:15)—*correctly* asserts Jesus' power. This insertion is unique to Luke's Gospel. While the Beelzebul teaching has parallels in the other Synoptic Gospels (cf. Mark 3:22–35 and Matt. 12:22–37), Luke's insertion of vv.27–28 is distinctive.[72] The unique addition of Luke 11:27–28 highlights Luke's particular interest in the theme of blessedness. This insertion also raises the question as to whether or not this is another example of Luke editing the Markan tradition in a more positive light, as was seen in Luke 8:19–21 (cf. Mark 3:31–35).

If in antiquity a mother is brought honour through the greatness of her sons,[73] then the woman's admiration ("Blessed is the one that bore you and nursed you", Luke 11:27), would have been viewed as a culturally accepted form of praise (Ovid, *Metam.* 4.320–24; Petronius, *Sat.* 94.1; *Inf. Gos. Thom.* 7.5–8; 17.3). As Wolter suggests, "The macarism with which a woman from the crowd reacts to Jesus applies to the mother of Jesus only on the surface of the text. It is actually Jesus to whom the praise refers".[74] The woman calls Jesus' mother blessed as a way of praising and affirming Jesus' power and authority. If blessedness is consistently spoken of in positive terms in Luke's Gospel, and this exclamation is a form of praise (Luke 11:27), then it, too, should be viewed in an affirmative sense. And if the responses from those in the crowd are to be read in parallel, the woman's response (Luke 11:27) stands in stark contrast to the crowd. The other characters in the crowd misunderstand Jesus entirely, accusing him of gaining his power from Beelzebul (Luke 11:15), but the woman recognises Jesus' authority and offers praise. Therefore, for Jesus to affirm the woman's declaration in Luke 11:28 is contextually plausible as this woman is aligning herself with Jesus, the one who has just proclaimed, "whoever is not with me is against me" (Luke 11:23).[75] Thus, the way Luke frames these verses makes it probable that Jesus' response in Luke 11: 28 should be read in the affirmative.

---

71 Other examples include Luke 1:46–55 and 1:68–79, Luke 8:41–42 and 8:43–46.

72 While this scene as depicted in Luke 11:27–28 does not appear in any of the other Synoptic Gospels it is echoed in the Gospel of Thomas (cf. *Gos. Thom.* 79). Scholars differ on their view of the relationship between these two sources. For instance, Gathercole argues that Thomas incorporates distinctive Lukan phraseology (Gathercole, *The Composition of the Gospel of* Thomas, 185–208) whereas Patterson makes the case that Thomas is not dependent on Luke but instead preserves sayings of Jesus that circulated independently in early Christian oral tradition. See Patterson, *The Gospel of Thomas and Christian Origins*, 100. While it is likely that an oral tradition preceded Luke's Gospel, my focus is on the literary presentation of this episode as found in Luke 11:27–28.

73 Bock, *Luke 9:51–24:53*, 1094.

74 Wolter, *The Gospel According to Luke*, 110. See also Kittel and Fredrich, s.v. μακάριος, 367–370.

75 For a discussion on Luke's inclusion of women in his narrative see, Embudo, "Women Vis-à-Vis Prophecy in Luke-Acts", 111; Karris, "Women and Discipleship in Luke", 1–20.

4. Theological Implications for Reading Luke 11:27–28 Positively

This brings us to the final part of this essay, where we will see the theological implications of a positive reading of Luke 11:27–28.

4.1. The Annunciation and the Embodied Discipleship of Mary

A significant aspect of Mary's life and mission is related to her biological role as the mother of Jesus.[76] For Mary to fulfil her call to bear "the Son of the Most High" (Luke 2:32) required her to give up her body as an instrument for God's intentions.[77] If we return to Luke 1:42, Elizabeth, filled with the Spirit, says that Mary is blessed among women, and blessed is the fruit of her *womb* (κοιλίας). Here we have the specific mention of the physical site of Jesus' conception: Mary's womb. It is the same part of her body that is called blessed by the woman in the crowd in Luke 11:27.[78] In fulfilling God's call (Luke 2:31–35), Mary allowed God to break into her physical body. In this case, her body is the very place in which her faithfulness and obedience to God are lived out. Without Mary's body, there is no obedience to her call and no place for the Son of God (Luke 2:35) to be conceived. Karen O'Donnell in *Broken Bodies* makes an apt observation that Jesus' birth[79] "cannot be separated from his mother, Mary […] it is dependent upon, and inseparable from, her".[80] This calling required Mary "to surrender her body as an act of faith".[81] Moreover, her calling required her to physically grow, bear, and nurse Jesus. It required her to give up her plans,[82] and endure the hardship of watching her son suffer, as Simeon foretold ("and a sword will pierce your own soul too", Luke 2:35b).[83]

There is no doubt in the minds of some feminist scholars that there is a significant element of trauma in Mary's bodily participation in God's salvation plan.[84] Though some scholars are firm

---

76 Elvey, *An Ecological Feminist Reading of the Gospel of Luke*, 121. See also Matthews-Green, *Mary as the Early Christians Knew Her*, 1; Gaventa, "Nothing Will Be Impossible with God", 23.

77 For a helpful discussion on Luke's narrative Christology and what it means for Jesus to be "Lord" in Luke's Gospel, see Rowe, *Early Narrative* Christology, 162, 197–207.

78 This is affirmed by Reid and Matthews who, in pointing to Elizabeth's words, emphasise that Mary is blessed not only for her obedience but because she physically bears Jesus. See Reid and Matthews, *Luke 1–9*, 56.

79 While later theology articulates this in terms of the "incarnation" and Mary as "Theotokos" it is important to note that Luke himself does not employ such categories. Instead, Luke presents Mary as a faithful servant whose embodied obedience enables God's salvific plan. For a discussion on the title "Theotokos" as used for Mary, see Kateusz, *Mary and Early Christian Women*, 113–120.

80 O'Donnell, *Broken Bodies*, 19.

81 Mulya, "Queering the Virgin/Whore Binary", 55.

82 Some suggest that Mary's question in Luke 1:34, "How can this be, since I do not know a man?" indicates that she took a vow to *never* "know a man"—one she had to forfeit in order to be obedient to the call of God. The theory is drawn from Num. 30:6–16 (cf. Mishnah, *Yom*. 8:1), suggesting that women took vows of sexual abstinence even in marriage, vows "denying" themselves. Documents from Qumran speak of similar vows taken by women in the home of their father or husband (11 Q Temple 53:16). See Pitre, *Jesus and the Jewish Roots of Mary*, 117. See also Sri, *Rethinking Mary in the New Testament*, 53–56; Brown, Donfried, Fitzmyer, and Reumann, *Mary in the New Testament*, 114–115. For an argument against this view see Shaker, "Sub Tuum Praesidium", 3–25.

83 Johnson, *The Gospel of Luke*, 61. It is recognised by most scholars that this is a difficult verse to understand. It may refer to the sorrow Mary will face when seeing her son crucified, but it could also refer to her own stumbling. See Stein, *Luke*, 24, 117. See also Chen, *Luke*, 40. Thinking of Mary watching her son's death is a sober reminder of what Shelly Rambo calls "the space of death", where death has occurred and there is not yet the hope of new life. This is the space Mary occupies at the cross. See Rambo, *Spirit and Trauma*, 56, 172.

84 According to O'Donnel, "To be traumatized is to have been made powerless in an experience or experiences. The traumatic event itself is one that overwhelms the resources a person might already have in place". O'Donnell, *The Dark* Womb, 48–49. See also Herman, *Trauma and Recovery*, 33.

in stating that Mary consents to what is done to her body,[85] others, such as Mulya, suggest that "Gabriel's use of the term *episkiasei*" conveys that Mary will be "overcome by God's spirit" and that, importantly, at no point is she asked for her consent. Therefore, Mary can only respond, "Here I am, the servant of the Lord; let it be with me according to your word" (Luke 1:38).[86] Likewise, Parks notes that though Mary accepts her call, she uses the language of being enslaved to God, which—for the original readership—would conjure up "all that would have come with being an enslaved woman pregnant with the child of her slave-owner".[87] Whether one believes that Mary did in fact give consent (willingly or somewhat powerlessly), it cannot be denied that her body was still overcome. Therefore, to ignore or downplay the bodily and somatic participation of Mary in the Gospel would be to downplay or ignore the physical cost of Mary's call and the lived ways in which she heard and obeyed God's word. Forbes and Harrower write, "Bearing God within oneself is perhaps the highest calling a human being could receive"[88] and the way she carries out this call is one of her greatest attributes. Likewise, to downplay Mary's bodily participation is to downplay the way that believers—the body of Christ—participate in God's work in the world.[89] It is for this reason that "Christianity's earliest and most persistent doctrines focus on embodiment".[90]

4.2. Jesus' Human Dependence on his Mother

Finally, if Jesus does in fact *rebuke* the woman in Luke 11:27, this not only negates Mary's physical participation in God's call and denies the bodily space in which God enacted his salvation plan, but it also shows Jesus denying his very real human dependence on his mother. In James MacGrath's work, *What Jesus Learned from Women,* he explains that, while many Christians today say they believe in the humanity of Jesus, when you ask them to picture dirty nappies and scraped knees, this notion is put to the test.[91] If Jesus was truly human, a child of flesh and blood,[92] he was born weak and vulnerable, fully dependent on his mother for all his needs (food, milk, bathing, nursing, someone to teach him to speak, walk, learn, and grow).[93] In his weakest and most dependent state, he required the faithful offering of Mary's body and life. If Jesus were not entirely dependent on Mary to carry him, nurse him, love him, teach him, and show him right from wrong, then Jesus would not be fully human.

---

85 See Pope, "Luke's Seminal Annunciation", 789–807. See also Webb, "Overcoming Fear with Mary of Nazareth", 98; Gaventa, "Nothing Will Be Impossible with God", 35.
86 Mulya, "Queering the Virgin/Whore Binary", 55. For a discussion on the virgin birth and what it might mean for Mary to be overcome by the Spirit, see Otobo, "The Holy Spirit and Luke's Infancy Narrative", 44–46.
87 Parks, Sheinfeld, and Warren, *Jewish and Christian Women in the Ancient Mediterranean*, 167. Mulya, however, makes a rather different point, suggesting that the worth of Mary is unhelpfully found in her *absence* of sex. It is through her eternal virginity that she embodies the patriarchal ideas of "female purity, obedience, and submission". Mulya, "Queering the Virgin/Whore Binary", 53.
88 Forbes and Harrower, *Raised from Obscurity*, 49.
89 A similar idea is observed by Green when speaking of embodied conversion in Luke–Acts and bodily participation in baptism. See Green, *Conversion in Luke–Acts*, 77.
90 O'Donnell, *Broken Bodies*, 1. The Gospel of John, for instance, goes to great lengths to emphasise the bodily and physical aspects of Jesus' humanity (the word became flesh, John 1:14). The writer to the Hebrews uses the humanity of Jesus as reasons for his ability to not only empathise with us but to show how he (paradoxically) conquered sin and death. Paul says that he exalts God in his body (Phil. 1:20) and claims in 1 Corinthians that to deny bodily resurrection is to deny the gospel (1 Cor. 15:13–17). See Gorman, *Participation*, 21.
91 McGrath, *What Jesus Learned from Women*, 21.
92 Seim, "The Virgin Mother", 99.
93 For a helpful reimagining of Mary's relationship with Jesus and how Mary may have influenced Jesus' ministry, see Bond and Taylor, *Women Remembered*, 128.

With this in mind, a positive reading of Luke 11:28 seems to lead to a more theologically coherent understanding of this passage. If Jesus *affirms* the proclamation, "Blessed is the womb that bore you and the breasts that nursed you!" (Luke 11:27) with the reply, "*Yes indeed*, blessed are the ones who hear the word of God and obey it!" (Luke 11:28)—with his mother as a leading example—we see Jesus recognising his own humanity, weakness, and dependence on his mother, and we note Jesus acknowledging the sacrifice that Mary made in allowing her body to be the physical place in which Jesus was carried, nurtured, and raised. We see Jesus admiring the faithful obedience of his mother as a source of life for him. We see Jesus acknowledging the way in which God fulfilled the salvation plan as prophesied by Gabriel—the son of the Most High conceived in the womb of a young virgin (Luke 2:31–32).

5. Conclusion

In conclusion, the long-standing negative interpretation of Luke 11:27–28, where Jesus is thought to dismiss the woman's praise and, by implication, diminish the role of his mother, warrants a fresh perspective. It has been demonstrated in this paper that it is linguistically feasible to interpret Luke 11:27–28 (and most importantly the particle μενοῦν) positively. Not only does the grammar allow for this, but contextually this aligns with Luke's portrayal of Mary. Within the broader framework of Luke's Gospel, Mary is portrayed as a model of blessedness, embodying the very qualities that Jesus praises in disciples—faithfulness, obedience, and a deep connection to God's word. Theologically, the positive reading not only restores Mary's rightful place as an exemplar of discipleship but also highlights the profound reality of Jesus' humanity, which was intimately tied to his relationship with his mother. Mary's physical and spiritual role in God's redemptive plan is not something to be downplayed but rather affirmed and celebrated. Examining Luke 11:27–28 through this lens invites us to move beyond doctrinal divides and instead see Mary not only as the mother of Jesus (which is important enough), but as a figure of faith and obedience in her own right, embodying the blessedness that Jesus himself affirms. In doing so, we arrive at a more theologically coherent understanding of both Mary's discipleship and the humanity of Christ.

Ali Robinson
arobinson@csu.edu.au
United Theological College
16 Masons Drive, North Parramatta NSW 2151

Bibliography

Bauckham, R. — *Gospel Women: Studies of the Named Women in the Gospels* (Grand Rapids, MI: Eerdmans, 2002).

Bock, D. L. — *Luke 9:51–24:53* (Baker Exegetical Commentary on the New Testament; Grand Rapids, MI: Baker Academic, 1996).

Bond, H. K. and J. Taylor — *Women Remembered: Jesus' Female Disciples* (London: Hodder & Stoughton, 2022).

Bovon, F. — *Luke 1: A Commentary on the Gospel of Luke 1:1—9:50* (Hermeneia; Christine M. Thomas trans.; Minneapolis, MN: Fortress, 2002).

Bovon, F. — *Luke 2: A Commentary on the Gospel of Luke 9:51–19:27* (Hermeneia; Christine M. Thomas trans.; Minneapolis, MN: Fortress, 2013).

Braaten, C. E., and R. W. Jenson (eds.) — *Mary Mother of God* (Grand Rapids, MI: Eerdmans, 2004).

Brown, R. E., K. P. Donfried, J. A. Fitzmyer, and J. Reumann (eds.) — *Mary in the New Testament: A Collaborative Assessment by Protestant and Roman Catholic Scholars* (Philadelphia, PA: Fortress/ New York, NY: Paulist, 1978).

Brown, R. E. — *The Birth of the Messiah: A Commentary on the Infancy Narrative in Matthew and Luke* (Garden City, NY: Image Books, 1979).

Calvin, J. — *Commentarii in Harmoniam Evangelicorum: Matthew, Mark, and Luke* (Vol. 45 of Calvini Opera; Brunswick–Berlin: Schwetschke & Sohn, 1863–1900).

Calvin, J. — *Commentary on a Harmony of the Evangelists, Matthew, Mark, and Luke* (Vol. 2; William Pringle, trans.; Edinburgh: Calvin Translation Society, 1846).

Carroll, J. T. — *Luke: A Commentary* (New Testament Library; Louisville, KY: Westminster John Knox, 2012).

Chen, D. G. — *Luke A New Covenant Commentary* (Eugene, OR: Cascade Books, 2017).

Coleridge, M. — *The Birth of the Lukan Narrative: Narrative as Christology in Luke 1–2* (JSNTSup 88; Sheffield: JSOT Press, 1993).

Denniston, J. D. — *The Greek Particles* (Oxford: Oxford University Press, 1996).

Edwards, J. R. — *The Gospel According to Luke* (Pillar New Testament Commentary; Grand Rapids, MI: Eerdmans, 2015).

Elvey, A. F. — *An Ecological Feminist Reading of the Gospel of Luke: A Gestational Paradigm* (New York, NY: Edwin Mellen, 2005).

Embudo, L. A. B. — "Women Vis-à-Vis Prophecy in Luke–Acts: Part 1", *Asian Journal of Pentecostal Studies* 20.2 (2017), 111–130.

Erasmus, D. — *Collected Works of Erasmus: Paraphrase on Luke 11–24* (Vol. 48; Jane E. Phillips, trans.; Toronto: University of Toronto Press, 2003).

Fitzmyer, J. A. *Luke the Theologian: Aspects of His Teaching* (New York, NY: Paulist, 1989).

Fitzmyer, J. A. *The Gospel According to Luke X–XXIV: A New Translation with Introduction and Commentary* (Anchor Bible 28A; Garden City, NY: Doubleday, 1985).

Forbes, G. W. and S. D. Harrower *Raised from Obscurity: A Narratival and Theological Study of the Characterization of Women in Luke–Acts* (Eugene, OR: Pickwick, 2015).

Gadenz, P. T. *The Gospel of Luke* (Catholic Commentary on Sacred Scripture; Grand Rapids, MI: Baker Academic, 2018).

Gathercole, S. J. *The Composition of the Gospel of Thomas: Original Language and Influences* (SNTSMS 151; Cambridge: Cambridge University Press, 2012).

Gaventa, B. R. *Mary: Glimpses of the Mother of Jesus* (Minneapolis, MN: Fortress, 1995).

Gaventa, B. R. "Nothing Will Be Impossible with God", in Carl E. Braaten and Robert W. Jeson (eds.), *Mary Mother of God* (Grand Rapids, MI: Eerdmans, 2004), 19–35.

Gaventa, B. R. and C. L. Rigby (eds.) *Blessed One: Protestant Perspectives on Mary* (Louisville, KY: Westminster John Knox, 2002).

Goodacre, M. S. *The Synoptic Problem: A Way through the Maze* (London: Sheffield Academic, 2001).

Gorman, M. J. *Participation: Paul's Vision of Life in Christ* (Grove Biblical Series 88; Cambridge: Grove Books, 2018).

Green, J. B. *Conversion in Luke–Acts: Divine Action, Human Cognition, and the People of God* (Grand Rapids, MI: Baker Academic, 2015).

Green, J. B. *The Gospel of Luke* (NICNT; Grand Rapids, MI: Eerdmans, 1997).

Green, J. B. "The Social Status of Mary in Luke 1:5–2:52: A Plea for Methodological Integration", *Biblica* 73 (1992), 457–71.

Herman, J. L. *Trauma and Recovery: The Aftermath of Violence—from Domestic Abuse to Political Terror* (London: Hachette, 2015).

Johnson, L. T. *The Gospel of Luke* (Sacra Pagina; Collegeville, MN: Liturgical, 1991).

Karris, R. J. "Women and Discipleship in Luke", *CBQ* 56 (1994), 1–20.

Kateusz, A. *Mary and Early Christian Women: Hidden Leadership* (Cham: Palgrave Macmillan, 2019).

Kempe, M. *The Book of Margery Kempe* (A Norton Critical Edition; Lynn Staley, trans. and ed.; London: Norton & Company, 2001).

Kreitzer, B., S. M. Manetsch, and T. George (eds.) *Luke* (Reformation Commentary on Scripture 3; Downers Grove, IL: IVP Academic, 2015).

Luther, M.	*D. Martin Luthers Werke: kritische Gesamtausgabe* (Vol. 17, pt. 2; Weimar: Hermann Böhlau, 1909).
Maas, A.	"The Blessed Virgin Mary", *The Catholic Encyclopedia, vol. 15* (New York: Robert Appleton Company, 1912. <https://www.newadvent.org/cathen/15464b.htm.> [accessed 1 March 2025].
MacCulloch, D.	*The Later Reformation in England, 1547–1603* (2nd ed; Cham: Palgrave, 2001).
Marshall, I. H.	*The Gospel of Luke* (NICNT; Grand Rapids, MI: Eerdmans, 1978).
Marshall, M. J.	"The Rise and Rise of James the Just in Luke–Acts", *JGAR* 6 (2022), 93–108.
Matthews-Green, F.	*Mary as the Early Christians Knew Her: The Mother of Jesus in Three Ancient Texts* (Brewster: Paraclete, 2013).
Maunder, C.	*Mary: Founder of Christianity* (London: Oneworld, 2022).
McGrath, J. F.	*What Jesus Learned from Women* (Eugene, OR: Cascade Books, 2021).
Morris, L. L.	*Luke* (Tyndale New Testament Commentaries; Downers Grove, IL: IVP, 1988).
Moule, C. F. D.	*An Idiom Book of New Testament Greek* (Cambridge: Cambridge University Press, 1959).
Mulya, T. W.	"Queering the Virgin/Whore Binary: The Virgin Mary, the Whore of Babylon, and Sexual Violence", in Caroline Blyth, Emily Colgan, and Katie Edwards (eds.), *Rape Culture, Gender Violence, and Religion: Biblical Perspectives* (Cham: Palgrave Macmillan, 2018), 57–73.
Myers, A. D.	*Blessed among Women? Mothers and Motherhood in the New Testament* (Oxford: Oxford University Press, 2017).
Nolland, J.	*Luke 9:21–18:34* (Word Biblical Commentary 35B; Waco, TX: Word, 1993).
O'Donnell, K.	*Broken Bodies: The Eucharist, Mary and the Body in Trauma Theology* (London: SCM, 2019).
O'Donnell, K.	*The Dark Womb: Re-Conceiving Theology through Reproductive Loss* (London: SCM, 2022).
Otobo, F.	"The Holy Spirit and Luke's Infancy Narrative: Reading a Legitimatory Role", *JGAR* 8 (2024), 37–56.
Painter, J.	*Just James: The Brother of Jesus in History and Tradition* (Edinburgh: T&T Clark, 1999).
Parsons, M. C.	*Luke* (Paideia; Grand Rapids, MI: Baker Academic, 2015).
Partridge, A. C.	*English Biblical Translation* (London: Deutsch, 1973).
Parks, S., S. Sheinfeld, and M. J. C. Warren	*Jewish and Christian Women in the Ancient Mediterranean* (Abingdon: Routledge, 2022).

Patterson, S. J.	*The Gospel of Thomas and Christian Origins: Essays on the Fifth Gospel* (Boston: Brill, 2013).
Peeler, A.	*Women and the Gender of God* (Grand Rapids, MI: Eerdmans, 2022).
Pitre, B.	*Jesus and the Jewish Roots of Mary: Unveiling the Mother of the Messiah* (New York, NY: Image, 2018).
Plummer, A.	*A Critical and Exegetical Commentary on the Gospel According to Saint Luke* (Edinburgh: T&T Clark, 1896).
Pope, M.	"Luke's Seminal Annunciation: An Embryological Reading of Mary's Conception", *JBL* 138.4 (2019), 789–807.
Ralston, T.	"The Virgin Mary: Reclaiming Our Respect", in S. Glahn (ed.), *Vindicating the Vixens: Revisiting Sexualized, Vilified, and Marginalized Women of the Bible* (Grand Rapids, MI: Kregel Academic, 2017), 187–200.
Rambo, S.	*Spirit and Trauma: A Theology of Remaining* (Louisville, KY: Westminster John Knox, 2010).
Reid, B. E. and S. Matthews	*Luke 1–9* (Wisdom Commentary 43A; Collegeville, MN: Liturgical, 2021).
Rowe, C. K.	*Early Narrative Christology: The Lord in the Gospel of Luke* (Berlin: de Gruyter, 2006).
Seim, T. K.	*The Double Message: Patterns of Gender in Luke and Acts* (Nashville, TN: Abingdon, 1994).
Seim, T. K.	"The Virgin Mother: Mary and Ascetic Discipleship in Luke", in Amy-Jill Levine and Marianne Blickenstaff (eds.), *A Feminist Companion to Luke* (London: Sheffield, 2002), 65–78.
Shaker, C.	"Sub Tuum Praesidium: A Reflection on the Protection of Mary, the Blessed Virgin Mother of God", *Magistra* 23.2 (2017), 3–25.
Schreiner, T. R.	*Commentary on Luke* (The Baker Illustrated Bible Commentary; Grand Rapids, MI: Baker Books, 2012).
Spencer, F. S.	*The Gospel of Luke and Acts of the Apostles* (Interpreting Biblical Texts; Nashville, TN: Abingdon, 2008).
Sri, E.	*Rethinking Mary in the New Testament* (San Francisco, CA: Ignatius, 2018).
Stein, R. H.	*Luke* (New American Commentary 24; Nashville, TN: B&H, 1992).
Thompson, A. J.	*Luke* (Exegetical Guide to the Greek New Testament; Nashville, TN: B&H Academic, 2018).
Thrall, M. E.	*Greek Particles in the New Testament: Linguistic and Exegetical Studies* (Vol. 3; Grand Rapids, MI: Eerdmans, 1962).

Vatican Council II	*Lumen Gentium* (21 November 1964), sec. 58 lines 291–292. <https://www.vatican.va/archive/hist_councils/ii_vatican_council/documents/vatii_const_19641121_lumen-gentium_en.html> [accessed 1 March 2025].
Webb, N.	"Overcoming Fear with Mary of Nazareth: Women's Experience Alongside Luke 1:26–56", *Review and Expositor* 115.1 (2018), 96–103.
Wilson, B. E.	"Pugnacious Precursors and the Bearer of Peace: Jael, Judith, and Mary in Luke 1:42", *CBQ* 68.3 (2006), 445–463.
Witherington III, B.	*Women in the Ministry of Jesus* (SNTS 51; Cambridge: Cambridge University Press, 1984).
Wittman, T.	"The Logic of Divine Blessedness and the Salvific Teleology of Christ", *International Journal of Systematic Theology* 18.2 (2016), 132–153.
Wolter, M.	*The Gospel According to Luke: Volume II (Luke 9:51–24)* (Baylor-Mohr Siebeck Studies in Early Christianity 5; Wayne Coppins and Christoph Heilig, trans.; Waco, TX: Baylor University Press, 2017).

Authentic worship in John and in Luke-Acts
Influence, interfluence, and resonance

PAUL N. ANDERSON[1]

Abstract
While most Johannine-Lukan analyses involve comparisons between the Third and the Fourth Gospels, including the Acts of the Apostles in the mix contributes new perspectives and insights. While several of John's theological themes and images are also carried over into the Lukan Gospel, echoes along the lines of authentic worship are especially pronounced when considering John and Acts together. Resonant themes include challenges to religious elites, the workings of the Holy Spirit, presentations of Samaritans and their worship, the place of women in religious leadership, and the character of authentic worship. An additional feature involves the presentation of the religious elite opposing Jesus and his later followers in Acts, which corroborates some of the same in the Fourth Gospel, reflecting earlier historical tensions as well as later engagements. This essay explores similarities and differences between the Johannine and Lukan traditions along these lines, tracing resonance and dissonance between them and sketching implications for understanding origins and developments of the Jesus movement and early Christianity accordingly.

1. The Johannine and Lukan Traditions: Influence, Interfluence, and Resonance

While the focus of the present essay is not to perform an overall history of Johannine and Lukan traditional developments and relations, some inferences of how to approach issues of intertraditional relationships are inescapable. In the light of John's dialogical autonomy,[2] we have here an independent Jesus tradition developing theologically within at least two or three different contexts. The Johannine tradition shows clear evidence of a Palestine phase of its origin and development, with knowledge of pre-70 CE Jerusalem, Judaea, and Samaria and demonstrating clear Galilean (northern) sympathies. A move to a Hellenistic context is also evidenced by the translation of Aramaic terms and Jewish customs into Greek, with a further transition from a

---

1 Paul N. Anderson serves as Professor of Biblical and Quaker Studies, George Fox University of Newberg, Oregon and as Extraordinary Professor of Religion at the North-West University of Potchefstroom, South Africa. A draft of this paper was presented at the Johannine Literature Seminar of the SNTS meetings held at Bard College, August 2011.
2 My overall Johannine theory, cf. Anderson, *Riddles*, 125–55.

particular Johannine community to a plurality of sister communities within the region—plausibly Asia Minor.[3] An earlier edition of John is likely to have been forged around 80–85 CE (and is thus *the second gospel*—the first after Mark, and arguably an augmentive and slightly corrective complement to Mark)—followed by the writing of the Johannine Epistles by the Johannine Elder (85–95 CE), who finalised the Johannine Gospel around the turn of the century (100 CE) shortly after the death of the Beloved Disciple (John 21:24).[4]

Luke-Acts is clearly a two-volume work, despite recent challenges to Cadbury's analysis nearly a century ago.[5] Differences of genre are factors of differences of subject, not purpose: Luke's account of Jesus and his ministry is followed directly by his report on the advances of the apostles. Among the most plausible inferences of New Testament studies, Luke and Acts were written by the same author, finalised in that order, although traditional features within both works may reflect earlier and/or later developments. For instance, one might guess that Luke's earliest report may well have begun with: (a) reports of Paul's journeys as a travelogue evidenced by the 'we' passages, as he appears to have accompanied Paul in his travels to Rome in Acts 16–28, (b) followed by his expanding upon Mark, Q (or Matthew), and even John in the writing of his Gospel, (c) after which he finalised his second volume, the Acts of the Apostles, adding further material to the travelogue. That would account for the lateness of the finalisation of Luke-Acts (around 100 CE), despite the fact that the last events recorded in Acts 28 antedate the passing of Paul (ca. 61 CE or so), even before his final imprisonment and martyrdom under Nero (ca. 64–67 CE).

Whatever the case, a basic continuity of perspective between Luke and Acts is plausible, even though a biographical narrative is a different genre than a history of the Jesus-movement's development. Given that Luke has used Mark as a source, the most plausible explanation for the over six-dozen Johannine-Lukan contacts is to see them as Luke's departures from Mark in Johannine directions, reflecting Johannine influence upon the Lukan tradition rather than inferring a Johannine dependence upon Luke or the use of a common (and unavailable!) source.[6] Despite Luke-Acts likely being completed around 95–100 CE, some familiarity with the Johannine tradition, probably in the oral stages of its development, is more plausible than inferring no contact at all, or John's dependence upon Luke.[7] The John–Acts relationship, however, is a different matter, as there is no parallel historical tradition (such as Mark provides for analyses of Luke) by which to compare similarities and differences between John and Acts. It also could be that John-echoes in Acts, or Acts-echoes in John, may simply reflect familiarity with historical tradition or developments of memory within the early Christian movement rather than intertraditional dialogue or text-based influence in either direction.

---

3   Note the primitive and archaeologically attested features in the Fourth Gospel, reflecting lived familiarity with the topography and mundane settings of the itinerary of Jesus in Galilee, Judaea, and Samaria. Anderson, 'Aspects'.
4   This set of theories is laid out in an overall paradigm I call 'the dialogical autonomy of the Fourth Gospel' in Anderson, *The Fourth Gospel*, 37–41, 101–126; Anderson, *Christology of the Fourth Gospel*, xxxvi-lxxxvi; Anderson, *Riddles*, 125–55.
5   Cadbury, *The Making of Luke/Acts*.
6   Whereas Bailey, *Traditions*, argued that the commonalities between John and Luke may be explicable on the basis of their uses of a common source, there is no evidence that such a source existed. More plausible is the inference of Luke's use of the Johannine tradition; see Cribbs, 'St. Luke and the Johannine Tradition', 422–50. His work was followed by Moody Smith and others; see the Appendix below for a fuller arguing of this thesis.
7   Note that the most characteristic features of Luke (and Luke/Matthew): the birth narrative and genealogy of Jesus, Jesus' inaugural sermon in the Nazareth synagogue, Beatitudes and the Lord's Prayer, parables of the Good Samaritan and the Prodigal Son, etc. are missing from John, whereas many of John's features have been added by Luke to his use of Mark: the great catch of fish, Peter's confession following the other feeding, changing a head-anointing to a foot-anointing, women named Mary and Martha, a parable of a man named Lazarus, etc.

For instance, one question that will remain unsolved by this essay is whether the narrator's comment in John 7:39, τοῦτο δὲ εἶπεν περὶ τοῦ πνεύματος οὗ ἔμελλον λαμβάνειν οἱ πιστεύσαντες εἰς αὐτόν· οὔπω γὰρ ἦν πνεῦμα, ὅτι Ἰησοῦς οὐδέπω ἐδοξάσθη ('Now he said this about the Spirit, which believers in him were to receive; for as yet there was no Spirit, because Jesus was not yet glorified'), refers to the post-resurrection bestowal of the Holy Spirit upon Jesus' followers in John 20:22, or whether it refers to the post-ascension outpouring of the Spirit upon believers in Acts 2:33, and even upon the Gentiles in Acts 10:45. So, it cannot be said that the Johannine evangelist was not aware either of Acts or its underlying tradition in his presentation of the bestowal of the Spirit, nor can it be said that the author of Acts was unaware of the 'Johannine Pentecost' in crafting his narrative; either, neither, or both may have been the case. Of course, even the earlier and later Pauline traditions were also aware of the theme (Rom. 5:5; Tit. 3:6), so the motif of the outpouring of the Spirit antedates in written form the finalisation of Johannine and Lukan traditions alike. At the least, what we have here is *resonance* between traditions—presenting a similar theme in distinctive ways—showing its importance in the minds of authors and their traditions. More important than the origin of the theme, of course, is what narrators actually do with it, rhetorically and theologically.

Therefore, the most important aspect of Johannine–Lukan comparative analyses is simply to note similarities and differences, making inferences as to the level and character of interaction between traditions, as well as allowing them to speak with their own voices when appropriate. While some Johannine influence upon the Lukan gospel tradition is apparent, it is not impossible to infer some interfluentiality between the Lukan and Johannine traditions overall, including Acts or its subjects. Whatever the case, resonance between the traditions may be a serviceable approach for analysis, as it is not simply the matching of words that is of interest (as some studies of intertextuality pursue, although I prefer the language of interfluentiality, as orality and aurality extend beyond textuality and literacy in media-critical perspective),[8] but aspects of conceptuality and theme will also be of interest in considering the theological content at hand. Of course, similarity also might not suggest text-based influence in either direction, and difference might not suggest the lack of contact; autonomous traditions may indeed echo similar themes rooted in historical events or in their renderings, and even historical memory at times asserts itself over and against other presentations in the interest of historicity, not simply theology.[9] As a result, a comparative analysis will primarily be concerned with similarities and differences between the Johannine and Lukan traditions, however they may have developed.

---

8   At this point, I prefer to speak in terms of interfluence, echoes, and resonance between traditions where directional influence is unclear rather than intertextuality. Indeed, as Julia Kristeva has developed a meaningful interpretive term and theory to back it up, based on Mikhail Bakhtin's dialogism, sometimes intertraditional dialogues are not about or involving 'texts' at all—they involve ideas, meanings, themes, and associations as well as textually similar words, and audiences and purveyors of texts are always people—human agents, who have their own perceptions, experiences, and interests in how they receive and transmit particular words and their meanings. See Kristeva, *Desire*, and Bakhtin, *Dialogic Imagination*. See also Anderson, 'Bakhtin's Dialogism'.

9   As Hayden White has asked with pointed incisiveness, 'Whose history is being rendered, here?' White, *Metahistory*. On these matters, not only are Mark and John well considered the Bi-Optic Gospels, reflecting two individuated sets of impressions regarding Jesus and his ministry from day one, they also reflect levels of intertraditional dialogue, whereby the first edition of John (at least) augments Mark chronologically and geographically and also pushes back in ways correctively regarding Mark's chronology, presentation of John the Baptist, and the valuation of the feeding narrative (Anderson, *Christology of the Fourth Gospel*, 110–36, 194–220).

2. Religion Versus the Revealer in Acts and John

While the tensions between Jesus and Judaean religious leaders in the Fourth Gospel have been largely seen as reflecting religious tensions between Johannine believers and synagogue leaders in post-70 CE diaspora settings rather than historical memories of Jesus and his uneven reception during his ministry, such is a flawed inference on several levels. First, the two-level reading of John argued by J. Louis Martyn, based upon the Signs-Gospel theory of his student, Robert T. Fortna, is factually flawed. As with the highly diachronic theory of Bultmann's inference of three major sources underlying the Gospel of John, which assumedly had been disordered and thus reordered by Bultmann—conveniently 'evidencing' the poetic/strophic features of an imagined Gnostic Revelation-Sayings Source under Bultmann's reconstruction—neither is there any compelling evidence for Fortna's imagined re-ordering and reconstruction of a foundational 'Signs Gospel' to which the evangelist has added theological content, including dialogues, discourses, and reflective expansions upon events. When all of Bultmann's stylistic, theological, and contextual evidence for alien material—either underlaying or overlaying the evangelist's work—is subjected to critical scrutiny using John 6 as a case study, there is no compelling evidence of non-Johannine material in the Gospel of John. Indeed, a final compiler likely finalised the narrative by adding the evangelist's later preaching material to an earlier edition; with Brown and others, the final compiler's contributions appear conservative rather than intrusive.[10]

Likewise, despite Fortna's reconstruction of an imagined narrative source underlying the evangelist's work that included the signs and the passion narrative, also disordered and reordered to fit Fortna's imagined 'original' sequence, the mere stripping of dialogues, discourses, and theological reflections upon events and their receptions does not imply, let alone confirm, an alien hand at work. While Fortna correctly notes uses of καὶ asyndeton and οὖν historicum in the narrative, this does not imply an alien hand at work. It simply reflects the way the narrator tells his story of Jesus, citing deeds and events, which are expanded upon within the narrative, leading into discussions and discourses by Jesus. Interestingly, the second critique of Mark by the Johannine Elder, as cited by Papias according to Eusebius (*Hist. Eccles.* 3.39) is that Mark's providing lists of Jesus-sayings, dislocated from events and dialogical contexts, is *not* actual history. Rather, the more coherent Johannine presentation of Jesus and his ministry expands upon historical events, followed by reactions and discussions leading into contextual teachings of Jesus as means of addressing adequate and inadequate responses to his works, reflects a *fuller historical memory of Jesus and his ministry*, in the opinion of the Johannine Elder and also in the judgement of Schleiermacher.[11]

The point, here, is that tensions between Jesus and religious leaders in Jerusalem, as presented in the Gospel of John, do not simply reflect later theological additions to non-Johannine narratives. Tensions between the Jesus-movement and Judaean leaders did not simply eventuate in post-70 CE diaspora situations, where Jesus-adherents were programmatically cast out of synagogues (John 9:22; 12:42; 16:2). No. These tensions may well have extended back into the ministry of Jesus itself, which then continued to be felt in the later Johannine situation, but did not originate thence.[12]

---

10   On precisely this point, the meaning of John 6:51c–58 reflects not the requirement of instrumental liturgical acts for salvation to be obtained—which would indeed reflect a departure from the evangelist's Christocentric soteriology, where Jesus himself is the way, the truth, and the life—rather, the call is for believers to be nourished by the suffering flesh and blood of Jesus on the cross, calling for the embracing of the way of the cross if they expect to be raised with him in the afterlife (Anderson, *Christology of the Fourth Gospel*, 206–20).

11   On the overturning of Strauss, *The Christ of Faith*, in favour of Schleiermacher, *The Life of Jesus*, see Anderson, 'The Jesus of History', 63–81.

12   Bernier, *Aposynagōgos and the Historical Jesus*.

Historically, the critique of religious leaders and their approaches to authentic Jewish faith and practice originated with Jesus and his ministry, and many of the Ἰουδαῖοι *believed* in John (see especially 8:31; 11:45; 12:11).[13] Thus, claims that the Johannine narrative is anti-Jewish are totally wrong, and Jesus himself proclaims that 'salvation is of the Jews' (4:22). Likewise, every reference to Israel or Judaism itself is positive in John, and the only times that Jewish persons are presented negatively are reports of Judaean leaders among the religious elite in Jerusalem being set against the works and teachings of Jesus due—in Johannine perspective—to the belief that they did not have God's love in their hearts (5:42) and did not really know intimately the ways of the Father (7:28; 8:55; 15:21; 16:3; 17:25) or what Jesus was doing (1:10; 3:11; 8:14; 13:7). While later reflections account for the uneven receptions of Jesus as factors of spiritual inattentiveness to the ways of God, they did not take place late-and-only-late. In Johannine perspective, this unevenness of reception at least went back to the actual ministry of Jesus, who, as the northern Galilean Prophet, was largely rejected by the Judaean religious elite. And of course, the history of Israel is itself rife with northern prophets being scorned and rejected by the Judaean elite, so the Prophet from Nazareth is no exception, here.

Second, the rejection of Jesus by the religious elite is also replicated in the Synoptics, and similar later tensions are also described in further detail in the Acts of the Apostles. Acts thus reflects initial and continuing pushback against the Jesus movement from the beginning of the apostolic era over the next three decades, before the destruction of the Jerusalem temple. Point: resistance to Jesus and his followers on the part of religious leaders is not limited to the Fourth Gospel alone; it is replicated in each of the Synoptics and even more fully referenced in the Acts of the Apostles, providing *corroborative impressions* of these historical tensions, wherein the Fourth Gospel is not alone. Consider, for instance, the resistance of the Judaean-based religious elite to the movement precipitated by the charismatic Prophet from Galilee—*the way*—in Luke's second volume:

a) Throughout the book of Acts, Jews and Gentiles alike come to believe in Jesus as the Jewish Messiah/Christ, and this is presented as a threat to the religious elite of Jerusalem and also in major cities in the Graeco-Roman world (Acts 1–28).

b) As Peter and John ministered in Jerusalem, healing the lame man by the Beautiful Gate near the temple, calling people to believe in Jesus as the Messiah/Christ, opposition arises among the Sadducees and Jerusalem leaders (Acts 3).

c) They bring Peter and John before the council under Annas and Caiaphas and order them not to preach about Jesus as the Messiah/Christ, putting them in prison (Acts 4).

d) Stephen's witness is opposed by the Synagogue of the Freedmen, and they accuse him of speaking against the temple (citing John 2:19, that Jesus will destroy the temple) and changing the customs of Moses; he is then stoned to death (Acts 6–7).

e) Saul begins persecuting Jesus-adherents—followers of *the way*—dragging people off to prison, and scattering them from Jerusalem throughout Judaea and Samaria; when he becomes a follower of Jesus, Jewish leaders in Damascus seek to kill him (Acts 9).

f) Under Herod, James the brother of John is put to death by the sword (44 CE), and seeing that this pleased the Jews, Herod then imprisons Peter (Acts 12).

g) When Paul and Barnabas preach in Pisidian Antioch, Iconium, Lystra, and Syrian Antioch, many Gentiles believe in Jesus as the Jewish Messiah/Christ, but they receive pushback by the Jewish leaders, who stir up opposition against them, whereupon Paul is stoned and left for dead (Acts 13–14).

---

13 Note the many times that the *Ioudaioi* and Jewish persons *do* believe in Jesus in the Fourth Gospel, all general references to Judaism and Israel are either positive or neutral. Anderson, 'Anti-Semitism and Religious Violence'.

h) As Paul and Silas (and Timothy) minister and preach in Thessalonica and Berea, they receive warm welcomes among the Gentiles and the Jewish leaders of Berea, but Jewish leaders of Thessalonica and Macedonia stir things up against them (Acts 17, 20).

i) Despite Paul's effective ministry in Corinth, Jewish leaders bring a civic case against Paul before Gallio, the proconsul of Achaia, charging him with speaking against the law of Moses (Acts 18).

j) Upon Paul's ministering effectively for two years in Ephesus, many Jews and Gentiles are reached with the gospel, while others oppose Paul, but some Jewish exorcists—the seven sons of Sceva—begin casting out demons 'in the name of Jesus whom Paul preaches', but this is rebuked by an evil spirit (Acts 19–20).

k) Upon Paul's final return to Jerusalem, despite purifying himself conservatively, when Asia-based Jews see him in the temple, they stir up the leaders and try to kill him, thinking that he had brought Gentiles (Trophimus the Ephesian) into the temple (Acts 21).

l) After speaking to the Jerusalem crowd in Aramaic, the crowd roars: 'Rid the earth of him! He's not fit to live!' Whereupon Paul receives protection by the Romans; and after addressing the Sadducees and Pharisees before the Sanhedrin, a conspiracy of forty Jewish men vow to neither eat nor drink until they had killed Paul (Acts 22–23).

m) Jewish leaders seek to bring Paul back to Jerusalem to stand trial, but under Roman protection—as Paul had appealed to have his case heard before Caesar—their plans to have him killed are foiled by his being under Roman custody, allowing him to preach in Rome under house arrest (Acts 24–28).

In something of a parallel fashion, the Johannine presentation of the reception of and opposition to Jesus of Nazareth by religious leaders in Galilee and Judaea shows some interesting parallels with mixed receptions of Paul and Jesus-adherents over the three decades of developments narrated in Acts. Note first the ways that the Johannine Christ-hymn—as an *Overture* added to the final edition of the Fourth Gospel's finalisation—comments upon the uneven reception of Jesus, who was rejected by some of his own, but by whom any and all who believe in him are empowered to become the children of God, welcomed into the divine family (John 1:9–13). This confessional response to the evangelist's narration over the years, likely by John the Elder (author of the Epistles and final compiler of the Beloved Disciple's witness after his death around 100 CE)[14] comments not only upon the uneven reception of Jesus *during* his ministry; it also denotes such *over the previous seven decades*, resembling many of the features referenced in Acts. Thus, note the resistance to Jesus and his followers by the Judaean religious elite in the Gospel of John, despite the fact that many of the Jews and Judaeans in Jerusalem indeed believed (2:23; 7:31; 8:31; 10:42; 11:45; 12:11,42) and his being portrayed as fulfilling the typologies of historic Israel as 'the King of Israel' (1:49; 12:13). Even his being taunted derisively as 'the King of Jews' by Pilate and his soldiers (18:39; 19:3, 19–21) poses an ironic witness to his perceived Jewishness. Note here, however, the character of opposition to Jesus in the Fourth Gospel by the religious leaders of Jerusalem:

a) Jewish leaders from Jerusalem—priests, Levites, and Pharisees—question John the Baptist, asking him if he were the Eschatological Prophet or Elijah, challenging his ministry, and by extension the one to whom he pointed (John 1).

---

14 For an analysis of 'the Johannine Question' and John's authorship, see Anderson, 'The Son of Zebedee', pp.17–82 and 241–49.

b) Upon clearing the temple of its sacrificial animals, money changers, and merchandising tables, Jewish leaders question Jesus as to what sign he might yet perform to demonstrate his authority, though many in Jerusalem for the Passover festival (and thus Jews) believe (John 2).

c) Nicodemus, a Pharisee and leader among the Jews, notes the divinely commissioned authority of Jesus because of his signs, but he fails to comprehend the spiritual character of the kingdom of God, what it means to be born from above, and the work of the Holy Sprit as felt-but-unseen wind; he later stands up for Jesus amongst other Jewish leaders and assists in taking down the body of Jesus at the cross (John 3, 7, 19).

d) Jesus returns to Galilee through Samaria, having learnt that the Pharisees noted that he was gaining more disciples than John, and many among the Samaritans believed in Jesus, as did those who had seen his signs performed in Jerusalem; people also believe in Galilee, having seen his signs in Jerusalem and in Capernaum, as well (John 4).

e) Upon the healing of the lame man in Jerusalem on the Sabbath, Jewish leaders oppose Jesus first for breaking the Sabbath, and then for claiming divine authorisation by God, his Father, whereupon the Jewish leaders plot to kill Jesus; they do not have God's love in their hearts. Later, Pharisees and priests also oppose Jesus, and the Jewish leaders attempt to stone Jesus to death for blasphemy (John 5, 7–8).

f) After the feeding of the five thousand, the Galilean crowd seeks to rush Jesus off for a royal coronation as a king like Moses, and Jewish leaders taunt Jesus, asking for another sign (as Moses provided in the wilderness) that they might believe, but Jesus calls for openness to being taught by God in the present, favouring eschatology over exegesis: it is not the bread that Moses gave that matters, but the nourishment that God gives in the here and now that counts (John 6).

g) Upon healing the blind man on the Sabbath, Jewish leaders—including Pharisees and priests—oppose Jesus and claim that he is a sinner for having done so; while some believe in him because of his signs, others seek to stone Jesus to death, but he escapes their grasp (John 9–10).

h) The raising of Lazarus again brings about a mixed reception amongst the Jewish populace of Judaea—which threatens the religious leaders—with many of the Jews believing; whereupon the chief priests and the Pharisees call for a council meeting of the Sanhedrin, lest all the Jews believe in Jesus, after Jesus was 'sacrificed' (politically) to the Romans, unwittingly (and ironically) becoming a universal sacrifice (eschatologically) for the entire world (John 11).

i) Many of the Jews in Judaea were believing in Jesus because of his raising of Lazarus from the tomb, and God-fearing Greeks coming to Jerusalem to worship at the festival sought to meet Jesus—whereupon Philip serves as a cross-cultural bridge, as he does in Acts 6, 8, 21[15]—following belief by some and unbelief by others, fulfilling Scriptures of Isaiah (John 12).

j) Jesus is received by some though rejected by others, and his followers even back then were cast out of synagogues if they confessed Jesus openly; but they are not to fear, as Jesus has overcome the world (John 9, 12, 16).

k) In the trans-Kidron garden, Jesus is arrested by the guards of the Jewish officials of Jerusalem and is tried before Annas, and then Caiaphas, whereupon he is turned over by the Jewish leaders to Pilate (the Roman procurator), claiming that Jesus was a criminal (John 18).

---

15 Anderson, 'Come and See!'

l) Despite Pilate's finding no fault in Jesus and seeking to release him, the Jewish leaders demand that Jesus be put to death for breaking the Jewish law and claiming to be the Son of God; after his death, the body of Jesus is taken down from the cross and buried in an unused tomb by Joseph of Arimathea and Nicodemus secretly, for fear of the Jews (John 19).

m) On the First Day of the week, Jesus appears to Mary Magdalene in the garden, and she conveys the news of the risen Lord to the disciples, who are gathered behind closed doors out of fear of the Jews, whereupon Jesus appears to them, breathes upon and inspires them, and imbues them with priestly authority to be forgivers of sins (John 20).

In doing a comparison-contrast between the tensions with religious leaders experienced by the apostles in Acts and by Jesus in the Fourth Gospel, a number of similarities emerge. First, the popularity of Jesus (and John the Baptist) and his followers, who reached and evangelised thousands, is reported as threatening to the religious leaders of Jerusalem. They seek to hold onto power and sway—whether they be priestly managers of temple practices or Pharisaic interpreters/adjudicators of the Mosaic law—against popular competitors. Second, the spiritual empowerment to produce signs, healings, and other wonders becomes a scandal to those who do not have such gifts. Institutional religious leaders are thus threatened by charisma-demonstrations. Third, Jesus and his followers challenge the hegemony of temple-based institutionalism, teaching a more universal and incarnational vision of God's presence and dwelling place being within and among authentic followers of God, thus extending the blessings of Abraham to the larger world. Fourth, Pharisaic keepers of the law are offended by Jesus' healings on the Sabbath and by Paul's mission to the Gentiles, where circumcision is not expected as the basis for being welcomed into Jewish fellowship as a believer in Jesus. And fifth, the claiming of divine authorisation by the Father as the divine Son is perceived as blasphemy, leading to attempts to stone Jesus and later his followers.

What we see here, in John and Luke-Acts, is a number of ways that the Revealer—and the eschatological divine initiative—becomes a scandal to religion—that which is of human origin as constructed means of apprehending and furthering contact with the divine—which poses an existential conflict within every religious tradition. Such is the case within Christianity as well as Judaism: the map is not the territory; the wineskins are not the wine; the body is not the soul or the spirit. And yet, new structures, ways, and means must be set up as modalities to contain and further the sodalities, which require attending, discerning, and heeding the working of the Spirit—the divine initiative—at work in eschatologically time-changing ways in the ministry of Jesus, the Christ Events, and the developing life of the Church. That being the case, though, the Johannine and the Lukan witnesses bear within themselves the capacity to restore vitality to sectors of the Christian movement every bit as much as the ministry of Jesus advanced a vision of the transformation of Judaism in the First Century, which changed the world then and continues to do so, at least potentially, in every generation since.

And indeed, every Christian tradition has as its founding basis a distinctive vision of the ministry of Jesus and the vitality of the early Christian movement: whether it be the legacy of Peter and the apostles, liturgical reminders of theological unity around the seven Ecumenical Councils, particular orders of Christian disciplines and vocations, the recovery of Scripture as the basis for faith and practice, movements of revivalism and social reform, missionary outreach to unreached groups, the charismatic recovery of Pentecostal life in the Spirit, and numerous other ways of seeking to follow Jesus in search of primitive Christianity revived.[16] At the heart, though, of

---

16 Note the description of the Quaker explosion in the Seventeenth Century in the title of William Penn's introduction to the 1696 publication of the *Journal* of George Fox: 'Primitive Christianity Revived'. See the revised edition by Buckley.

meaningful application of these visions is the presentation of authentic worship in John, Luke, and Acts: the key to spiritual vitality and religious renewal.

3. Authentic Worship in John, Luke, and Acts

As a key to spiritual renewal and vitality, authentic worship is put forth in the Gospel of John and Luke, and also in the Acts of the Apostles, as the heart of the spirituality that Jesus came to instantiate in his teachings and ministry. In his challenging conventional approaches to faith and practice of his day —in Galilee, Samaria, and Judaea—the Jesus movement continued to challenge other approaches to religion in the Graeco-Roman world, finding resonance with Jewish and Samaritan audiences, as well as non-Jewish God-fearers, as followers of Jesus proclaimed the advent of the kingdom and leadership of God, eschatologically available to all.[17]

3.1 Authentic Worship in the Gospel of John

One of the primary themes of the Fourth Gospel is that of *authentic worship*, and while the purpose of the Fourth Gospel has been thought to be expressed in John 20:30–31, C. K. Barrett puts it well:

> I suggest, however, that it may be profitable to consider John 4:19–26 as a further summary of what John intended to achieve in writing his book. The Father himself seeks men [sic] who will worship him in Spirit and in truth: this then was God's purpose in the incarnation, and John certainly wrote with the intention of furthering the divine purpose, whatever that may have been.[18]

In the Samaritan woman's acknowledging Jesus as a prophet (v.19; later she confesses him to be the Messiah, v.29), the spatial and formal debates about worship between Jews and Samaritans are about to be dissolved. Acknowledging longstanding differences regarding whether Jerusalem or Gerizim is the fitting mountain on which effective worship is to be transacted, despite professing that 'salvation is of the Jews' (John 4:22), Jesus declares: ἀλλὰ ἔρχεται ὥρα καὶ νῦν ἐστιν, ὅτε οἱ ἀληθινοὶ προσκυνηταὶ προσκυνήσουσιν τῷ πατρὶ ἐν πνεύματι καὶ ἀληθείᾳ, καὶ γὰρ ὁ πατὴρ τοιούτους ζητεῖ τοὺς προσκυνοῦντας αὐτόν· πνεῦμα ὁ θεός, καὶ τοὺς προσκυνοῦντας αὐτὸν ἐν πνεύματι καὶ ἀληθείᾳ δεῖ προσκυνεῖν. ('But the hour is coming, and is now here, when the true worshippers will worship the Father in spirit and truth, for the Father seeks such as these to worship him. God is spirit, and those who worship him must worship in spirit and truth' John 4:23–24).

Again, having asserted that true worship is limited neither to a designated worship site nor a liturgical form, Jesus expands on his earlier assertion regarding the new *topos* of the temple in John 2:14–21.[19] In John 4, the meaning of Jesus' actions in chapter 2 becomes apparent. Rather than simply seeing his prophetic action in the temple as a demonstration against the commercialisation of sacrifice, the institutionalisation of cultic procedures, or the unjust leveraging of economic

---

17 In his proclamation of the God's kingdom being at hand (Mark 1:15: ἡ βασιλεία τοῦ θεοῦ), a helpful way to think about God's *basileic activity* is to see it as God's dynamic leadership being available to all, if people will attend, discern, and heed the present activity of God—inaugurated by Jesus and effected through the Holy Spirit—within and among Christ's followers (Luke 17:21).

18 Barrett, *Essays on John*, 14.

19 For an incarnational view (my language) of God's dwelling place being not in Jerusalem but in the lives and communities of believers, see Coloe, *God's Temple*; Coloe, *Dwelling*. For a view of this incarnational transference in the post-70 CE Mediterranean world, see Porter, *Johannine Social Identity Theory*.

requirements in the attainment of ritual purity, Jesus may have been doing something far more profound. Perhaps he was declaring the entire temple system to have run its course, making way for a new age—a new eschatological reality in which access to the divine presence and means of grace is availed directly to humanity without cultic intermediaries—a new spiritual reality not only for Judaism, but for the entire world. Incarnationally, the new temple is the body of Jesus (John 2:21), and likewise the body of believers who gather in any place and at any time, worshipping in Spirit and in truth (John 4:21–24).

Along these lines, Mark's narrating the rending of the veil in the temple conveys a similar meaning; *all* now have access to the holy of holies in the temple as a result of the Christ events (Mark 15:38, followed by Matt. 27:51 and Luke 23:45).[20] A Matthean echo of the accessibility of the divine presence is found in Matthew 18:18–20, as wherever two or three are gathered in the name of Jesus, he is present in their midst. Likewise, the spiritual presence of Christ, availed through the Holy Spirit, is developed more fully in John 14–16, echoing this new era and developing it further into the lives and communities of his followers. Just as Jesus challenges topocentric understanding of worship in Jerusalem, he does the same at Gerizim; effective worship is no longer tied to outward features of settings or forms, but to inward factors of truth and authenticity.

Apparent also in this passage is the emphasis upon eschatology, and with some tension: the hour *is coming when…*; the hour is coming *and now is here* (John 4:21,23). One reason for the fair degree of tension within Johannine presentations of eschatological themes is that the timing of 'the hour' refers to different realities. Jesus' hour is not yet come for him to perform signs in John 2:4 (although he then does so, directly); the hour of Jesus' arrest and glorification is not yet come during his third visit to Jerusalem (John 7:6,8,30; 8:20), but finally it does come, signalling his glorification and departure (John 12:23,27; 13:1; 17:1). Jesus also declares that the hour is coming in the future, when Jesus' followers are persecuted by those thinking they are doing God's service (John 16:2–4). Whereas the first set of statements references the timing of eventualities during the ministry of Jesus, now eschatological statements involve predictions to be experienced by Jesus' followers in the future.

More pointedly, several passages emphasise that the *hour/time* (ὥρα) is coming and that it now is here, announcing the presence of the future; it is in this category that the John 4 statement belongs. The hour is coming—and is now here—when:

- Jesus' followers will be scattered facing persecution in the world, but he has overcome the world (John 16:32–33)
- Jesus will speak plainly of the Father and not in figures of speech (John 16:23–31)
- the dead will hear the voice of God's Son and those in graves will be judged in the resurrection (John 5:24–29)
- authentic followers of God will worship neither in Jerusalem nor Samaria but in Spirit and in truth (John 4:21–23).

---

20 Jesus speaks of this temple (ναός), tearing it down and building it up John 2:19,20,21, and while not narrated directly in Mark, Jesus' having spoken such words is cited twice in Mark (Mark 14:58; 15:29). Interestingly, the reference to the temple (ναός) not made with human hands is both made by Stephen (in Acts 7:48 with reference to the temple in Jerusalem) and by Paul (in Acts 17:24 with reference to the Areopagus), and Paul asserts in Acts 19:26 that gods made by human hands are not real gods. In Acts 19:24 Luke uses the word ναός with reference to the shrine to Diana of Ephesus. The theme of the dwelling place of God not made with human hands is also referenced in 2 Cor. 5:1 and Heb. 9:11,24, so the theme apparently circulated broadly among various traditions.

The primary function of these proleptic eschatological passages is that they connect an earlier proleptic saying of Jesus with the actualised experience of later believers. Hence, later followers of Jesus indeed suffer persecution at the hand of otherwise well-meaning religious leaders, Jesus' otherwise veiled language is understood with eventual clarity, promise of fitting judgement in the afterlife is embraced with hope, and authentic worship in the Diaspora is on a spiritual par with historic centres of Jewish and Samaritan cultic life. One can imagine members of the mission-churches in middle and later decades of first-century Christianity nodding with knowing approval at such a proleptic statement of Jesus; they were experiencing its eschatological realisation as communities of the new 'temple'—an *incarnational* dwelling place—of God.

Another feature of authentic worship involves the reminder that it is not only humans who seek the life of the Spirit, but it is those who desire to worship authentically whom the Father actively seeks to draw into worship (John 4:23).[21] Here, the divine–human dialectic is described with eschatological force. As God has spoken to humanity at many times and many ways, and now through his Son Jesus Christ (Heb. 1:1–4; Col. 1:15–20; Phil. 2:6–11; John 1:1–18), the divine address also invites a human response of faith.[22] Thus, the mission of the divine *Logos* implies not a monologue, but a dialogue. Not only is it humans who seek the Divine, but the Divine also is seeking out humanity as a double search.[23] Herein the polarities of John's universalism (John 1:9) and particularity (John 14:6) are held in tension by the assertion that no one can come to God except one be drawn by the Father (John 6:44), the eschatological means of which the Father's Son is.[24]

Luke presents this motif distinctively by asserting that the Son of Man is come to seek and save the lost (Luke 19:10). Elsewhere in John, the divine initiative is carried further by the work of ὁ δὲ παράκλητος, the *Advocate*, the Holy Spirit, who will teach Jesus' followers, remind them of his words, testify on his behalf, and convict the world authentically of both sin and of righteousness (John 14:26; 15:26; 16:7–11). In Lukan terms, the comfort (παράκλησιν) of God is offered by the work of the Spirit (Luke 2:25; Acts 9:31; 13:15; 15:31; cf. also 1 Cor. 14:3; 2 Cor. 1:5; 8:17; Phil. 2:1; 1 Thess. 2:4; 2 Thess. 2:16; Philm. 7; Heb. 6:19; 1 John 2:1). As the world's rejection of the Revealer in John results from revelation's scandalising of all that is of human initiative and origin, Jesus describes the having-sent-me-Father as seeking those who will respond receptively in faith to the divine initiative in worship. Therefore, it is because God *is* spirit that authentic worship can only be actualised in spirit and in truth (John 4:24).

3.2 Authentic Worship in Luke

Authentic worship in Luke is addressed indirectly and with less prevalence. Following the Lukan birth narrative, the prophetess Anna is presented as worshipping in the temple and fasting day and night. Upon seeing the infant Jesus, she begins praising God and speaking to those who hoped for the redemption of Jerusalem (Luke 2:36–38). This is followed by Jesus' returning to Jerusalem as a twelve-year-old and impressing the Jewish teachers with his wisdom (Luke 2:41–52). Aside from the Q temptation narrative in Luke 4:1–13, where Jesus asserts that worship is reserved for God alone, worship is not mentioned as a theme in Luke until the last two verses. After his appearing to his disciples and ascending near Bethany, his disciples worshipped Jesus

---

21 Barrett develops this theme thoughtfully in his *Essays on John*.
22 Note also the anti-imperial thrust of each of the New Testament Christ-hymns: Anderson, 'The Johannine *Logos*.'
23 Jones, *The Double Search*; see also Anderson, 'On Seeking Truth'.
24 This theme is developed more fully in Anderson, *Riddles*, 34–35, 183–86. On Johannine universalism and particularity, see Anderson, 'Universal Light'.

and returned to Jerusalem, where they are continually blessing God in the temple (Luke 24:52–53). While the temple is not presented as the required place for effective worship to be offered in Luke, it is associated with authentic worship—even in relation to the honouring of Jesus and worshipping him in the temple.

3.3 Authentic Worship in Acts

Authentic worship in Acts is developed more fully than in the Gospel of Luke, and it is featured centrally in the witness of Stephen in Acts 7. God's promise of blessing to Abraham centres on the promise that he and his descendents would come out and worship God in the land he is given (Acts 7:2–7). Then, Moses' encounter with Yhwh in the wilderness before the angel and the burning bush is described as taking place on holy ground (Acts 7:31–34), but Israel rejected Moses and took after other gods, leading to their removal beyond Babylon (Acts 7:35–43). Then Stephen backs up and refers to the tent of testimony in the wilderness which God instructed Moses to erect, pointing out that Joshua brought it into the promised land and that it was honoured through the reign of David until Solomon built a dwelling place for the God (or 'house', some mss.) of Jacob (Acts 7:44–47).

In the next paragraph, the basis for the accusation that Stephen was speaking blasphemous words against Moses and God and against the holy place and the law (Acts 6:11–13): God does not live in houses built by human hands, but heaven is his throne, and the earth is his footstool. Stephen then speaks pointedly at the religious leaders of Jerusalem, calling them 'You stiff-necked people, uncircumcised in heart and ears, you are forever opposing the Holy Spirit, just as your ancestors used to do', and linking their betraying and murdering of the Righteous One with the persecuting of the prophets in days of old (Acts 7:48–52; citing Isa. 66:1). Therefore, rather than being guilty of the earlier charge that he was speaking against the law, Stephen accuses the Jerusalem authorities of not heeding the law, which they had received from angels, in their rejecting of the promised one (Acts 7:53).

This leads directly to the stoning of Stephen, who is then portrayed by Luke as a Christ-figure, in that he both receives a vision of God and Jesus—the Son of Man at the right hand of God— and he asks, as Jesus did, that this sin not be held against them (Acts 7:54–60; Luke 23:34). In Luke's analysis, Stephen is killed, ironically, for speaking against the law and the temple, when he actually is presented as upholding the spiritual worship of God as developed in Jewish Scripture, associating the temple authorities who also put Jesus to death with the stiff-necked Israelites who went after other gods and forsaking the God of Israel and the Holy Spirit. One can also understand why Jerusalem authorities would have been offended by such a critique, as they doubtless saw themselves as fulfilling divine ordinances, not violating them.

Some have wondered whether Stephen's critique of the temple, distinguishing the building and its systems from the spiritual presence of God not bound by houses made with human hands, suggests that he was a Samaritan.[25] Such a critique of Judaean cultic institutions, however, need not have been confined to Samaria, although the apparent dissension over the authorisation of Gerizim versus Jerusalem in John 4 poses a possible basis for the connection. Still, one can imagine Galileans also sharing anti-Judaean sympathies (after all, they go back to the divided kingdom a full millennium and even earlier), as would more distanced sectors of the Jewish family in the Diaspora. Nonetheless, the narrative in Acts here moves directly into the Samaria mission,

---

25 See, for instance, Spiro, 'Stephen's Samaritan Background'.

as the new wave of persecution in Acts 8:1 scatters believers into the Judaean countryside and Samaria. This is followed directly by Philip's ministry in Samaria, proclaiming the Messiah and performing signs. As a result, many in Samaria believed, even Simon the magician (Acts 8:5–13). Following this news, Peter and John are also sent to minister in Samaria, because some had been baptised in the name of the Lord Jesus but had not yet received the Holy Spirit. When Peter and John laid hands on them and prayed for them, though, they did receive the Holy Spirit (Acts 8:14–17). At this, Simon desired to receive such powers himself and offered money to procure them. Peter denounced him, however, for his wickedness, and Peter and John continued their gospel ministry through Samaria on their way back to Jerusalem (Acts 8:18–25).

Here authentic spiritual empowerment is connected not to water baptism in the name of Jesus but to the laying on of hands and prayer. A similar scenario arises in Acts 18:24—19:7, where Apollos of Alexandria preaches powerfully in the Synagogue of Ephesus, winning disciples for Jesus. These some twelve men were baptised by Apollos, who only knew the baptism of John. When Paul encountered them upon his next visit, he asked if they had received the Holy Spirit; they replied that they had not, and that they did not know there was a Holy Spirit. At this Paul baptised them in the name of the Lord Jesus and laid his hands upon them, whereupon they received the Holy Spirit, spoke in tongues, and prophesied. Therefore, in Luke's presentation of the early Christian movement's development, there appear to have been issues surrounding the efficacy of spiritual transformation regarding outward forms (water baptism, the charisma of the individual, laying on of hands, etc.) and the workings of the Spirit. Sometimes people receive the Holy Spirit, and sometimes they do not.[26]

This may even have contributed to the partisan spirit in 1 Corinthians 1:12; the effectiveness of Apollos' preaching may have been in competition with the Spirit-imbuing ministries of Peter and Paul, and perhaps others simply claiming to be Christ-followers.[27] Interesting here is the fact that authentic spiritual empowerment is sometimes associated directly with water baptism, but sometimes spiritual baptism happens as a result of the laying on of hands and prayer; it is not always conveyed by means of water. Therefore, in Luke's understanding, the authentic operation of the Spirit is a gift conveyed by incarnational means rather than formal ones, and there is some variety of giftedness among Christian leaders themselves, affecting also their ministries.

Overall, the presentation of the temple in John and in Luke-Acts is quite similar. Parallel to John 12:20, where Philip effectively points to Jesus the Hellenists who had come to worship in the Jerusalem temple, in Acts 8:27 Philip also ministers effectively to the Ethiopian eunuch, who had also come to Jerusalem to worship in the temple (note that Paul also describes having gone to the Jerusalem temple to worship in Acts 24:11, and to purify himself Acts 21:24,26; 24:18, as did the Jews in John 11:55). Elsewhere in Acts, Jerusalem and its temple complex are presented as the hub of the Jewish persecution of Christians, somewhat parallel to rejection of the northern prophet by the southern *Ioudaioi* in John; and yet Jerusalem is also featured as the headquarters of the growing Christian movement, just as in John, Jesus first appears to his followers in Jerusalem.

---

26 And of course, the whole point of Paul's listing spiritual gifts alongside the imagery of the one body, one head, and many parts is to emphasise unity amongst diversity and diversity amongst the unity of believers. The greater gifts are those that edify others (preaching/teaching, etc.) versus those that edify only the individual. Cf. Anderson, *From Crisis to Christ*, 252–53.

27 It cannot be ruled out that the so-called Christ-party might have been influenced by Johannine ethos and teaching even as early as the Pauline mission throughout Greece and Asia Minor, although Acts does not present John travelling beyond Judaea and Samaria.

Clearly at stake here is the sociological tension between religious establishment and innovation; put theologically, understandings of ways God has spoken in the past, through Scripture and tradition, are challenged by understandings of how God is speaking in the present, through Jesus as the Messiah, as confirmed by Scripture, tradition, and experience in the minds of some, but not others; put eschatologically, the experience of God's saving-revealing workings in the present find their greatest challenges from the memory and honouring of God's workings in the past. Indeed, Jesus' followers are to tarry in Jerusalem until they are baptised with the Holy Spirit; and, when the Holy Spirit comes upon them, they will be his witnesses in Jerusalem, Judaea, Samaria, and the remotest parts of the earth (Acts 1:4–8). This unfolding history of God's irruption into human history through the workings of Christ and the Holy Spirit, as lived out by Jesus' witnesses, is the main thrust of the Acts of the Apostles.

At this point, Acts introduces important information regarding the development of the early Jesus movement and tensions between circumcised believers and the mission to the Gentiles. After Peter's receiving a vision at Joppa and Gentiles' receiving the gospel, he receives strong criticism among believers in Jerusalem in Acts 11. And, following Paul's first mission, dissention from the Jewish leaders in Jerusalem necessitated the council meeting in Acts 15. While many instances of authentic worship are narrated as a factor of Christian fellowship in Acts (see especially chs. 1–6 and 15), the theme comes in again as a religious thrust in Acts 16 and following. For instance, Lydia, a worshipper of God in Thyatira (Acts 16:14), receives the gospel, and after she and her household were baptised, she opens her home to the ministry of Paul and others. Throughout Asia Minor and Greece, as Jews and Gentiles alike hear the gospel, some of them respond and become authentic worshippers of God as a result.

3.4 Overall Resonance of Authentic Worship in John and Luke-Acts

Overall, authentic worship in Luke-Acts carries a good deal of resonance with John, perhaps with a bit of interfluentiality between these traditions. While Jerusalem with its temple is the historic and religious centre of the Jewish faith and practice, within the Second Covenant, God's saving-revealing work is not bound to Jerusalem nor its cultic institutions. While people come to Jerusalem to worship authentically, some keepers of the religious institutions and their forms are presented as resistant to God's time-changing work in Jesus as the Christ, where others are more open in their responses to Jesus and the work of his followers. Where people respond authentically to God's presence and manifestations, even in the Diaspora, they are presented as receptive and responsive to the divine initiative as proclaimed in the gospel message.

In the light of the Romans' destruction of Jerusalem and the temple in 70 CE, God's transformative presence and work in the Jerusalem temple is now understood to be accessible more universally —wherever believers worship in Spirit and in truth—as an incarnational reality to be experienced in gathered meetings for worship (Matt. 18:18–20). This would have rung true both in synagogues throughout the Mediterranean world meeting on the Sabbath as well as the gathering of believers in house churches and other venues on First Day within apostolic and other missions to the larger world. Thus, the Jerusalem temple becomes a typology the New Covenant (developed more fully in Hebrews), and it is also prefigured in the Johannine writings as well as Luke's second volume. On the topics of the Holy Spirit, Samaritans, and women, the Gospel of John can thus be seen to have contributed also to at least some of Luke's content, echoed further in Acts.

4. John's Theological Contributions to Luke-Acts

While Luke departs from Mark and coincides with John extensively in terms of narrative detail, its presentation of John the Baptist, aspects of narrative content, presentations of Jesus' teachings and ministry, presentations of disciples, and associative links, Luke also conflates John and Mark together at several points. Some Johannine content is also found in Acts—or vice-versa—and these features include presentations of the Holy Spirit, Samaritans, and women.

4.1 The Work of the Holy Spirit in John and in Luke-Acts

The work of the Holy Spirit is a centrally featured theme in John and Luke-Acts, and it is fair to say that Luke expands the theme as presented in Mark in Johannine directions. As one of the central themes in the great discourses of Jesus in John is that the Holy Spirit will continue to teach Jesus' followers after his departure (John 14:26; 16:13), leading them into truth and reminding them of his words in timely ways, this theme is added by Luke to the promise of Jesus in Mark. Mark's Jesus promises that when facing trials before synagogues and leaders, his followers will be given the words to say at the appointed time (Mark 13:9–11); Luke expands on this promise in ways Johannine, promising that 'the Holy Spirit will teach you at that very hour what you ought to say' (Luke 12:12). Paul also refers to the teaching ministry of the Spirit (1 Cor. 2:13), so Pauline influence is not out of the question, but in Acts, the Spirit clearly instructs Philip (Acts 8:29), Peter (Acts 10:19), the believers at Antioch (Acts 13:2), Paul (Acts 20:23), and Agabus (Acts 21:11). Therefore, the promise of Jesus in John 14–16, that the Holy Spirit will continue to teach and guide his followers, is also sounded amply in Luke-Acts as a proleptic and actualised reality.

Another interesting feature about the Holy Spirit is that only in John and in Acts is the Spirit associated directly with *wind*. In John 3:8 Jesus declares: τὸ πνεῦμα ὅπου θέλει πνεῖ, καὶ τὴν φωνὴν αὐτοῦ ἀκούεις, ἀλλ' οὐκ οἶδας πόθεν ἔρχεται καὶ ποῦ ὑπάγει· οὕτως ἐστὶν πᾶς ὁ γεγεννημένος ἐκ τοῦ πνεύματος ('The wind blows where it chooses, and you hear the sound of it, but you do not know where it comes from or where it goes. So it is with everyone who is born of the Spirit'). The point is that the reality of the wind is felt by its impact, rather than its visibility; such is the character of the kingdom of God. Its workings might not be outwardly visible, but its effects attest to its potency and reality. In Acts 2:2–4, the Spirit descends on the gathering of believers on Pentecost, making a sound like that of a rushing wind. Here the incapacity of humanity to contain the workings of God is evident; humans are called to respond to the divine initiative and to set their sails to the wind of the Spirit. This is precisely the sort of spiritual reality that confounds religious authorities, as revelation—the Creator's disclosure of convicting truth and instructive guidance—is ever a scandal to the creaturely constructs of religion, conventionally helpful though they may be.

A third feature common to the Johannine and Lukan presentations of the Holy Spirit is that John's Jesus promises his followers that he will send the παράκλητος—the comforting Holy Spirit—who will be in and with his followers (John 14:17). Luke describes the comfort and consolation of God as παράκλησιν, effected by the work of the Spirit who is with and among his followers (Luke 2:25; Acts 9:31; 13:15; 15:31). Thus, the Holy Spirit carries forth two further works in the Johannine and Lukan traditions. First, believers are led into liberating truth, as Jesus speaks the truth (John 8:40,45,46; 16:7; Luke 4:25) and speaks truly (John 1:47; 6:55; 8:31; 17:8; Luke 9:27; 12:44; 21:3), resulting in believers knowing truly (John 7:26; 17:8; Acts 12:11). Further, Jesus' followers bear witness in John, and they also do so in Luke-Acts (John 1:7,8,15,32,35; 4:39; 15:27; 19:35; 21:24; Luke 11:48; 21:13; Acts 10:39–42; 13:31; 14:3; 20:21; 22:15; 23:11; 26:16). Thus, such ministries are presented as a function of the Spirit's filling and empowerment, predicted by the risen Lord in Acts 1:8.

Therefore, in John and Luke-Acts, the Holy Spirit teaches and guides followers of Jesus into truth dynamically, presented distinctively as wind, and the Spirit also comforts and empowers believers in their time of need. Luke thus reports his understanding of the work of the Spirit beyond the gospel narrative as actualised in the experiences of the apostles, but the Johannine contribution to Luke's perspective is clearly palpable.

4.2 The Presentation of Samaritans in John and Luke-Acts

Samaritans are presented in the Johannine and Lukan traditions distinctively as being objects of Jesus' mission (rather than neglected by the Matthean Jesus: Matt. 10:5) and included among his followers. Such may be coincidental, but for Luke's departure from Mark in directions that *embrace* the Samaritan mission implies a traditional basis, such as is found only in John. Note several features of general agreement. First, within the New Testament 'Samaria' as a location is found only in John and Luke-Acts (John 4:4,9; Luke 17:11; Acts 1:8; 8:1,5,9, 4; 9:31; 15:3), and in contrast to the other Synoptics, Jesus ministers in Samaria as well as Galilee (John 4:4–42; Luke 17:11). Jesus' followers are also reported as travelling through Samaria in the Johannine and Lukan traditions alone (John 4:8,27–38; Luke 9:51–56; Acts 8:1–25; 15:3). While none of the particular visits to or travelling through Samaria in Luke-Acts are identifiable as having a direct connection with John 4, there is at least a degree of geographical resonance and perspectival unity between the traditions.

A second common feature is that Samaritan characters are presented in John and Luke in exemplary ways, despite a common acknowledgment that Jews ordinarily have no dealings with Samaritans (John 4:9; implicit in Luke 10:33–37). Such a mention acknowledges also the irony of such presentations. In John 4, not only does *the Samaritan woman* become a believer in Jesus as the Messiah/Christ, but she also heralds the news among her townspeople, and they too come to believe in Jesus for themselves (John 4:1–42). Therefore, she becomes an apostolic figure of outreach—the Apostle to the Samaritans—despite the ironic fact of her social identity. Further, while Jesus is rejected by some of the Judaean leaders and as a spurned prophet in his own hometown, note how he is accepted warmly and offered hospitality among the Samaritans and other Galileans, aside from his rejection in Nazareth (Mark 6:4 counterbalanced by John 4:39–45). Likewise in Luke, the Parable of the Good Samaritan (Luke 10:25–37), while the priest and the Levite should have stopped to help the victim on the road to Jericho, it is *the Samaritan* who proves to be the good neighbour. And, amongst the ten lepers who where healed, the one that returned and thanked Jesus was *a Samaritan* (Luke 17:16). Therefore, in both the teaching of Jesus and in the following developments in the narrative, Samaritan characters play ironically exemplary roles for later audiences uniquely in John and Luke. Such presentations also command potent rhetorical capacity, as these narratives are delivered later in their respective traditions, inviting inclusiveness and cross-cultural/religious outreach.

A third common feature between the Johannine and Lukan presentations of Samaritans involves the inclusion of Samaritans into the Jesus movement. In John 4, many among the Samaritans of Sychar come to believe in Jesus, and they offer him and his followers hospitality among them for two days, which they reportedly accept (John 4:40). Implicitly, Jesus' fellowship among the Samaritans evokes a disparaging accusation among the Judaean leaders, accusing him of being 'a Samaritan and having a demon' (John 8:48). Interestingly, Jesus denies having a demon but does not explicitly counter the allegation that he is a Samaritan. Might that reflect Samaritan sympathies within the very mission of Jesus? In Luke, Jesus is also received among the Samaritans (Luke 17:11–19), and in Acts 8:5–25 Philip and Peter and John travel through Samaria, and their mission is successful, though Philip's encounters with Simon the magician are presented as problematic. Apparently, believers had scattered into Samaria from Jerusalem after the martyrdom of Stephen (Acts 8:1–4), and overall, Jesus' prophecy that his followers would become witnesses in Jerusalem, Judaea, Samaria, and the remotest parts of the earth (Acts 1:8) is taken at face value by Luke.

What is striking about the Johannine and Lukan presentations of the mission to the Samaritans by Jesus and his followers is that this feature is unique in the New Testament. Neither in the other Gospels, nor in any of the Epistles, nor in the Apocalypse is anything said of Samaria or the Samaritan people, so such a feature is unlikely to have been simply concocted out of the blue. However, given that most trips between Galilee and Judaea would have involved traversing Samaria, it is also highly unlikely that neither Jesus nor his followers had *any* dealings with Samaritans whatsoever. That they reportedly did so is a strong historical likelihood, given that Samaritans are presented sympathetically in John and Luke-Acts. Cutting against ethnocentric and religiocentric investments, the Johannine and Lukan Jesus and his followers show themselves to be inclusive of disparaged peoples—individually and collectively—resulting from the power of authentic human–divine encounter and its resultant loving fellowship.

4.3 The Elevation of Women in John and Luke-Acts

A further interesting fact is that women in the Johannine and Lukan traditions are also presented with the highest status anywhere in the New Testament, and certainly Luke reflects Johannine influence along these lines. While the associations between John and Acts are less pronounced on this theme, the resonance is still clear; the Holy Spirit is poured out on young and old, male and female, and Jews and Gentiles (fulfilling Joel 2:28–32 in Acts 2 and beyond) as the new age of the Spirit transforms the known world. First, *the mother of Jesus* is featured prominently in John and Luke. In John, the mother of Jesus is featured for the opening and closing of his ministry in Cana and on Golgotha (John 2:1–12; 19:25–27). She is also known to the crowd in John 6:42 and is entrusted to the beloved disciple at the foot of the cross as a typology of familial ecclesiology and relational value.[28] Luke's birth narrative especially features Mary's situation and her pondering things in her heart (Luke 1:26—2:51). At the cross, Luke describes Mary also as 'the mother of James', featuring not only her connection to Jesus but her continuing influence on the familial approach to church leadership, exemplified in Acts 15 by James, whose caliphate leadership advanced the Jesus movement for its first three decades. Therefore, the mother of Jesus plays pivotal roles in both the Johannine and Lukan traditions.

Second, the connection between *Mary and Martha* in John 11:1—12:8 and Luke 10:38–42 presents an inescapable inference regarding some sort of intertraditional contact. As Martha and her sister are presented as 'loved' by Jesus in John 11:5 (as also is Lazarus), and his staying in their home in Bethany and receiving an anointing by Mary after the raising of Lazarus are pivotal within the Johannine narrative. That Luke builds upon the Johannine tradition is suggested by the following features: (a) Luke presents two sisters, Mary and Martha, who are known by Jesus and who serve him earnestly, displaying roles similar to those presented in John 11–12. Mary sits at the feet of Jesus, while Martha cares for domestic duties. Jesus ends up blessing the relational intimacy exemplified by Mary (Luke 10:42), suggesting also familiarity with Mary's anointing the feet of Jesus in John 12:1–8. (b) Luke betrays familiarity with (and dependence upon?) the Johannine rendering of the anointing of Jesus (while shifting it earlier in the narrative than it is

---

28 On the implications her (and the beloved disciple's) non-named appellation in John, see Anderson, 'Anonymous Appellations'.

in Mark and John, associating the event with the Son of Man's being a friend of tax collectors and sinners, Luke 7:34) in that he moves the more royal head anointing of Mark 14:3–9 (followed by Matt. 26:6–13) to an anointing of Jesus' feet as it is in John (Luke 7:36–50). While a move away from a servile anointing to a royal one could be imagined as fulfilling rhetorical interests, movement in the other direction makes it a highly unlikely departure from Mark (and Matthew?) without a traditional basis, which John alone provides. Here Luke shows further evidence of familiarity with the Johannine tradition (likely an oral-aural connection rather than written-read familiarity) in that he introduces another 'Mary' directly in the following paragraph (Mary Magdalene, Luke 8:2), which may also account for his adding the parabolic interpolation suggesting the woman's motivation.[29] Rather than gratitude for the raising of Lazarus, a conjectural inference of gratitude for sins forgiven is what lies behind Luke's embellishing the anointing narrative with a moralising flourish, which also accounts for his moving the report earlier in the narrative. (c) A third didactic embellishment of the Johannine Bethany account is implied by Luke's featuring a dead-man-yet-living—*Lazarus*—as the central figure in a parable regarding poverty and riches (Luke 16:19–31). While such a feature does not imply direct familiarity with the Johannine raising of Lazarus narrative, Luke does add also a second resurrection account (the son of the widow of Nain, Luke 7:11–15) and opportunistically employs the memory of the poor, departed Lazarus and afterlife consequences of economics and ethic, serving one of Luke's predominant theological interests.[30]

A third feature of Luke's aligning his narrative with the Johannine tradition, though having less direct associations, is the presentation of *women as apostolic leaders* in the Jesus movement. (a) Women make pivotal christological confessions in both John and Luke, as Martha declares climactically in John 11:27: 'Yes, Lord, I believe that you are the Messiah, the Son of God, the one coming into the world'. This is the closest statement in the narrative to the rhetorical purpose of the Fourth Gospel as stated clearly in John 20:31. In Luke 11:27 a woman in the crowd breaks in and confesses: 'Blessed is the womb that bore you and the breasts that nursed you', although Jesus turns the confession toward a blessing of those who hear God's word and obey it. (b) Women play important roles in Jesus' teaching, as a woman in childbirth is associated with the birth pangs of the new age (John 16:21), and a woman searching for her lost coin plays the role of God searching for those who are lost and rejoicing when one is found (Luke 15:8–10). (c) Women are also reported as being important witnesses to the resurrected Lord in both traditions, as women report having seen messengers in radiant clothes at the empty tomb (John 20:12; Luke 24:23).

The featuring of women in leadership is carried further in Acts, as such women as Tabitha (Dorcas), Mary (mother of John Mark), Lydia, Priscilla, Damaris, and even Paul's sister play active roles in the rise and progress of the Christian movement. The Spirit is poured out upon women and men alike, and certainly the Johannine and Lukan traditions feature women as being central within the leadership of the early church. While Luke to some degree mutes the more radical presentation of the likes of the woman at the well as being *the Apostle to the Samaritans* in John 4 and Mary Magdalene as being *the Apostle to the Apostles* in John 20, he still features women prominently and adds his own contributions to the Johannine account.

---

29 Nowhere in the New Testament is Mary Magdalene presented directly as a promiscuous woman; those inferences several centuries later result from connecting Luke 8:2 with the preceding paragraph.
30 Note a number of Johannine features in the background of Luke 7: the healing of a Roman official's servant in Capernaum from afar (vv.1–10—cf. John 4:46–54); the raising of a young Judean man from the dead (vv.11–17; cf. John 11:1–45); the questioning if John the Baptist or Jesus is the Messiah, including John's pointing to Jesus as the coming one (vv.18–35; cf. John 3:22–36). While Luke's literary access to the written Johannine account seems unlikely on these similarities, at least echoes of content found distinctively in John implies some form of intertraditional familiarity.

In addition to dozens of details and textual features where Luke departs from Mark and coincides with John, these more theologically laden themes show Luke's following John's trajectory in presenting his 'orderly account' with deference to 'those who from the beginning were eyewitnesses and servants of the *Logos*' (Luke 1:2, οἱ ἀπ' ἀρχῆς αὐτόπται καὶ ὑπηρέται γενόμενοι τοῦ λόγου). That being the case, Johannine influence upon Luke is apparent, though the fact that many of John's features are not followed by Luke suggests that he is not working from a text but may have been familiar with a formative stage of the tradition, or even the oral rendering of at least some of the Johannine witness, before its final completion around 100 CE. On connections between John and Acts, particular overlaps are fewer, but some general similarities suggest either influence, interfluence, or echoes of resonance between these two traditions. Of course, one reason for the lack of overlap may also involve the fact of differing foci as two distinctive subjects (Jesus of Nazareth and the acts of the apostles), and that may simply reflect their distinctive historical thrusts overall. What is clear, however, is that the trajectories set by Luke's use of the Johannine tradition in setting forth his Gospel narrative continue on in his second volume, especially with reference to the Holy Spirit, Samaritans, and women. Thus, Luke's 'orderly account' not only reflects the employment of Johannine features in his expansion upon Mark; it also furthers his understanding of Jesus and the movement he founded, carried forth by the works of the apostles.

5. Conclusion: Jesus, the Spirit, and the Emergent Christian Movement

Authentic worship comes through clearly as one of the leading themes in the Fourth Gospel, showing itself to be one of John's key means of declaring the evangelist's purpose. If the purpose of John's first edition is to convince hearers/readers that Jesus indeed is the Jewish Messiah/Christ, and if the later material supplementing the final edition of John calls for abiding in Christ and his community under the fellowship and empowerment of the Holy Spirit,[31] the emphasis on authentic worship in John 4 furthers both of these purposes extremely well. Not only is it humans that seek after God, but God is actively at work, seeking any and all who will worship him in Spirit and in truth. Such an endeavour, while rooted in Jewish faith and practice, is finally actualised in temples made not with human hands but within the changed and changing lives of those who are receptive and responsive to the activity of God's Spirit, independent of place and form. Such a time is coming, and now is, when the presence of the future is actualised in believers' understanding and experience.

As these themes are played out in the Gospels of John and Luke and also in Acts, their developments show at least a good deal of intertraditional resonance, and at times a bit of influence or even interfluence. Especially with reference to such theological themes as the work of the Holy Spirit, the meaningful role of women, and the hospitable presentation of Samaritans, John's influence upon Luke is palpable. Though somewhat distinctive in Acts, these themes are also further developed in Luke's second volume, although some degree of Johannine–Lukan interfluence along the way cannot be ruled out entirely. Given the development of the emergent Christian movement, while its Jewish roots and identity remain clear within the Johannine and

---

31 See my analysis of the apologetic and pastoral 'purposes' of the first and final editions of the Johannine evangel in Anderson, *Riddles*, 85–87, 141–4.

Lukan traditions alike, the ministry of the Jewish Messiah brings the blessings of Abraham to the greater world beyond, not by inculcating proselytes into its religious practices, but by extending the mission and message of the Revealer to Jerusalem, Judaea, Samaria, and the remotest parts of the earth (Acts 1:8). Such a message of the divine initiative, of course, always scandalises that which is of human origin, but so it is with Jesus, the Spirit, and the emerging Christian movement. And, the Johannine and Lukan traditions alike bear witness to the growing pains of such a development.

Appendix

Luke's Dependence upon the Johannine Tradition and an Overlooked First-Century Clue to Johannine Authorship (Acts 4:19–20)[32]

In lecturing on a Bi-Optic Hypothesis in a variety of settings around Europe the summer of 2010, the most common questions related to the Johannine-Lukan relationship. Because the Fourth Gospel was finalised last among the canonical Gospels (I believe ca. 100 CE is a plausible inference), it is assumed that John borrowed from Luke rather than Luke's drawing from the oral stages of the Johannine tradition.[33] This view, however, is highly problematic. Just because John may have been finalised late, its tradition did not originate late. John contains a good deal of primitive material, and thus the Johannine tradition would have been available to Luke as a gatherer of gospel material long before the finalisation of either Gospel.

The answer to this issue, however, depends on the questions one asks. Indeed, the Fourth Evangelist expands on biblical themes and events within the narrative, but does this mean that all contacts with Luke imply Johannine dependence and expansion? Not necessarily. Three questions seem important in considering the Johannine-Lukan relationship. First, why are Luke's most characteristic features missing from John? Second, why does Luke coincide (or side?) with John against Mark at least six dozen times?[34] And third, what might the discovery of an overlooked first-century Lukan clue to John's authorship contribute to a critical rethinking of scholarly approaches to the longstanding riddles of the Fourth Gospel?

1. Johannine Dependence on Luke?

While scholars correctly note that the Fourth Evangelist often expands upon features of a biblical text or on details emerging from the story of Jesus' ministry, the assumption that Johannine-Lukan contacts reflect John's dependence on Luke falls flat when considering the particulars. If one were to catalogue the dozen most memorable features of Luke, for instance, these would have to include the likes of: (a) shepherds, angels, and the birth narrative; (b) the hymns of Zechariah, Mary, and Simeon; (c) perhaps a genealogy (also in Matthew); (d) baby Jesus and young Jesus in the Temple; (e) the threefold temptation of Jesus in the wilderness (also in Matthew); (f) the Nazareth inaugural address of Jesus; (g) the Lord's prayer and the beatitudes (also in Matthew); (f) commandments to turn the other cheek and to love one's enemies (also in Matthew) and to love God and neighbour (in all three Synoptics); (h) the parables of the Good Samaritan and the Prodigal Son; (i) the story of Zacchaeus; (j) Jesus' agony in the garden (sweating drops of blood) and his appearance before Herod; and (k) post-resurrection encounters on the road to Emmaus. *None* of these distinctive Lukan features, however, appear in John; so, if John knew Luke, it seems

---

32 An earlier form of this appendix appeared as an essay in *Bible and Interpretation* (September 2010): https://bibleinterp.arizona.edu/opeds/acts357920.

33 Scholars arguing John's dependence on Luke have largely followed the erroneous speculation of Streeter (*The Four Gospels*) who wrongly followed the factually unsubstantiated view that John the Apostle died early, and therefore could not have written anything ascribed to him. Cf. Anderson, 'The Son of Zebedee'.

34 Having first noted three dozen ways in which Luke departs from Mark in Johannine directions in Appendix VIII of Anderson, *Christology*, 274–77, I was in consultation with Raymond Brown on this perspective, and he was in the process of changing his mind on the Johannine-Lukan relationship before he passed away in 1998. I later laid out some of these features also in Part III of Anderson, *Fourth Gospel* (pp.112–17); and, this list may grow as I continue the analysis further.

odd that none of Luke's most memorable features were remembered by John.[35]

Additionally, the twelve chapters in Luke that are most distinctively Lukan (Luke 1–2 and 10–19) show very few contacts with the Gospel of John. So, if the Johannine evangelist knew and used the Lukan tradition, he drew only from incidental details and not from the most characteristic of Luke's features or sections. Such an inference is thus highly unlikely from a literary-critical standpoint.

2. Lukan Dependence on John

Conversely, and critically, a better way to assess the relationship is to move from most likely inferences to others. Given that Luke depended on Mark, as nearly all biblical scholars believe was the case, the incisive question is better put: *why* did Luke *depart from Mark* at least six dozen times in ways that *coincide, or side, with the Johannine tradition*? Lamar Cribbs, Mark Matson, and Barbara Shellard have argued this case,[36] and the literary evidence favours this approach over Johannine dependence upon Luke. While it is unlikely that Luke had access to the Johannine written tradition, either in its first-edition or final forms (after all, Luke does not change the order of the temple incident, and he locates the great catch of fish at the beginning instead of the end of Jesus' ministry), it does seem that at least some form of general familiarity with the Johannine formative tradition, whether it be oral-aural familiarity (hearing some of the narrative rendered, either from a text or performed otherwise) would best account for the presence of Johannine details and emphases in Luke's 'orderly account'. Noting Luke's multiple departures from Mark and sidings with John becomes the *second and strongest basis* for ascertaining the character of the Johannine-Lukan relationship.

While the present appendix cannot take the space to lay out the full extent of the parallels, consider these notable instances, where Luke appears to draw from the Johannine tradition in both his Gospel narrative and in Acts:

1) Johannine detail is included in Luke-Acts:

- The beholding of Jesus' glory (*doxa*) is added to the transfiguration scene (John 1:14; Luke 9:32)
- Bethlehem is described as the city of David only in John and Luke (John 7:42; Luke 2:4)
- Jesus is described as the son of Joseph only in Luke and John (John 1:45; 6:42; Luke 3:23; 4:22)
- Stoning and fear of stoning by Jewish leaders or the crowd (especially in Jerusalem) is mentioned only in John and Luke-Acts (John 8:59; 10:31–33; 11:8; Luke 13:34; 20:6; Acts 5:26; 7:58; 14:5,19)
- The *Ioudaioi* seek to kill Jesus and his followers (John 5:18; 7:1; Acts 9:23; 26:21)
- The crowd acclaims Jesus as 'king' at the triumphal entry (John 12:13; Luke 19:38)
- The place Jesus went to on the Mount of Olives was known and frequented (John 18:2; Luke 21:37; 22:39)
- The 'right' ear of the servant was severed by Peter (John 18:10; Luke 22:50)
- The court/house of the high priest was entered by Jesus (John 18:15; Luke 22:54)
- Annas is uniquely mentioned in John and Luke-Acts, as is his association with Caiaphas (John 18:13,24; Luke 3:2; Acts 4:6)

---

35 See above, note 7.
36 In addition to Cribbs, 'St Luke', see Cribbs, 'A Study of the Contacts', Matson, *In Dialogue*; Shellard, *New Light*. D. Moody Smith, a leading authority on John and the Synoptics, also concurred with Cribbs along these lines: Smith, *John Among the Gospels*.

- Pilate's instructing the words to be written in Hebrew, Greek, and Latin is a detail common only to John and Luke (John 19:20; Luke 23:38—in some mss.)
- The tomb is one in which no one had ever been laid (John 19:41; Luke 23:53)
- Two messengers in white or dazzling clothes are mentioned at the empty tomb (John 20:12; Luke 24:4)

2) The Johannine presentation of John the Baptist is replicated in Luke and Acts:

- People question outwardly or in their hearts about John the Baptist, regarding whether he was the Christ (John 1:20; Luke 3:15)
- John declares himself *not* to be the Messiah in John and Acts (John 1:20; 3:28; Acts 13:25)
- John has a more extensive itinerant ministry (John 1:19–42; 3:22—4:3; 10:40–42; Luke 3:1–22; 7:18–35; 11:1) than portrayed in Mark
- In both John and Acts, spiritual birth involves not just water, but the Spirit (John 3:5; Acts 8:12–17; 18:24—19:7)

3) Luke adds Johannine narrative and content:

- The age of Jesus is alluded to (albeit differently) in John and Luke (John 8:57; Luke 3:23)
- 'The law of Moses' is referred to distinctively in John and Luke-Acts (John 1:17,45; 7:23; Luke 2:22; 24:44; Acts 13:39; 15:5; 28:23)
- Mary and Martha are mentioned as sisters and are presented as having similar roles (John 11:1–45; 12:1–11; Luke 10:38–42)
- A man named Lazarus is presented in both John and Luke and in both cases is associated with death and the testimony of after-death experiences—Luke expands a narrative into a parable (John 11:1—12:17; Luke 16:19–31)
- A distinctive story about a dead man being raised by Jesus is included in John and Luke (John 11:1–45; Luke 7:11–17)
- Pilate declares Jesus' innocence three times (John 18:38; 19:4,6; Luke 23:4,14,22)
- The crowd desires to give tribute to Caesar in their double demand for his crucifixion (John 19:1–16; Luke 23:2–33)
- The day was the day of Preparation for the Sabbath, explaining the haste of the burial (John 19:42; Luke 23:54)
- The great catch of fish is climactically mentioned as something of a calling or re-calling narrative (John 21:1–14; Luke 5:1–11)
- Concern is expressed at whether the nets might break (John 21:11; Luke 5:6–7)
- Jesus eats fish and bread with the disciples after the resurrection (John 21:9–13; Luke 24:28–43)

4) Presentations of Jesus' teachings and ministry in John are replicated in Luke:

- The 'word of God' is an embellished Lukan theme (John 1:1–2; 10:35; Luke 3:2; 5:1; 8:11,21; 11:28; Acts 4:31; 6:2,7; 8:14; 11:1; 12:24; 13:5,7,46; 17:13; 18:11)
- Only in John and Luke-Acts is Jesus referred to as 'saviour' (John 4:42; Luke 1:69; 2:11; Acts 5:31; 13:23)
- Double questions are asked regarding Jesus' Messiahship and Sonship (John 10:24,33–36; Luke 22:67,70)
- The ascension is alluded to or mentioned (John 20:17; Luke 24:51; Acts 1:9–11)

- Jesus suddenly appears to his disciples after the resurrection, standing among them (John 20:19; Luke 24:36)
- Jesus invites his followers to see and touch his hands (John 20:20,27; Luke 24:39–40)
- Jesus bestows peace upon his followers after the resurrection (John 20:19,21; Luke 24:36)
- Luke uniquely connects the beginning of feeding of the multitude with Bethsaida, the home of Philip, whom Jesus in John asked to find the crowds something to eat (John 1:44; 6:5; 12:21; Luke 9:10)
- The citation of Isaiah 6:9–10 is distinctively associated with the reaching of the Gentiles in John and Acts (John 12:20–41; Acts 28:25–28)
- 'Israelites' are portrayed as people in whom there is nothing false, and amongst whom God is at work in John and Acts (John 1:47; Acts 2:22,29; 3:12; 5:35; 13:16; 21:28)
- Jesus is presented explicitly as the prophet predicted by Moses (Deut. 18:15–22) in John and Acts (John 5:46; 6:14; Acts 3:22; 7:37; 26:22–23)
- Jesus refers to 'my kingdom' only in John and Luke (John 18:36; Luke 22:30)
- Jesus prays for his disciples, that they might not fail during the time of trial (John 17:15; Luke 22:31–32)

5) Presentations of disciples in John are repeated in Luke-Acts:
- The disciples question who would be the betrayer (John 13:22–24; Luke 22:23)
- Satan enters Judas (John 13:27; Luke 22:3)
- Only John and Luke mention a second Judas who is *not* Iscariot (John 14:22; Luke 6:16; Acts 1:13)
- Mary Magdalene becomes a link between the risen Lord and the apostles (John 20:18; Luke 24:10)
- Peter runs to the tomb after Mary's report (John 20:4; Luke 24:12)
- Peter arrives at the tomb and sees the linen cloths lying there (John 20:5; Luke 24:12)
- Peter is reported as having returned to his 'home' (John 20:10; Luke 24:12) after seeing the empty tomb
- The unbelief of Thomas in John 20:24–28 is alluded to as the unbelief of the apostles in Luke 24:11 following Mary's report
- Simon Peter is the primary disciple associated with the great catch of fish (John 21:2–11; Luke 5:3–8)
- Philip is presented as one who evangelises aliens, including Hellenists, Samaritans, and Ethiopians (John 12:20–22; Acts 8:5–40)

6) Luke follows John's order and presentation several times, against Mark:
- Luke begins Jesus' ministry in ways reminiscent of John's rendering: the countryside of Galilee in the area around Nazareth (John 1:43—2:11; Luke 4:14–16)
- Only one sea-crossing is used in Luke rather than Mark's two (John 6:16–21; Luke 8:22–26)
- Only one feeding is mentioned in Luke, and this is the feeding of the 5,000, as it is in John (John 6:1–15; Luke 9:10–17)
- Luke relocates the confession of Peter after the feeding of the 5,000 as a contrast to its following the feeding of the 4,000 as it does in Mark (John 6:68–69; Luke 9:20)
- Luke moves the servanthood discussion to the Last Supper, where it is in John (John 13:1–17; Luke 22:24–30)

- Jesus extols and exemplifies the greatness of servant leadership *at the table* (John 13:1–17; Luke 12:37; 22:24–30)
- Luke moves the prediction of Peter's denial to the Last Supper (John 13:38; Luke 22:34)
- Jesus' post-resurrection appearances begin in or near Jerusalem (John 20:19–29; Luke 24:13–53)

7) At times Luke conflates John's and Mark's presentations together:

- Peter's confession is 'the Christ of God' conflating 'the Christ' with 'the Holy One of God' (Mark 8:29 and John 6:69; Luke 9:20)
- Luke departs from Mark's presentation of the anointing of Jesus' head, and presents the event as the anointing of Jesus' feet—an unlikely move to make without a traditional basis; John provides such a basis (Mark 14:1–11 and John 12:1–8; Luke 7:36–50)

8) Sometimes associative links (not strong contacts, but distinctive similarities nonetheless) appear between John and Luke-Acts:

- 'Levites' are mentioned only in John and Luke-Acts (John 1:19; Luke 10:32; Acts 4:36)
- The claim by Jerusalem leaders that Jesus' or his disciples' lack of formal education is mentioned in John and Acts (John 7:15; Acts 4:13)
- 'Siloam' is only mentioned in John and Luke (John 9:7,11; Luke 13:4)
- Speaking against Caesar is used rhetorically against Jesus and his followers by surrogates of Jewish leaders (John 19:12; Luke 23:2; Acts 17:7)
- Jesus is described as a 'king' and a threat to Caesar before Pilate (John 19:14–15; Luke 23:2)
- Solomon's portico in the Jerusalem temple is mentioned only in John and Acts (John 10:23; Acts 3:11; 5:12), and this is one of the places Jesus and his followers witnessed to Jewish leaders

9) The Holy Spirit references emphasised in John are repeated in Luke-Acts:

- The Holy Spirit will teach believers what they need to know and say (John 14:26; Luke 12:12)
- The Holy Spirit is presented distinctively as 'wind' (John 3:8; Acts 2:2)
- The work of the Holy Spirit is described as 'comfort' (*paraklēsis*) provided by the Comforter (*Paraklētos*) in John and Luke-Acts (John 14:16,26; 15:26; 16:7; Luke 2:25; Acts 9:31)

10) Women are presented in similar ways in John and Luke-Acts:

- Jesus enters the home of Mary and Martha and is served by Martha (John 12:1–8; Luke 10:38–42)
- The mother of Jesus is featured prominently in John and Luke (John 2:1–12; 19:25–27; Luke 1:26—2:51)
- Women make confessions in John and Luke (John 11:27; Luke 11:27)
- Women are reported as having seen angels/men in radiant clothes at the empty tomb (John 20:12; Luke 24:23)

11) Samaritans are presented in similar ways in John and Luke-Acts:

- 'Samaria' is only mentioned in John and Luke-Acts in the New Testament (John 4:4,9; Luke 17:11; Acts 1:8; 8:1,5,9,14; 9:31; 15:3)
- Jesus ministers in Samaria as well as Galilee (John 4:4–42; Luke 17:11)

- Jesus' followers (versus Jesus' instructions in Matthew 10:5) are reported as travelling through Samaria (John 4:8,27–38; Luke 9:51–56; Acts 8:1–25; 15:3)
- A Samaritan person is presented as a favourable example for later audiences (John 4:39–42; Luke 10:25–37; 17:11–19)
- Jews having no dealings with Samaritans is declared or suggested (John 4:9; Luke 10:33–37)
- Samaritans are reported as believing that Jesus was the Messiah or receiving his ministry with gratitude (John 4:39–42; Luke 17:16; Acts 8:7–8,13–17)

12) Events reported only in John are alluded to in Luke-Acts:
- The 'idle tale' told by Mary Magdalene to the apostles in Luke 24:10–11 appears to be a reference to the account in John 20:2, where she reported the empty tomb to Peter and the beloved disciple
- The disciples' visit to the tomb in John 20:3–9 is alluded to in the disciples' report on the road to Emmaus in Luke 24:24
- The Lord's post-resurrection appearance to Simon Peter in John 21:2–21 is alluded to in Luke 24:34

While many of these similarities may be only incidental and might not prove direct contact between traditions, the preponderance of these features does imply some sort of intertraditional contact between the Johannine and Lukan traditions. While John Bailey argued that Luke and John may have shared a common, unavailable source,[37] there is no evidence of such a document. What we do have are the Gospels of Mark and John, and Luke clearly departs from Mark in ways that cohere with the Johannine witness at multiple times and in multiple ways.

3. Luke's Omissions and Rearranging of Mark Coinciding with John's Orderly Account

As Lamar Cribbs also noted, where John is silent with relation to Mark, Luke also omits many of those Markan sections, and most striking instance is Luke's 'Great Omission', whereby much of Mark 6–8 is omitted (Mark 6:47—8:26), while content from John 6 is included, followed by Luke's 'Little Omission', whereby some of Mark 9–10 is omitted (Mark 9:41—10:12).[38] While silence never provides as strong an argument as positive evidence, Luke's again cohering with John over and against Mark is conspicuous on three accounts: Luke's 'Great Omission', Luke's 'Little Omission', and Luke's Reconfiguration of Mark 6 and 8 along the lines of John 6.

1) Luke's 'Great Omission' (of Mark 6:47—8:26)—preferring the account of John 6
- Jesus walks on water (Mark 6:47–52; not in John, omitted by Luke)
- Healings in Gennesaret (Mark 6:53–56; not in John, omitted by Luke)
- Eating with defiled hands (Mark 7:1–23; not in John, omitted by Luke)
- The Syrophonecian woman's faith (Mark 7:24–30; not in John, omitted by Luke)
- Healing of deaf man (Mark 7:31–37; not in John, omitted by Luke)
- Feeding of the four thousand (Mark 8:1–10; not in John, omitted by Luke)
- Pharisees ask for a sign (Mark 8:11–13; not in John, omitted by Luke)

---

37 Bailey, *Traditions Common to Luke and John*.
38 Powell, '8.3. Passages from Mark Omitted by Luke'.

- Discourse on bread and leaven (Mark 8:14–21; not in John, omitted by Luke)
- Healing of blind man of Bethsaida (Mark 8:22–26; not in John, omitted by Luke and also Matthew)

While it would have served Luke's rhetorical interests in his presentation of Acts 6:1–6, where the seven Greek-serving deacons would have matched the seven basketfuls of bread morsels that were gathered in Mark 8:8 and 20, Luke presents a single feeding—not two—as presented in John, against both Mark and Matthew (if Luke knew Matthew also). Luke also omits several of Mark's healings and debates with Jewish leaders reported in Mark 6:47—8:26, which might also raise questions as to whether this material might reflect a diachronic history of the Markan text itself, especially if the feeding of the 4,000 narrative reflects ways that story was circulated among the Gentile churches.[39] Critical concerns over Mark's duplications, however, are apparent in Eusebius (Papias' citation of the Johannine Elder) as well as the Gospels of John and Luke. If Luke did have a full text of Mark, though, these omissions are indeed conspicuous, given that they cohere with the Johannine account.

2) Luke's 'Little Omissions (of Mark 9:41–10:12)—cohering with the Larger Johannine account

- Elijah must come first (Mark 9:9–13, not in John, omitted by Luke)
- Temptations to sin (Mark 9:42–48, not in John, omitted by Luke)
- Salted with fire (Mark 9:49, not in John, omitted by Luke)
- On marriage and divorce (Mark 10:1–9, not in John, omitted by Luke, though see Luke 16:18)
- Question from the sons of Zebedee (Mark 10:35–40, not in John, omitted by Luke)
- Cursing of the fig tree (Mark 11:12–14, not in John, omitted by Luke)
- Lesson of the fig tree (Mark 11:20–25, not in John, omitted by Luke)
- Anointing in Bethany (Mark 14:3–9; but see Luke 7:36–50 and John 12:1–10)
- Mocking of Jesus by soldiers (Mark 15:16–20, not in John, omitted by Luke)

While these distributed passages in the final ministry of Jesus in Mark, omitted by Luke, are not in John, this might be explicable on the basis that Luke's inclusion of Johannine material coheres especially with the Johannine Passion Narrative as well as John 6.[40] This could be explicable on the basis of Luke's having had fuller access to, or preference for, at least these two sections of John (John 6 and 13–21), for whatever reason. In addition to these distributed omissions (assuming Luke had access to Mark's account along these lines), some passages are omitted also by Matthew as well as Luke (also coinciding with John's silence): Jesus' family coming to restrain him (Mark 3:21; note, however, that both Mark 3:21 and John 10:20 report people—and different ones—claiming that Jesus was 'out of his mind'), the Parable of Seed Growing Secretly (Mark 4:26–29), and the naked man fleeing in the courtyard (Mark 15:51–52; note that Peter is naked in John 21:7). Along these lines, their double exclusion by Matthew and Luke (although they are also not in John) may simply reflect their being perceived to be odd and not worth reporting.

---

39 Apparently, the Johannine Elder is also critical of Mark's duplications—plausibly multiple feedings and sea crossings, likely reflecting Mark's gathering his material from more than one source, Petrine or otherwise—as the Elder (cited by Papias in Eusebius *Eccles. Hist.* 3.39), excuses Mark's duplications, as he was simply seeking to leave nothing out.

40 See Matson, *In Dialogue*.

3) Luke's Modification of Mark 6—8, and Lukan details in keeping with John 6

- Luke moves Peter's confession to the other Feeding (the 5,000, not the 4,000) as it is in John 6 rather than Mark 8
- Luke harmonises Peter's confession in Mark 8:29 ('You are the Christ') with his confession in John 6:69 ('You are the Holy One of God') as 'You are the Christ of God' (Luke 9:20)
- Luke reports only one sea-crossing (as in John, Luke 8:22–25) but having already reported such, Luke stays with Mark 4:35–41 rather than resorting to the sea crossing in John 6:16–21
- Luke includes additional details found in John 6, though not all that similar:
  - Jesus looked up and saw (people coming toward him, John 6:5; rich people putting gifts in the treasury, Luke 21:1)
  - Jesus had given thanks (John 6:11,23; Luke 22:19)
  - Jesus is tempted to produce bread (citing Scripture by the religious leaders, John 6:27–31; citing Scripture by the devil, Matt. 4:1–11; Luke 4:1–13)
  - People ask if this is not the son of Joseph (John 6:42; Luke 4:22)
  - Whoever 'comes to me' (says Jesus) faithfully will find life (John 6:35,37,45; Luke 6:47–48)
  - Jewish ancestors died (John 6:49,58; Acts 7:15)
  - To eat and drink of/with Jesus is blessed (his flesh and blood, John 6:53–58; at his table, Luke 22:28–30)

In addition to Luke's apparent borrowing from the Johannine Passion Narrative, it appears that Luke may have had some form of access to John 6, given that he follows John's lead over and against Mark numerous times. Then again, he does not go with John's sea-crossing account, as he has apparently already incorporated the account in Mark 4 in Luke 8; that might even reflect Luke's authorial development of his Gospel narrative as ground (water) already covered. While some of these features are noted in the above list of a dozen ways in which Luke departs from Mark coinciding with Johannine features, these changes of sequence and inclusion in ways cohering with John 6 cannot have been simply incidental; they reflect familiarity with, and preference for, the Johannine account over against Mark, and Matthew (or Q), depending on how one addresses Luke's double-tradition material. Also, if John 6 and 21 were added to the later stages of the Fourth Gospel's finalisation, Luke's familiarity with these two chapters, at least, reflects either Luke's later contact with the Johannine witness, or even its later-finalised material having been developing—and accessible—earlier.

While arguments from silence are a weaker form of reasoning than arguments from evidence, Luke *does* appear to include Johannine material in his incorporation of Mark, although it is doubtful that he had a full Johannine text available, as he clearly did with Mark and either Matthew or Q. Luke's prologue, however, might even acknowledge his use of the Johannine tradition in expressing appreciation to what was 'handed on to us by those who from the beginning were *eyewitnesses and servants of the word*' (Luke 1:2). Such is all the more likely, as Luke also provides an overlooked first-century clue to Johannine authorship.

4. An Overlooked First-Century Lukan Clue to Johannine Authorship?

The fourth consideration is the fact that Luke explicitly connects the apostle John with a Johannine saying in Acts 4:19–20, a fact that has been totally overlooked on all sides of the debate. Of course, Johannine authorship has been a knotty problem amongst scholars for two centuries, but one reason for excluding John the Apostle from authorship is the view that Irenaeus was the first to make the connection, which he explicitly does around 180 CE. This is problematic for two reasons: first, there is no other person connected with the authorship of the Johannine Gospel other than John the Apostle, except, perhaps John the Elder, both of whom Papias and others claim were buried in Ephesus. Hence the distinctions: 'the elder' and 'the disciple' (or 'the apostle' or 'the beloved disciple' or 'the theologian') identifying two leaders sharing the same name. Irenaeus may be the clearest one to connect John the Apostle with the Fourth Gospel, but he is not the first, as Charles Hill demonstrates.[41] Second, the only time John the Apostle speaks in Acts, he says something *with an unmistakably Johannine ring*, and this connection is made *a full century before Irenaeus*.

More specifically, 'Peter and John' speak in Acts 4:19–20, but it is in the form of two statements, not one, *a composite citation*, as the research of Sean Adams has elucidated.[42] The first statement appears to be made by Peter, and it is echoed by two other Petrine statements in Acts 5:29 and 11:17.

'Whether it is right in God's sight to listen to *you rather than to God*, you must judge' (Acts 4:19).

'We must obey *God rather than any human authority*' (Acts 5:29).

'If then *God* gave them the same gift that he gave us when we believed in the Lord Jesus Christ, *who was I that I could hinder God*?" (Acts 11:17).

Whether or not the historical Peter actually spoke this way, he is presented as speaking in characteristically Socratic rhetoric, appealing to divine rather than human authority. One could also argue the case that Peter—the bold apostle—likely employed loaded rhetoric, and the power-oriented legacy of Peter and his leadership style would not have been far off from such a presentation. Such, however, is not the present claim. Whatever the case, it must at least be acknowledged that Peter is presented several times in Acts, including 4:19, as appealing characteristically to divine authority rather than human authority. Luke thus presents Peter knowingly in a characteristic way.

The next statement, in verse 20, however, is *thoroughly Johannine*, and this fact has been totally missed within larger discussions, critical and otherwise.[43] While Luke uses seeing verbs over 250 times and hearing verbs over 150 times in his two-volume work, this is the only time he does so in this particular order, in the first person plural, and in the past tense; thus, the closest parallel in the New Testament is 1 John 1:3. When Acts 4:20 is considered in the light of the Johannine writings, Luke's connecting of John the Apostle with a characteristically Johannine saying is unmistakable.

'For we cannot keep from speaking about *what we have seen and heard*' (Acts 4:20).

'We declare to you *what we have seen and heard* so that you also may have fellowship with us' (1 John 1:3).

Jesus 'testifies to what he has *seen and heard*, yet no one accepts his testimony' (John 3:32).

Of course, this does not prove that John the Apostle spoke in these terms, or that Luke was correct in connecting him with a Johannine saying. Indeed, there are many other reasons scholars have

---

41   Hill, *Johannine Corpus*.
42   Adams and Ehorn, *Composite Citations*.
43   Craig Keener, though, has noted this characteristic Johannine link, agreeing with the present analysis, in the second volume of his four-volume commentary on Acts: *Acts: An Exegetical Commentary*, ad loc.

excluded an eyewitness, one of the twelve, and particularly the son of Zebedee from eligibility as the Fourth Evangelist, and these are laid out elsewhere (along with thirty-six theological, historical, and literary Johannine riddles).[44] However, given the facts that Luke appears to have drawn from the Johannine tradition in addition to Mark, and that he acknowledges his indebtedness to those who were *'from the beginning eyewitnesses* and servants of the *Logos'*, the fact of his connecting of John the Apostle with a distinctively Johannine phrase in Acts 4:19–20 calls for a critical reopening of an otherwise 'open-and-shut' case on the origin and character of the Johannine witness.[45]

Given the additional facts that there is no compelling evidence for either John's dependence on alien sources (à la Bultmann and Fortna) or the Synoptics (à la Streeter and Barrett), Luke's testimony regarding the Johannine witness calls for a new paradigm for addressing the Johannine riddles.[46] The Fourth Gospel is neither a derivative narrative (versus the Jesus Seminar) nor a fictive imitation of reality.[47] While theologically developed and engaged, it represents an autonomous and dialogical Jesus-tradition deserving of critical consideration within the historical quest for Jesus. This is what a Bi-Optic Hypothesis seeks to provide, and what the John, Jesus, and History Project seek to explore. Perhaps this new century and millennium will avail a way forward for that to happen—both critically and reflectively—posing new critical and compelling approaches to the Jesus of history, the Christ of faith, and the Gospel of John.

Paul N. Anderson
Professor of Biblical and Quaker Studies, George Fox University of Newberg, Oregon
and Extraordinary Professor of Religion at the North-West University of Potchefstroom, South Africa

---

44 Anderson, *Riddles*.
45 Anderson, 'The Son of Zebedee'.
46 My analyses of Bultmann's and Barrett's approaches, as well as others, are laid out in Anderson, *Christology of the Fourth Gospel*, Appendix VIII, which argues the implications of Acts 4:19–20 for Johannine authorship (pp.274_77).
47 Anderson, 'John: The Mundane Gospel'.

Bibliography

Adams, Sean A. and Seth M. Ehorn   *Composite Citations in Antiquity: Jewish, Graeco-Roman, and Early Christian Uses* (LNTS 1/525; London: Bloomsbury: T&T Clark, 2016).

Anderson, Paul N.   'Anonymous Appellations in the Fourth Gospel—Confirming the Non-Identity of the Beloved Disciple AND the Mother of Jesus?', in David B. Capes (ed.), *Does It Matter Who Wrote the Bible? The Pastoral Implications of Pseudonymity and Anonymity in the New Testament* (Eugene, OR: Pickwick Publications, 2025), 45–75.

Anderson, Paul N.   'The Universal Light, or the Only Way to the Father? Universalism and Exclusivism in John's Provocative Christology', *Religions* 15 (2), 204 (January 2024): https://doi.org/10.3390/rel15020204.

Anderson, Paul N.   'John: The Mundane Gospel and Its Archaeology-Related Features', *The Bible and Interpretation* (July 2020): https://bibleinterp.arizona.edu/articles/john-mundane-gospel-and-its-archaeology-related-features

Anderson, Paul N.   'The Son of Zebedee and the Fourth Gospel: Some Clues on John's Authorship and the State of the Johannine Question,' in Bernardo Estrada and Luis Guillermo Sarasa (eds.), *El Evangelio de Juan. Origen, Contenido, Perspectivas – The Gospel of John. Origin, Content, Perspectives* (Colección Teología Hoy No. 80; Bogota: Editorial Pontificia Universidad Javeriana / Studiorum Novi Testamenti Societas, 2018), 17–82 and 241–49.

Anderson, Paul N.   'Anti-Semitism and Religious Violence as Flawed Interpretations of the Gospel of John', in R. Alan Culpepper and Paul N. Anderson (eds.), *John and Judaism: A Contested Relationship in Context* (Resources for Biblical Study 87; Atlanta: SBL Press, 2017), 265–311. A longer edition was published in *The Bible and Interpretation,* October 2017. https://bibleinterp.arizona.edu/articles/2017/10/and418017).

Anderson, Paul N.   'The Johannine *Logos*-Hymn: A Cross-Cultural Celebration of God's Creative-Redemptive Work', in edited by R. Alan Culpepper and Jan van der Watt (eds.), *Creation Stories in Dialogue: The Bible, Science, and Folk Traditions* (Radboud Prestige Lecture Series by Alan Culpepper; BINS 139; Leiden: Brill, 2016), 219–42.

Anderson, Paul N.   'On Seeking Truth (and Being Found by It) – A Christocentric Double Search', in Jeffrey Dudiak (ed.), *Befriending Truth: Quaker Perspectives* (Quakers and the Disciplines 2; Longmeadow, MA: Full Media Services, 2015), 182–95.

Anderson, Paul N.   *From Crisis to Christ: A Contextual Introduction to the New Testament* (Nashville, TN: Abingdon, 2014).

Anderson, Paul N.   '"Come and See!" Philip as a Connective Figure in the Fourth Gospel in Polyvalent Perspective', in Steven A. Hunt, D. François Tolmie, and Ruben Zimmermann (eds.), *Character Studies in the Fourth Gospel* (WUNT 1/314; Tübingen: Mohr Siebeck, 2013), 162–82.

Anderson, Paul N.	'The Jesus of History, the Christ of Faith, and the Gospel of John', in Bernardo Estrada, Ermenegildo Manicardi, and Armand Puig i Tarrech (eds.), *The Gospels: History and Christology; the Search of Joseph Ratzinger – Benedict XVI, Vol. 2* (Rome: Libreria Editrice Vaticana, 2013), 63–81.
Anderson, Paul N.	*The Riddles of the Fourth Gospel: An Introduction to John* (Minneapolis, MN: Fortress, 2011).
Anderson, Paul N.	'Bakhtin's Dialogism and the Corrective Rhetoric of the Johannine Misunderstanding Dialogue: Exposing Seven Crises in the Johannine Situation', in Roland Boer (ed.), *Bakhtin and Genre Theory in Biblical Studies* (Semeia 63; Atlanta, GA: SBL Press, 2007), 133–59.
Anderson, Paul N.	'Aspects of historicity in John: Implications for Archaeological and Jesus Studies', in James H. Charlesworth (ed.), *Jesus and Archaeology* (Grand Rapids, MI: Eerdmans, 2006), 587–618.
Anderson, Paul N.	*The Fourth Gospel and the Quest for Jesus; Modern Foundations Reconsidered* (LNTS 321; London: T. & T. Clark 2006).
Anderson, Paul N.	*The Christology of the Fourth Gospel; Its Unity and Disunity in the Light of John 6* (WUNT 2/78; [Tübingen: Mohr Siebeck 1996]; third printing with a new introduction, outlines, and epilogue; Eugene, OR: Cascade, 2010).
Bakhtin, Mikhail	*The Dialogic Imagination—Four Essays* (edited by Michael Holquist; Austin, TX; University of Texas Press, 1981).
Bailey, John A.	*The Traditions Common to the Gospels of Luke and John* (NovTSup 7; Leiden: Brill, 1963).
Barrett, C. K.	*Essays on John* (Philadelphia, PA: Westminster, 1982).
Bernier, Jonathan	*Aposynagōgos and the Historical Jesus in John: Rethinking the Historicity of the Johannine Expulsion Passages* (Biblical Interpretation Series 122; Leiden: Brill, 2013).
Cadbury, Henry J.	*The Making of Luke/Acts* ([1927], 2nd edn. 1958; Peabody, MA: Hendrickson 1999).
Coloe, Mary L. P.V.B.M.	*Dwelling in the Household of God: Johannine Ecclesiology and Spirituality* (Collegeville, MT: Liturgical Press, 2007).
Coloe Mary L. P.V.B.M.	*God's Temple Dwells with Us: Temple Symbolism in the Fourth Gospel* (Collegeville, MT: Liturgical Press, 2001).
Cribbs, F. Lamar	'A Study of the Contacts That Exist Between St. Luke and St. John', *Society of Biblical Literature: 1973 Seminar Papers* (edited by George MacRae; vol. 2; Cambridge, MA: SBL, 1973), 1–93.
Cribbs, F. Lamar	'St. Luke and the Johannine Tradition', *JBL* 90/4 (1971), 422–50.
Hill, Charles E.	*The Johannine Corpus in the Early Church* (Oxford: Oxford University Press, 2004).

Jones, Rufus	*The Double Search: Studies in Atonement and Prayer* (Philadelphia, PA: John Winston Company, 1906).
Keener, Craig S.	*Acts: An Exegetical Commentary: Volume 2 Acts 3:1—14:28* (Grand Rapids, MI: Baker, 2013).
Kristeva, Julia	*Desire in Language: A Semiotic Approach to Literature and Art* (New York, NY: Columbia University Press, 1980).
Matson, Mark A.	*In Dialogue with Another Gospel?* (Atlanta, GA: SBL, 2001).
Penn, William	'Primitive Christianity Revived. Introduction to the 1696 publication of the *Journal* of George Fox', (revised by Paul Buckley; Newberg, OR: Inner Light Books, 2018).
Porter, Christopher A.	*Johannine Social Identity Theory after the Fall of the Jerusalem Temple* (Biblical Interpretation Series 194; Leiden: Brill, 2021).
Powell, Mark Allan	'8.3. Passages from Mark Omitted by Luke', in Mark Allan Powell, Supplement to *Introducing the New Testament* (2nd edn; Grand Rapids, MI: Baker, 2018), 852.
Schleiermacher, Friedrich	*The Life of Jesus* (S. Maclean Gilmour, trans.; Jack C. Verheyden, intro.; Philadelphia, PA: Fortress, 1975).
Shellard, Barbara	*New Light on Luke; Its Purpose, Sources and Literary Context* (London: T&T Clark, 2004).
Smith, D. Moody	*John Among the Gospels* (2nd edn; Columbia, SC: University of South Carolina Press, 2001).
Spiro, Abram	'Stephen's Samaritan Background', in *The Acts of the Apostles* (AB 31; New York, NY: Doubleday, 1967), 285–300.
Strauss, David F.	*The Christ of Faith and the Jesus of History* (Leander E. Keck, trans. and intro.; Philadelphia, PA: Fortress, 1977).
Streeter, B. H.	*The Four Gospels* (London: Macmillan, 1924).
White, Hayden	*Metahistory: The Historical Imagination in Nineteenth-Century Europe* (Baltimore, MD: John Hopkins, 1973).

Bad smells at a religious gathering[1]

ALAN H. CADWALLADER

Abstract

Smell tends to be placed at the bottom of the rung of attention in analyses of the ancient world. When it gains attention it tends either to be heavily regulated (into taboo, periphery, comedy) or burdened with symbolism. This paper takes up an apocryphal addition to the story of Lazarus in the remarkable illumination found in Codex Rossanensis—a slave covering his nose as he leads Lazarus out from the grave. It explores the meaning and control of odour in occupational and religious settings, with special attention to death and curses, beans and garlic. The resultant insight suggests that there may be something radical being explored in early Christian negotiations of smell (with special attention to Jn 11:17–44, Acts 10:5–18 and 2 Cor 2:14–15).

In the ancient Graeco-Roman world, the senses, like so many aspects of life, were configured into a hierarchy of relationships. The so-called 'intellectual' senses—the visual and the aural, sight and hearing—were placed at the apex. These received the overwhelming concentration of literary attention and cultivation. The so-called 'animalistic' senses—touch and taste and smell—trailed off in the coverage to the point where, according to Mark Bradley, the most remarkable base-line of the hierarchy, that is smell, 'is its very transitoriness and elision from the record, as well as its ambiguities and complexities'.[2] In academic circles, and this essay cannot escape the charge, we are pulled into the continued dominance of sight and sound, our own reiteration of the ancient hierarchy that privileges the 'intellectual' over the 'animalistic' senses.[3] Indeed, the dominance of the intellectual senses infects the treatment of the animalistic in that there is a rapid, almost-escapist transformation of the actual often-tardy material realms into the symbolic. So, for example, Dorothy Lee, in a laudable desire to harness the five senses to an exposition of the incarnation in the Fourth Gospel, yet flicks the realm of smell into a theological contrast between death and life, a compounding, deodorising transition.[4] In her words, 'olfaction' (the fancy word for smell) 'functions as symbolic of both life and death'.[5] However much this may be true of the

---

1   This essay originated as the 'After-Dinner Address' for the Sydney College of Divinity Centre for Gospels and Acts Research, December 2024.
2   Bradley, *Smell*, 2–3.
3   See Corbin, *The Foul and the Fragrant*, 6–8.
4   Tullett, *Smell and the Past*, 17, relying on the insights of Barthes, *Sade, Fourier, Loyola*, 137.
5   Lee, 'The Gospel of John', 125.

Gospel of John (and a caveat does yet need to be placed here), we are allowed, even encouraged to slide quickly away from the assault on our noses into an ethereal world of symbolic imagination where such odorous offenses are either barred by an air-tight window or covered over with some sickly-sweet air sanitiser.

We see such an erasure even in the movement of English translations of John 11:39 from the very earthy Authorised Version 'Lord, he stinketh' to the Revised Version margin 'the body decayeth' to the ever-so-genteel RSV paraphrase 'there will be an odor', or 'he will smell' in the New Matthew Bible, beefed up slightly by the NIV as 'a bad odor' or 'bad smell' in the New Life Version. A number do lash out with 'there is a stench' (NRSV, NKJV) or even 'the stench will be unbearable' (Voice). No translation, as far as I can find, simply says 'he'll be on the nose', though this has a nice homophonic link to the Greek word used: ὄζειν.

In fact, this 'being on the nose' is precisely what is captured in one of the earliest illuminations of the Lazarus scene—that contained in Codex Rossanensis, a glorious sixth-century purple vellum Gospel book, now held in the cathedral museum at Rossano in southern Italy but probably rendered, at least in its illuminations, at a school in Beirut.[6] The illumination of the raising of Lazarus seeks to express the entire narrative in a rolling sequence of two parts, embellished in a lower polyptych with salient quotations from the Greek Old Testament headed by their reputed composers: David (for *Odes* 3:6, even though it contains a line from the prayer of Hannah), Hosea (for Hos. 13:14), David again (as composer of the entire Psalter, as in Heb. 4:7—here Ps. 76:15, though credited in the Masoretic Text as a song of Asaph) and Isaiah (for Isa. 26:19).[7] These harness First Testament testimonies to the resurrection of the dead, arranged, through the signalling, right hands, as now fulfilled in this Gospel episode.

But the illumination of the scene also adds some details not found in the text but thought, at least by the limner, to be implied. Firstly, the two sisters, Martha and Mary, *both* prostrate before Jesus, though the Gospel only mentions Mary falling at his feet (John 11:32 ἔπεσεν αὐτοῦ πρὸς τοὺς πόδας). Secondly, and more importantly for our purposes, Lazarus is accompanied from the cave-tomb by a figure whose short chiton dress and unkempt hair mark him as a slave, as also the two properly-grieving slaves immediately in front of him. This alone is striking when compared to another artistic representation from about the same time (that is, Sixth Century CE) in the magnificent cycle of events from the life of Christ given in mosaic form in the Chiesa di Sant'Apollinare Nuovo at Ravenna in northern Italy.[8] Here there are no slaves and Jesus is accompanied only by a quite Romanised evangelist, John. But the Gospel-book illuminator adds a further element to the slave presenting Lazarus at the mouth of the tomb—the neck-line to his chiton is raised over his nose, a visual signal of how much Lazarus was in need of cleansing bath!!! Lazarus was 'on the nose' which no aromatic herbs, spices and ointments could assuage—even if they had been used.[9]

This remarkable illumination lays the foundation for what I'd like to explore—what it meant in the ancient world to be 'on the nose', especially in religious contexts and how it was dealt with, or even engineered, in those settings. The extra-canonical slave in the Lazarus illumination will pop in and out to remind us of the significance of the great stink.

---

6   For the illumination, with the added function of magnification, see https://www.codexrossanensis.it/detail.php?lang=en&id=1.
7   See Hixson, 'Forty Excerpts', 513. Hixson over-reads the specificity of the pointing hands, claiming that the two Davids point to Christ, the two prophets to Lazarus (pp.528, 532).
8   On the utilisation of the Lazarus motif on early Christian sarcophagi, see Fox, 'Burial and Resurrection'.
9   Compare Plautus *Curc.* 101–3; Tacitus *Ann.* 16.6; Diodorus Siculus *Hist.* 18.26.3.

Ancient olfactory—an overview

Most writers who venture into the smell factory—or olfactory as they like to call it—remind readers that the ancient world was full of smells. The daily life of temple sacrifices,[10] fish and meat markets, and the public latrines where tanners, dyers, and fullers would sometimes harvest the liquid effluent for use in the industrial process,[11] meant that noxious, offensive, at least potent smells were part of everyday life, certainly in the cities.[12] Pompeii holds a number of graffiti that boast of defecating against the walls of houses or city-gates. One graffito to the left of the door of the House of Pascius Hermes unleashes a curse against the offender: 'Look out you wretched defecator. Ignore this warning and you might be dumped upon—by Jove's fury.'[13] The *Martyrdom of Bartholomew* speaks of another stench at the walls—that of a leper.[14] Whole towns might attract a name from their offensive atmosphere—so Puteoli (famous as a maritime stop for Paul [Acts 28:13]) means, on one etymology, 'putrid' (from *puteo* 'I stink').[15] Of course, this panorama of pungency was concentrated if you were unfortunate enough to be chained up in prison—like Paul for example.[16] However, change the setting to a farm, and excrement is prized as a fertiliser to improve yields. Columella, the Roman guru of agriculture, devoted an entire section to manure.[17]

The early-third-century Jewish rabbinical text, the Mishnah, admits that some smells were odious enough to allow divorce: 'And these are the men whom we compel to divorce their wives [if they apply]: A man smitten with boils, a man who has polypus [that is, halitosis, or in the view of some ancients, "snake-breath"],[18] a gatherer of handfuls of excrement [also used in the maceration step of the tanning process], a refiner of copper and a tanner.' (m. Ketubot 7.10; bt. Ketubot 77a). The explanation for such a non-fault divorce is that, quite simply, the husband stinks. But the range of warrantable offences points, at least in the last three instances, to recognised occupations in the ancient world that frequently drew odium because of their otiose odours.

A pincer movement of stench—tanning and fishing

As an aside, this raises the old question of Paul's supposed tent-making (Acts 18:3 cf. 1 Cor. 4:12), or perhaps more strictly, leather-working (σκηνοποιός, often, but not exclusively, having an objective of making a tent). Did it mean that Paul was actually involved in the tanning process or simply as the value-adding recipient of the product?[19] More pointedly, what does it say about Peter's lengthy stay with Simon the tanner at Joppa in Acts 10, most especially if, as frequently, the tanning workshop

---

10   On the pervading stench of sacrifice, see Warrior, *Roman Religion*, 41.
11   Martial *Ep.* 6.93. See Flohr, *The World of the Fullo*, 185–86; Kaster, 'The Dynamics of Fastidium', 176–7. On the efforts to deal with problems of sewerage see Koloski-Ostrow, '*Ita pestilens est odore taeterrimo*'.
12   See Classen et al., *Aroma*, 17.
13   *Cacator cave malum | aut si contempseris habeas | Iove iratum* CIL 4.7716. On the offence to the gods of toileting 'out of place', see Harrison, 'Finding the Right Spot', 348–49.
14   *Martyrdom of Bartholomew* 1.2
15   So Strabo *Geography* C245, from the foul waters that dot the region. He allows that others construed the name from *putei*, 'wells'.
16   See the description of a cell in Lucian *Tox.* 29.
17   Columella *Re Rust.* 2.14.1ff.
18   Virgil *Aen.* 7.351; Ovid *Meta.* 4.498. The problems of bad breath apparently attracted the notice of the physician, Rufus of Ephesus: 'On the stench of the mouth'. It seems also to figure as a matter of concern in magic-medicine: see Aramaic Incantation Text 16:9 (Montgomery, *Aramaic Incantation Texts*, 94).
19   See Hock, *The Social Context*, 21–25.

was part of the seaside establishment (Acts 10:5–18). The meeting must have been an odour-drenched nightmare—'what a nuisance they are to the public nose' as Plautus in his play *The Captives* described fishmongers.[20] 'Putridity does characterize the seaside', affirmed Saara Lilja.[21]

Likewise, tanning was infamous—and parodied—for its stench, which even infiltrated the dream-world.[22] Indeed, if the satirist Martial is anything to go by, the manufacture of purple dye from the murex shell at workshops down the eastern Mediterranean coastline meant that one of the most obnoxious nuisances of the coastal cities was the stench (Martial *Ep.* 4.4.6). It was, as Ephraim Lytle comments, 'penetrating',[23] even moreso when urine was used in the process (Pliny *NH* 9.127).[24] Perhaps a fisherman and a tanner were somewhat immune to the disagreeable reek that emanated from their skin, hair, and clothes.[25] Even so, this did not necessarily transfer to others—Artemidoros the dream-guide constructed the regulation of obnoxious tanners by removing them outside of townships—preferably downwind or on an exposed outcrop, I suspect![26] The Mishnah prescribed putting such establishments on the east side of town (m. Batra 2.9), that is, furthest away from the prevailing westerly winds. One early Attic inscription forbade the tanning of hides and the discharge of waste products on the banks of the Illisus River upstream from the temple of Heracles (*IG* I³ 257, 440–430 BCE), a place (Kynosarges) south of the city but filled with religious institutions.[27]

This suggests that the modern circumspection about how much ancient peoples were sensitive to smells that we find disagreeable needs to be tempered.[28] Certainly, how a smell is labelled can affect how it is experienced but not exclusively determine reactions to pungency.[29] The proliferation of household incense burners, of oils, unguents, and perfumes indicates that at least those above subsistence levels tried to overlay local smells,[30] especially those emanating from those working at subsistence levels or below. Smells readily offered a taxonomy of social status. Even so a number of towns seem to have fullonica and tanning establishments within their precincts, and one seating allocation at the stadium at Aphrodisias is given to the βυρσέων συντεχνία.[31] Tanners' associations were also active in inscribing the familiar honorifics for the elite.[32] And if the Mishnah was followed in Joppa, the traditional site of Simon's house may be mis-placed (that is, squarely in the township)! The differences in this range of material supports John Bodel's repeated emphasis that valorisations and denigrations found a variety of expressions and applications across the Mediterranean.[33] No one place or region necessarily transfers to another in its particular values.

20 *alieno naso quam exhibeant molestiam*: Plautus *Capt.* 817.
21 Lilja, *The Treatment of Odours*, 166.
22 Aristophanes *Eq.* 892, *Vesp.* 38.
23 Lytle, 'The Delian Purple', 255.
24 There is evoked the irony that purple is the esteemed dye for clothing, apparently bequeathing a 'lingering odour' even after the finished textile is on-sold. See Quiles, 'There's Something Fishy', 82.
25 Fish was the prototype of stench in ancient Egypt providing a taxonomic range of noxious odours. See Goldsmith, 'Fish, Fowl, and Stench'.
26 Artemidoros *Oneir.* 1.51, 2.20. Artemidoros implies that the handling of dead bodies (as part of the process of tanning) was a compounding pollution requiring distance, similar to those involved in the funerary industry (*UPZ* II.192 col. 4.28–9). This provides a further component in seeking to understand the complexity of Peter's stay with Simon.
27 See Fabiani, 'La concia delle pelli'. She includes a description of the steps in the tanning process (pp.380–84).
28 So a caveat on the argument of Morley, 'Urban smells', 116–19.
29 See Iatropoulos et al., 'The language of smell'.
30 Compare Homer *Od.* 4.445–6.
31 Roueché, *Partisans and Performers*. Unfortunately the survival of inscriptions on this row (and those behind and in front) is limited so that we do not know with whom the association of tanners was grouped.
32 For example *I.Kybira* 63 (mid 2nd century CE); *TAM* V,2 986 (Thyateira, c. 220 CE); *CIL* 6.1682 (Rome, 334 CE).
33 Bodel, 'Dealing with the Dead'.

All this certainly adds an olfactory dimension to the implications of 'clean', just as Peter felt at liberty to extend the semantic reference from food (Acts 10:10–16) to people in his encounter with Cornelius the centurion (κἀμοὶ ὁ θεὸς ἔδειξεν μηδένα κοινὸν ἢ ἀκάθαρτον λέγειν ἄνθρωπον Acts 10:28). Given that clean and unclean were frequently interwoven with status implications and elitist stereotypes,[34] the 'all things clean' (πάντα τὰ βρώματα Mark 7:19)[35] certainly contained a socially disruptive component and can work to break down the usual polarity of foul and fragrant. Indeed, Celsus' scathing critique of early Christians laces his invective with the houses that Christians frequent—wool-workers, leather-cutters, and fullers—probably intentionally constructed not for historical accuracy so much as designating the (smelly) foulness of the Christ adherents.[36]

This brief overview has given us a sense of the potency of smell, perhaps even inviting some to turn up their nose, or imagine covering it like the slave in the Rossanensis illumination. But it behoves us to probe further some of the religious dimensions of smell. From the beginning, we need to recognise that there was no inherent classification in smells. Practical and religious usage are two poles that become possible of recognition, depending on the context that is provided for this or that smell and its generation. To gain an appreciation of this, we turn to the malevolent pungency of and in ancient curses, to the flatulence of beans and to the acridity of garlic.

An Ancient Curse on Land Expropriation

Recently there has been published a most important new edition of a short Latin text that had been buried in a collection of writings that were, pragmatically if inaccurately, assigned to Virgil. The *Dirae* (that is, 'Curses') is a short poem gathering together a series of incantations that curse a rural estate.[37] It is set as an invective laid out by a farmer who has had his farm confiscated in order that it be handed over to veteran soldiers of Caesar; the transfer would seem to be a compensation not only for military service but for the assassination of their beloved general. Octavian had been senatorially authorised to apportion settlements for the veterans and he or Mark Antony (as enemies of the Republic) may be coded in the text as the despised Thracian king, Lycurgus. These hints help to assign a date of 41–40 BCE to the poetic curse.[38] But the hatred dispensed is primarily directed to the harm of the unnamed soldier who received the property wrenched from the farmer's hand. The curse is not directed at the soldier per se but on the beloved land itself that had been treasured by the now-dispossessed farmer.

The editor, Boris Kayachev, notes that the bucolic poem operates similarly to the curse tablets, the *tabellae defixionum* that regularly crop up across the ancient Mediterranean. The aim is harm to an offender, usually by tying her / him to catastrophic judgement, often involving the interventions of gods, spirits, or other beings that have contact with the underworld. In this case, there is an elaborate inversion of the beauty of farm life, culminating in a destructive fire and flood. One gains the sense of what the farmer had celebrated in his farm; for his successor, he wants the opposite. Section after section proceeds through the glories of farm life, but now the contrary is sought—each section often opened with 'let us repeat this incantation more grimly'. To give a sample of this unravelling of the expected order and nature of things, I give one excerpt:

---

34 See Beerden, 'Evoking Empathy', 143; Rizakis, 'Town and Country', 256.
35 Note one Nubian Greek manuscript reads here σώματα for βρώματα. See Plumley, 'An Uncial Text of St. Mark', 34–5.
36 Origen *Cels.* 3.55.
37 Kayachev, *Dirae*.
38 Kayachev, *Dirae*, 35–6.

May the wheat furrow raise barren oats, may the meadows wilt and pale as they thirst with drought, may fruits fall unripe from branches on which they grow, may leaves disappear from the woods and water from the springs.[39]

For our present purposes, the pleasant smells of farm become cursed into harmful stenches:

These meadows, blossoming with Venus' motley adornment, which in spring paint the plains with purple (from them sweet breezes, from them pleasant scent comes to the fields), may they spread pestilential fumes and foul poisons.[40]

Here the *pestiferos aestus et taetra uenena*, 'the pestilential fumes and foul poisons' become an eschatological judgement upon the new owner, a complete inversion of the expected fragrant natural order. It is of a piece with the collapse of cosmic order in the apocalyptic passages of the Gospels (Mark 13:24–5 // Matt. 24:29) and throughout Revelation. It may be that the pestilence in view is malaria, a common scourge besetting Roman rural estates—here a farm apparently secure from the horrific experience of malaria, is now made its haven. The sweet scent of flowers was frequently used, much as today, to obviate the creeping odour of death. Here the intent is subverted with the meadows becoming an agent of miasma, the pollution that was a constant concern of religious purity requirements, here compounded by poisonous vapours characteristic of Medusa and her vipers.

These curses not only were an inversion of life, conjuring harm on some intended victim, but they harnessed a combination of divinities and death, an inexorable, execrable onset of destitution. Although this is a stylised curse, whatever may have been its realistic hope of retribution for the loss of propertied well-being, most curses known from the curse tablets enacted a ritual placement in the tombs of others, especially those who had been buried after an untimely death.[41] The thought appears to have been that this somehow harnessed the power of death from the dead, and those divinities associated with death, to empower the discretely deposited curse tablet.[42]

This suggests that the slave in the Rossanensis illumination is not a dupe of the death-dealing odour—collateral damage as it were for the performance of a Jesus' marvel. Rather he can be seen as a bold venturer into the grave to assist the still-linen-bound Lazarus from the realm of Hades. He has, as it were, become a believer that death and its stench cannot infect him, even though the smell still requires some nasal barrier. 'Scent marks the boundary lines of the living and the dead', observes Peter McLellan,[43] and it is the slave who, suitably protecting his nose, has breached that liminal zone.

This transfers us from occultic religion to an expression of religion that addresses the necessity of dealing with these poisonous and pestilent situations—particularly pressing when emanating from the land. Here the earth-belching stench could not be overcome by lathering layers of aromatic counters upon it. In the ancient world, those places where noxious fumes erupted seem to have become focal points of religious attention, fencing off the poison by making the site a numinous centre. So various sites in Italy (such as in the Ampsanctus Valley of the Apennines in the south) that house sulphurous pools of water became sacred to Mefitis. Ingrid Edlund-Berry dubs her the 'goddess of stench'.[44]

---

39 *effetas Cereris sulcus producat auenas | pallida flaccescant aestu sitientia prata, | immuratura cadant ramis pendentia poma, | deficient siluis fronds et fontibus umor. Dirae* ll. 15–18 (translation by Kayachev).
40 *haec Veneris uario florentia prata decore | purpureo campos quae pingunt uerna colore | (hinc aurae dulces, hinc suauis spiritus agris) | mittant pestiferous aestus et taetra uenena. Dirae* ll. 20–23.
41 Jordan, 'A Survey of Greek Defixiones', 152.
42 See Cadwallader, *Colossae, Colossians, Philemon*, 371–74.
43 McLellan, *The Gospel of Mark*, 76.
44 See Edlund-Berry, 'Hot, cold, or smelly', 175–78. See generally, Mele (ed.), *Il culto della dea Mefite*.

At some sites, the smell was so powerful that it killed those who ventured too close. Thus taboos and officials governing approach were attached to the location, not only for protection but to harness for benefit the obvious potency of the site and its connected deity—where water was involved, this was frequently for healing. At Hierapolis in the Lycus Valley, the pungent sulphuric fumes that erupted from a cavity in the pitted limestone landscape cultivated a sense that here was an entrance to the underworld—a Ploutonion, carefully walled to enclose a 2000 square metre sanctuary.

The eunuch priests of Cybele were alone supposed to be able to cope with the vapours emitted from the bowels of the earth, unlike the sparrows and bulls sacrificed to the foul air. The wonder attracted reports from various ancient writers;[45] even today it has been proposed as the image behind Christ's descent into the depths in Ephesians 4:9.[46] But the temple of Apollo was also connected on the same noxious fault line and so prophetic oracles, healing, and control over death were all linked together in a religious extravaganza, albeit built on attendance and ritual that pre-date the city itself.[47] So important was the site to the city, that the Ploutonion was celebrated in coinage.[48] Here, foul smells became a profitable, if religiously imbued, venture.

The control of access and behaviour within these sanctuaries and in dedicated gatherings covered a range of aspects including dress, requirements after birth, sex, death, and ritual and festal contributions. Many of these Sacred Laws also contain hints at the effort to control smells, both welcome and unwelcome. I want to turn to two particular, if curious, regulations that occasionally find their way into these *Leges Sacrae*.

The Flatulence of Beans

Many years ago now, a number of us were exploring parts of Mark's Gospel. We puzzled over the name Boanerges, an epithet given according to Mark to the brothers James and John (Mark 3:17). Usually the name is translated 'Sons of Thunder' though a couple of translations venture 'Thunderbolts' (CEV; 'God's Word'). It is traced by some to a transliteration of the Aramaic, but most acknowledge that it is a long stretch from the Hebrew Ben-hadad through the Aramaic to the Greek βοανεργές. Etymologically, βοανεργές is closer to 'workers of bellows' or 'cattle-bawling' (cf. Mark 1:3) or perhaps 'war-shouts'. One sixth-century inscription from Ephesus recalled that John was not only θεολόγος but a son of thunder (βροντῆς υἱός).[49] So popular was this epithet that it was conferred on Philip in the fourth-century stories of Philip the evangelist-apostle. In these stories—the *Acts* and the *Martyrdom of Philip*—the apostle-prophet (as blended in Hierapolitan imagination) is called 'Son of Thunder', probably induced by the anger that he unleashes on demons and unbelief (*APhil* 11.6, *MPhil* 23). This would seem to be confirmed by a 'voice from heaven' (Christ) in *APhil* 2.17 which holds that 'son of thunder' was his former way, but now he is a son 'of gentleness'. Those who are inclined to merge Gospel texts into a Tatianic amalgam might cite the 'fire from heaven' that the brothers offered to summon in Luke 9:54.

One can see that the efforts to pin down the name and so exonerate Mark's own flamboyant translation have yielded no agreement. Consequently, it seems that one of our study group felt

---

45 See Strabo *Geog*. 13.4.14; Cassius Dio 68.27; Ammianus Marcellinlus 23.6.17–18.
46 Kreitzer, 'The Plutonium of Hierapolis'; *Hierapolis in the Heavens*. See the somewhat scathing review by Beryl Burrell in *CBQ* 70.4.
47 See d'Andria, 'Nature and Cult'; Rojas, *The Pasts of Roman Anatolia*, 88–93.
48 See *RPC* 1.2982; https://gallica.bnf.fr/ark:/12148/btv1b8527115t.
49 *I.Ephesos* 1.45, ll.6–7.

he might as well toss in his own speculation. Ray Barraclough, sometime Senior Lecturer at St George's Anglican College in Jerusalem, and no mean New Testament scholar, suggested that the name might simply have been conferred because the brothers ate too many beans! Here the spectre of the famous baked bean scene from Mel Brooks' film 'Blazing Saddles' wafts into view, if not atmosphere. I'm sure Ray was playing for laughs—an objective in which he was successful. However, the connection between thunder and flatulence had already been made in the ancient world, also for humour, by Strabo the Geographer no less.[50]

But it raises the question of the use of beans and lentils in the ancient world and how the inevitable digestive effects were dealt with. Certainly, beans were a common part of the everyday diet, covering a variety of legumes, some of which (for example, vetches) required considerable cooking to make them edible and reduce the flatulent after-effects.[51] These after-effects seem to be implied in a comedy called *The Wren* (τροχίλος) by the little-known Middle Comedy writer Heniochus, where amusement is garnered from the question:

> Why does bean soup so greatly fill the stomach,
> And why do those who know this Pauson's habits
> Dislike the fire? For this great philosopher
> Is always occupied in eating beans.[52]

Here both the bloatedness and flammability wrought by a methane build-up seem to be harnessed for comic intent. This connection between beans and flatulence is not played often in the comic writers, though breaking wind—'anal emissions' as Lilja delicately puts it—by itself certainly is a familiar trope of ancient comedy.[53] It is the comic bawdiness however that gives a clue to the unseemliness that the elite associated with flatulence, something to be laughed at rather than admitted. After all, it was the slave whose body odour was a characteristic of his position in society,[54] which adds further point to the extremes of stench emanating from Lazarus, if a *slave* should react the way he is represented in the Rossanensis illumination.

The orator Quintilian even advised against the use of some words precisely because in the division of their syllables they might conjure an offence against modesty, let alone amusement that would be distracting from the argumentative intent. He gives an example of *intercapedinis*, which he circumspectly puts in the genitive so he can avoid the final stem of the nominative –*pedo*, the Latin for breaking wind.[55] In such circles, flatulence was seen as a sign of an uncontrolled lifestyle, especially evident in gluttony.[56] Of course, the Cynics couldn't care less about such finesse in manners, at least according to Epictetus.[57] And disdain may be behind Suetonius' note that Claudius, albeit in response to someone who contorted himself to near-death in holding it in, considered passing an edict allowing anyone to give vent whilst dining with others.[58]

Yet beans also appear in religous contexts. Indeed there was an Athenian festival called the

---

50 See Strabo *Geog.* 14.5.14 (πομδαὶ δὲ γερόντων ... βρονταὶ δὲ γερόντων).
51 Koder, '*Stew and salted meat*', 65.
52 fr. *apud* Athenaeus *Deip.* 7.74. 'Pauson' became a stock character of limited ability, as in Aristophanes *Thes.* 947 where a penchant for gluttony is suggested.
53 See Aristophanes *Eccl.* 76–9, *Ran.* 1045, *Pax* 150, 615, *Vesp.* 381, *Ach.* 1; Plautus *Poen.* 3.2.33; Martial *Ep.* 12.77, 78. Lilja, *The Treatment of Odours*, 142.
54 Plautus *Amph.* 321.
55 Quintilian *Orat.* 8.3.
56 Plutarch *Brut.* 8.
57 Epictetus *Disc.* 3.22.
58 Suetonius *Claudius* 32.

Pyanepsia, dedicated to Apollo, celebrated in late October. It was supposedly named from the practice of eating beans (here the word used is πυάνοι) at the feast which seems to have been an ancient agricultural celebration.[59] This makes the mention of required abstention from beans all the more noticeable.

The religio-philosophical group, the Pythagoreans, for all their avowed vegetarianism, nonetheless repudiated dining on beans.[60] Indeed, Iamblichus' *Life of Pythagoras* features the philosopher convincing an ox to give up eating that particular food.[61] Pliny the Elder wandered through a number of explanations for the practice, ranging from a health issue (dulling the senses or inducing bad dreams) to religious scruples, namely that the souls of the dead were therein enclosed.[62] Cicero however was quite pragmatic, namely, that 'the food produces great flatulence and induces a condition at war with a soul in search of truth'.[63] Whether the soul struggles with bloat or smell or simply noisy thunderclaps, he was less forthcoming on revelatory detail.

This makes the prohibition of beans in some religious contexts of particular interest. The Eleusinian Mysteries banned their consumption in the lead up to and during the celebrations, according to Pausanias (1.37.4). But this is not found consistently in the celebrations of Demeter and Kore / Persephone, at least in some early sanctuaries. One highly fragmentary inscription of Sacred Laws from Athens has beans as one of the ingredients for the celebration or provision for the priests.[64] Stephen Lambert notes that, at least for Athens, the festivities were diffused, 'celebrated separately in individual demes'.[65] This suggests that one factor guiding the admission or rejection of beans might simply be a desire to differentiate one group's celebration from another. Robert Parker has warned against treating ritual norms from around the Mediterranean as if they were an homogenous group.[66]

The prohibition is also found elsewhere in some surviving Sacred Laws. One from Rhodes (dated to the First Century CE) seems to tie beans to a sexual stimulant (ἀπὸ ἀφροδισίων, ἀπὸ κυάμων, ἀπὸ καρδίας 'from lust, from beans, from desire').[67] This possibly opens another aspect of bean consumption and the possible rationale for its prohibition in religious gatherings, namely beans as a sexual stimulant. However, beans are used metaphorically for the development of breasts at puberty—which would be more coordinate with the other two items.[68] Significantly, the concern in the twelve-line fragment is about inner rather than outer purity: οὐ λουτροῖ ἀλλὰ νόῳ καθαρόν (ll. 6–7) so it may well be that bean abstinence is not, or not confined to sweet-smelling devotees.[69] It is not clear which deity/-ies are the focus of such ascetic observance, although Franciszek Sokolowski, the esteemed collator of ritual texts, suggested Asclepios or Sarapis.[70] Another cult regulation similarly advocating abstention from beans (without reference to sexual desires), comes from Smyrna, but it relates to the acceptable worship of Dionysos Bromios.[71]

---

59 Athenaeus *Deip.* 7.73.
60 Plutarch *Quaest. conv.* 9.10 (*Mor.* 728f)—attributed to adoption of Egyptian scruples; Epiphanius, *Pan.* de Fide 9.12.
61 Iamblichus *VPyth.* 13.61.
62 Pliny *NH* 18.30. This resurfaces allegorically in Manichean teaching—see Epiphanius *Pan.* Manicheans 28.2–5. Epiphanius is unimpressed (34.1–2).
63 Cicero *Div.* 1.32.
64 *IG* 1³ 232 = *CGRN* 7 (510–470 BCE?).
65 Lambert, *Attic Inscriptions*, 12.
66 Parker, 'Regionality'.
67 *LSS* 108, ll. 2–4.
68 Pollux *Onom.* 2.163; Rufus *Onom.* 92.
69 On the concerns over inner purity in Greek religion, see Petrovic, *Inner Purity*.
70 *LSS* 108, commentary.
71 *LSA* 84, l. 15

Sokolowski considers this regulation to be similar to that governing Pythagoreans and the Egyptian Orphic cults. He is careful to note that various reasons seem to govern the requirement.[72]

So whilst we may be sympathetic to Cicero's mundane explanation, that body bloat wars with soul search, it seems that a range of possiblities present themselves, obviating certainty in any particular case. What is clear however, is that abstention from beans is not ubiquitous in the Sacred Law regulations even for groups devoted to the same deity. Bodel's observation that particular localities developed their own particular emphases holds here, which may suggest that concerns about distinction from the practices of other religious groups in the neighbourhood may be a relevant consideration.

The Acridity of Garlic

Garlic was a common addition to cooking in the ancient world.[73] It was important enough to crop up in Diocletian's Price edict, specifically described as Italian garlic and selling at sixty denarii per modius.[74] It frequently, like mustard and a variety of cabbage, grew wild on the wayside—a tempting chora food for those struggling to subsist. But the potency of garlic is that its oil can seep into the skin and, when consumed, can pervade breath and body odour alike. Plautus, the Roman comic playwright, captured in the course of some pretty basic humour the trials of garlic consumption. One slave, Tranio, impugns another slave, Grumio, for his stench, providing the header 'You stink of garlic' (*oboluisti alium*) which is then unpacked in a series of offensive pejoratives. Grumio moans back that not everyone 'can reek of expensive perfume ... or dine on fancy foods like you ... just let my lot be nourished on garlic' (*non omnes possunt olere unguenta exotica ... sine me aliato fungi fortunas meas*).[75] Here the asymmetry of the slaves is played out against a backdrop of food and smells. Garlic readily became an insult against enemies, always suggestive of class differentials, the urbane over against the stinking rustic. And yet, according to Suetonius, when confronting a young soldier who oozed of perfume, Vespasian withdrew his commission, castigating him with 'I'd rather you smelled of garlic'.[76]

So offensive could the smell of garlic be, there was even a magical recipe designed to evaporate the stink. The remedy? 'Bake beetroots and eat them'.[77] This however was almost certainly a scam. The same group of recipes recommended that the cure for an old woman chattering or drinking too much was to mix minced pine with her wine. And if you were highly reticent about public gatherings, apply a gum mixed with wine and honey to your face! Garlic, according to another spell, could also bring down chariots by mixing it with snake's slough, using an incantation written down with the charioteer's name and deposited for three days in the grave of someone who had suffered an untimely death.[78] Garlic was frequently associated with dark creatures, like harpies, as a term that aimed to indicate their stench.[79]

---

72 *LSA* 84 commentary, p. 189.
73 See Athenaeus *Deip*. 7.16, 9.67.
74 *IG* VII 22, I.29 (Megara, 301 CE) cf. a grafitto on a pottery fragment reading σκόρδων μναῖ, a minas of garlic (*AEMTh* 16 (2002): 615).
75 Plautus *Most*. 38, 45.
76 Suetonius *Vesp*. 8.3.
77 *PGM* 7.167 (cf. Athenaeus *Deip*. 3.84c).
78 *PGM* 4.2211–16.
79 See Ager, 'Magic Perfumes and Deadly Herbs'.

To gain a sense of its potency, the Roman historian at Arizona State University, Britta Ager, decided to test a magical recipe at least for its odorous pungency.[80] The spell was designed to bend the moon-goddess Selene to one's intent of inflicting harm upon an enemy if standard entreaties had failed. The trick to gaining the goddess's attention was to blend together dog poo, mouse guts, and garlic. She regretted the experiment: 'It was hands down the most disgusting thing I've ever smelled in my life'.[81]

It would be easy to understand that this combination of smell and association with the occult would disbar the bulb and its imbibers from any religious gathering. Yet there is one early (sixth-century BCE) mention of garlic among various foodstuffs (provisions for the celebrations?) offered apparently to Dionysos, at Miletos.[82] And a fragment of the third-century (BCE) historian Philochorus suggests that women at a festival of Demeter at Attic Skira deliberately ate garlic in order to make themselves sexually unenticing.[83] Similar, two centuries later, is one for the Thesmophoric celebrations in honour of Demeter and Persephone at Cholargos in Egypt.[84] Elsewhere, garlic is specifically excluded from the offerings.[85] Generally, garlic was a *holus non gratus* in the sanctuary.[86] Indeed, one regulation governing access to the sanctuary of an unknown goddess prohibited not only eating garlic (which required a three-day time lapse before access could be granted), but even touching it (which required a washing and a day's wait).[87]

Conclusion: Christian Olfactory Reconfigurations

Garlic, beans, death—these are but a few samples of the olfactory factory of the ancient world, potent ones certainly but not readily distilled into an over-arching schema of stench. But we have seen that even though smell could be used as a status designation, space protection, and religious signifier, there was no absolute uniformity, whether it be Vespasian's preference for garlic over perfume in a soldier's body-odour, or beans as an ingredient of sacred festival dining. The difficulty for me has remained throughout that the stink can only be conveyed by textual and visual evocation, a tacit deodorisation that I could not avoid but have wanted to problematise as a means to challenge the oral and visual as the pre-eminent senses. The pungent malodorous infusion of death conveyed by the slave in the Rossanensis illumination of the raising of Lazarus has yet managed to convey that a ponky slave (the ancients often called it 'goatish') has challenged the stink of death to assist Lazarus from the mouth of the tomb. He has joined his own stink to that of the raised Lazarus. In this sense, he has registered his own silent belief in line with Martha's affirmation in John 11:27. But there is more to it. Rather than there being an oppositional contrast between the the stench of death in John 11:17–44 and the pervading fragrance of ointment in John 12:1–8, the slave of the illumination stands as a witness to a reconfiguration of death, as we find in

---

80 See Ager, *The Scent of Ancient Magic*.
81 ABC news report 11/10/2022; link: https://www.abc.net.au/news/2022-10-11/britta-ager-says-smell-in-ancient-rome-greece-can-teach-us-a-lot/101489650.
82 *CGRN* 6, l.A5 (525–500 BCE).
83 Philochorus *FGrH* 328 F 89: 'in order to abstain from sex, so they would not smell of perfume'. See Parker, 'The New Purity Law', 180.
84 *CGRN* 79, l.15 (334/3 BCE).
85 *CGRN* 225, l.A47 (perhaps honouring the Syrian goddess, otherwise unnamed, at Marmarina, near Larisa, 225–150 BCE); *IG* II² 1366 = *LSCG* 55 ll. 10–11 (cult of Mên Tyrannios at Laurion). See Carbon, 'The Place of Purity', 108–109.
86 See Athenaeus Deip. 7.19 (referring to a temple of the Mother of the Gods).
87 Malay-Petzl *Lydia* 497, ll. 7–9 (2nd century BCE).

John 11:25–6. To touch death, as Jesus invites others to do—of Lazarus with the polluting bindings of John 11:43–44 and Thomas in the command to place your finger and hand here in John 20:27—indicates that death for all its stink is forever changed. This meant for early Christians a linguistic and thence materialist shift in the contact with death. Paul caught this in an intensely evocative image of death and the Roman triumph in 2 Corinthians 2:14–15. The smell of Christians (and he was under no illusion that Christians smell, not just metaphorically, to opponents) could be both death to unbelievers and beautifully fragrant (εὐωδία) to those being saved.[88] This becomes important when we confront some early Christian hagiographies that assert pleasant aromas where one would normally expect the opposite.) So, for example, in Prudentius' *Hymn to St. Lawrence* the holocaust death of the saint (being barbecued) is smelled as obnoxious to pagans and ambrosiaic to Christians.[89] In this sense, scents are not only brought to the foreground of human awareness and knowledge, but a resistance to deodorisation is made whether that deodorisation be by metaphorical re-reading into some metaphysical realm or by the introduction of perfume into actual Christian gatherings. Whatever may be the value of both these literary and material condiments, to prioritise them as a means to sacrifice odours makes us not only less than human, but incompletely resurrected.

Alan H. Cadwallader

---

[88] See Attridge, 'Making Scents of Paul'.
[89] The ambiguity in the meaning-making over offensive smells however, is seen in Theodoret of Cyrrhus's *History of the Monks of Syria*, Marcianus 21, where a certain monk named Sabinus prepared his nourishment a month in advance so that its putrefaction would extinguish any pleasure to be gained from eating (cf. *Argonautica* 2.187–93).

Bibliography

ABC	ABC news report 11/10/2022; link: https://www.abc.net.au/news/2022-10-11/britta-ager-says-smell-in-ancient-rome-greece-can-teach-us-a-lot/101489650.
Ager, B. K.	'Magic Perfumes and Deadly Herbs: The Scent of Witches' Magic in Classical Literature', *Preternature* 8 (2019), 1–34.
Ager, B. K.	*The Scent of Ancient Magic* (Ann Arbor, MI: University of Michigan Press, 2022).
Attridge, H. W.	'Making Scents of Paul: The Background and Sense of 2 Cor 2:14–17', in J. T. Fitzgerald, T. H. Olbricht and L. M. White (eds.), *Early Christianity and Classical Culture: Comparative Studies in Honor of Abraham J. Malherbe* (Leiden: Brill, 2003), 71–88.
Barthes, Roland	*Sade, Fourier, Loyola* (trans R. Miller; Berkeley: University of California Press, 1989), 137.
Beerden, K.	'Evoking Empathy: Smell in the Twenty-First Century Reception of Antiquity', in A. Grand-Clément and C. Ribeyrol (eds.), *The Smells and Senses of Antiquity in the Modern Imagination* (London: Bloomsbury, 2023), 138–52.
Bodel, J.	'Dealing with the Dead: Undertakers, Executioners and Potter's Fields in Ancient Rome', in V. Hope and E. Marshall (eds.), *Death and Disease in the Ancient City* (London/New York: Routledge, 2000), 128–51.
Bradley, M. (ed.)	*Smell and the Ancient Senses* (London/New York: Routledge, 2015).
Burrell, Beryl	Review of J. Kreitzer, *Hierapolis in the Heavens: Studies in the Letter to the Ephesians* (Library of New Testament Studies 368), *CBQ* 70.4 (2008), 836–38.
Cadwallader, A. H.	*Colossae, Colossians, Philemon: The Interface* (Göttingen: Vandenhoeck & Ruprecht, 2023).
Carbon, J.-M.	'The Place of Purity: Groups and Associations Authority and Sanctuaries', in V. Gabrielsen and M. C. D. Paganini (eds.), *Private Associations in the Ancient World* (Cambridge: Cambridge University Press, 2023), 86–116.
Classen, C., D. Howes, and A. Synnott.	*Aroma: The cultural history of smell* (London: Routledge, 1994).
Corbin, A.	*The Foul and the Fragrant: Odor and the French Social Imagination* (trans. M. Kochan; New York: Berg, 1986).
d'Andria, F.	'Nature and Cult in the Ploutonion of Hierapolis. Before and After the Colony', in C. Şimşek and F. d'Andria (eds.), *Landscape and History in the Lykos Valley: Laodikeia and Hierapolis in Phrygia* (Cambridge: Cambridge Scholars Publishing, 2016), 189–217.
Edlund-Berry, I.	'Hot, Cold, or Smelly: The Power of Sacred Water in Roman Religion, 400–100 BCE', in C. E. Schultz and P. B. Harvey, Jr (eds.), *Religion in Republican Italy* (Cambridge: Cambridge University Press, 2006), 175–78.

Fabiani, R.	'La concia delle pelli e le acque dell'Ilisso: osservazioni su un document normative a caraterre religioso (*IG* I³ 257)', *Hormos* 10 (2018), 371–406.
Flohr, M.	*The World of the* Fullo: *Work, Society and Economy in Rome* (Oxford: Oxford University Press, 2013).
Fox, A. L. B.	'Burial and Resurrection: The Sculpted Sarcophagi of Ravenna and Visions of Perpetuity in an Age of Flux, (Ph.D thesis, University of North Carolina, Chapel Hill, 2013).
Goldsmith, D.	'Fish, Fowl, and Stench in Ancient Egypt', in A. Schellenberg and T. Krüger (eds.), *Sounding Sensory Profiles in the Ancient Near East* (Atlanta, GA: SBL, 2019), 335–60.
Harrison, J. R.	'Finding the Right Spot to Take a Leak', in J. R. Harrison and B. J. Bitner (eds.), *New Documents Illustrating Early Christianity 11A: Texts from Ephesus* (Atlanta, GA: SBL, 2024), 347–55.
Hixson, E.	'Forty Excerpts from the Greek Old Testament in Codex Rossanensis (Rossano, Museo Diocesano, S.N.), a Sixth-Century Gospels Manuscript', *JTS* 67 (2016), 507–41.
Hock, R.	*The Social Context of Paul's Ministry: Tentmaking and Apostleship* (Minneapolis, MN: Fortress, 1980).
Iatropoulos, G., et al.	'The Language of Smell: Connecting Linguistic and Psychophysical Properties of Odor Descriptors', *Cognition* 178 (2018), 37–49.
Jordan, D. R.	'A Survey of Greek Defixiones Not Included in the Special Corpora', *GBRS* 26 (1985), 151–97.
Kaster, R.	'The Dynamics of Fastidium and the Ideology of Disgust', *TAPA* 131 (2001), 143–89.
Kayachev, B.	*Dirae: A Poem from the Appendix Vergiliana: Introduction, Text, Translation and Commentary* (Swansea: Classical Press of Wales, 2024).
Koder, J.	'*Stew and Salted Meat*—Opulent Normality in the Diet of Every Day?" in L. Brubaker and K. Linardou (eds.), *Eat, Drink, and Be Merry (Luke 12:19)—Food and Wine in Byzantium* (Aldershot: Ashgate, 2007), 59–72.
Koloski-Ostrow, A. O.	'*ita pestilens est odore taeterrimo*', *Classical Outlook* 93 (2018), 53–61.
Kreitzer, L.	*Hierapolis in the Heavens: Studies in the Letter to the Ephesians* (London: T & T Clark, 2007).
Kreitzer, L.	'The Plutonium of Hierapolis and the Descent of Christ into the "Lowermost Parts of the Earth" (Ephesians 4,9)', *Biblica* 79 (1998), 381–93.
Lambert, S.	*Attic Inscriptions in UK Collections: British Museum: Cult Provisions* (AIUK 4.1; London: British Museum, 2019).
Lee, D.	'The Gospel of John and the Five Senses', *JBL* 129 (2010), 115–27.

Lilja, S.	*The Treatment of Odours in the Poetry of Antiquity* (Helsinki: Societas Scientarum Fennica, 1972).
Lytle, E.	'The Delian Purple and the *lex portus Asiae*', *Phoenix* 61 (2007), 247–69.
McLellan, P. N.	*The Gospel of Mark and Other Haunted Places* (Piscataway, NJ: Gorgias Press, 2023).
Mele, A. (ed.)	*Il culto della dea Mefite e la valle d'Ansanto: ricerche su un giacimento archaeologico e culturale del Samnites Hirpini* (Avellino: Sellino, 2008).
Montgomery, J. A.	*Aramaic Incantation Texts from Nippur* (Philadelphia, PA: University Museum, 1913).
Morley, N.	'Urban smells and Roman noses', in M. Bradley (ed.) *Smell and the Ancient Senses* (London/New York: Routledge, 2015), 110–19.
Parker, R.	'The New Purity Law from Thyateira', *ZPE* 205 (2018), 178–83.
Parker, R.	'Regionality and Greek Ritual Norms', *Kernos* 31 (2018), 73–81.
Petrovic, A., and I. Petrovic	*Inner Purity and Pollution in Greek Religion, Volume 1, Early Greek Religion* (Oxford: Oxford University Press, 2016).
Plumley, M. J.	'An Uncial Text of St. Mark in Greek from Nubia', *JTS* 27 (1976), 34–35.
Quiles, D. L.-C.	'There's Something Fishy about Philaenis: Martial 9.62 and Related Epigrams', *Euphrosyne* 47 (2019), 69–92.
Rizakis, A. D.	'Town and Country in Early Greece', *Pharos* 20 (2014), 241–67.
Rojas, F.	*The Pasts of Roman Anatolia: Interpreters, Traces, Horizons* (Cambridge: Cambridge University Press, 2019).
Roueché, C.	*Partisans and Performers at Aphrodisias* (London: Society for the Promotion of Roman Studies, 1993), nr. 45.12D.
Tullett, W.	*Smell and the Past: Noses, Archives, Narratives* (London: Bloomsbury, 2023).
Warrior, V.	*Roman Religion: A Sourcebook* (Indianapolis, IN: Hackett, 2002).

'Signs on the earth below' (Acts 2:19b)
Luke-Acts and the Miraculous in the Graeco-Roman World

JAMES R. HARRISON

Abstract

This article explores Luke's reference to the phrase σημεῖα ἐπὶ τῆς γῆς κάτω ('signs on the earth below') in Acts 2:19b within its wider Graeco-Roman context. Five strands of Graeco-Roman evidence regarding the miraculous, each of differing genres and from different historical periods, will be examined and their intersection with Luke-Acts explored, comparing their claims to legitimation where possible. The literature and documents are Philostratus' *Life of Apollonius of Tyana*, Lucian's *Alexander the False Prophet* and *The Passing of Peregrinus*, the writings of Apollonius the paradoxographer, the miracles of Asclepius at Epidauros and other sanctuaries, and, last, the magical papyri. It will be argued that Luke-Acts consistently highlights the distinctiveness of the approach of Jesus and the first Christian missionaries to the miraculous. Nevertheless, Luke is alert to local Graeco-Roman expressions of the miraculous in the eastern Mediterranean basin, which, by virtue of their similarity to some of the early Christian phenomena, help us to see the emerging conflict between both religious traditions.

Prolegomenon

In the eschatological outpouring of the Spirit of God by the exalted Lord and Messiah Jesus—which is legitimised textually by Peter's (or Luke's) exposition and adaptation of LXX Joel 2:28–32 (Acts 2:16–21)—the phrase σημεῖα ἐπὶ τῆς γῆς κάτω ('signs on the earth below': Acts 2:19b) is employed by Luke to designate one of Pentecost's ongoing pneumatic effects.[1] The narrative of Acts is replete with Luke's distillation of miraculous acts 'on the earth below', ranging from individual miraculous phenomena[2] to collective miraculous phenomena.[3] At various junctures in

---

1   For the Petrine (or Lukan) additions to and emendations of LXX Joel 2:28–32 in Acts 2:16–21, see Harrison, 'Prophecy, Divination, and Oneirology', 106–11.
2   For general discussion of the Acts material, see Dawson, *Healing, Weakness and Power*, 132–52. Resuscitations from the dead: Acts 9:36–42; 20:9–12. Miraculous curses and exorcisms: 3:1–16; 9:17–18; 9:33–35; 14:7–9; 14:19; 16:16–18; 28:7–8. Punitive miracles and afflictions: 5:5–11; 9:8–9; 12:23; 13:9–12. Nature and cosmic miracles: 2:2–6; 4:31; 5:17–25; 8:3; 12:5–11; 16:25–30; 28:3–6. On punitive miracles, see Reimer, *Miracle and Magic*, 107–11.
3   Apostolic and first-generation miracles inside and outside Jerusalem: Acts 2:43; 5:12,15,16; 6:8; 8:6–8,13; 14:3; 15:12; 19:11–12; 28:9.

Acts, Luke narratively reinforces the progression and legitimation of the miraculous articulated in Joel's prophecy by means of the repetition of σημεῖα καὶ τέρατα, τέρατα καὶ σημεῖα, and σημεῖον.[4] It is beyond the scope of this essay to discuss Luke's historiographical and apologetic intent in employing pivotal LXX texts to introduce Jesus' ministry in the Gospel (Luke 4:18–19 [Isa. 61:1–2a]) and his continued ministry through the Spirit via the apostles and first believers in Acts (2:16–21 [Joel 2:28–32]). Nor can we be diverted by important exegetical questions as to whether 'signs and wonders' in Luke-Acts (a) only contextually appear with the 'word' (Acts 2:14,19,22,40–41,43; 4:29–31; 5:12,17,20; 6:7–8; 7:35 38; 8:4,6,13–14; 14:3; 15:7,12);[5] (b) are specifically 'messianic' signs; (c) are amazement- and faith-evoking events (Acts 2:7,12,41; 3:9–12; 8:8–13; 9:35,42; 10:45; 12:16; 13:12; 14:11; 28:6);[6] or (d) 'function as a sign of God's eschatological Spirit through Acts',[7] among other interpretative options. Our focus will be on situating the σημεῖα ἐπὶ τῆς γῆς κάτω of Luke-Acts in their Graeco-Roman context, with a view to understanding what is both distinctive and similar about Christ's pneumatic acts of power against the backdrop of the first-century imperial world and seeing what kind of legitimation of the miraculous is sponsored in both traditions.[8]

In approaching the Lukan view of the miraculous in its Graeco-Roman context, we are confronted by several problems. While Luke's perspective on miracles has generated substantial discussion over the years,[9] his portrait of Spirit-endowed miracle-workers has not been sufficiently analysed against the backdrop of the diverse genres of Graeco-Roman evidence relating to the 'miraculous' in antiquity. A possible reason for this was that in the 1970s and 1980s a specific literary genre for the miraculous in antiquity was proposed as the starting point for future study on the issue. New Testament scholarship at the time was engaged in a spirited debate over the existence of the literary genre of 'aretalogy'—allegedly a specialised form of Hellenistic biography recounting the deeds of a θεῖος ἀνήρ ('divine man')—and its purported implications for understanding the Gospels and Acts as literature and for the theological, historical, and apologetic intent of their healing narratives.

A detailed examination of this debate is beyond the scope of this essay. Suffice it to say, Morton Smith and Moses Hadas extended the use of aretalogus in antiquity from a 'narrator' of miracle stories to a formal literary genre, which purportedly recounted miracle stories in praise of the deity, even though there was an absence of any surviving text labelled 'aretalogy'.[10] Consequently,

---

4   See n.21 *infra* for the Acts references.
5   O'Reilly, *Word and Sign in the Acts of the Apostles*, 191–206.
6   Reimer, *Miracle and Magic*, 88–95.
7   Keener, *The Spirit in the Gospels and Acts*, 196.
8   For recent discussion of miracles in the ancient world, see Gerolemou (ed.), *Recognizing Miracles in Antiquity and Beyond*.
9   See Lampe, 'Miracles in the Acts of the Apostles'; Fenton, 'The Order of the Miracles performed by Peter and Paul in Acts'; Hamblin, 'Miracles in the Book of Acts'; Achtemeier, 'The Lucan Perspective on the Miracles of Jesus'; Neirynck, 'The Miracle Stories in the Acts of the Apostles'; Nolland, 'Classical and Rabbinic Parallels to "Physician, Heal Yourself" (Lk. IV 23)'; Kirchschläger, *Jesu exorzistisches Wirken aus der Sicht des Lukas: Ein Beitrag zur Lukanischen Redaktion*; Hamm, 'Acts 3,1–10: The Healing of the Temple Beggar as Lucan Theology'; Hamm, 'The Freeing of the Bent Woman and the Restoration of Israel'; Garrett, *The Demise of the Devil*; Hemer, *The Book of Acts in the Setting of Hellenistic History*, 433–38; Pilch, 'Sickness and Healing in Luke–Acts'; Klauk, *Magic and Paganism in Early Christianity*; Reimer, *Miracle and Magic*; Weissenrieder, *Images of Illness in the Gospel of Luke*; Klutz, *The Exorcism Stories in Luke–Acts*; Dawson, *Healing, Weakness and Power*, 101–59; Porter, 'Magic in the Book of Acts'; Chad Hartsock, *Sight and Blindness in Luke–Acts*; Roberts, *Conflicts of ΜΑΓΕΙΑ and Miracles in the Acts of the Apostles*; Grafton, *Health and Healing in the Documentary Papyri*; Wasiac, 'Miracle Stories and Praise'; Stanley, *Paul and Asklepios*.
10 Hadas and Smith, *Heroes and Gods*, 3; cf. Kee, 'Aretalogy and Gospel', 403. For other scholars arguing this, see Bultmann, 'The Gospels (Form)'; Dibelius, 'The Structure and Literary Character of the Gospels'; Votaw, *The Gospel and Contemporary Biographies in the GraecoRoman World*; Koester, 'One Jesus and Four Primitive Gospels'; Betz, 'Jesus as Divine Man'; Georgi, *The Opponents of Paul in Second Corinthians*; Smith, 'Good News Is No New News: Aretalogy and Gospel'.

as Smith argues, Luke's Gospel, Porphyry's *Life of Pythagoras* (AD third cent.), Philo's *Life of Moses* (AD 39–50), and Philostratus' *Life of Apollonius of Tyana* (AD 220s/230s) are to be categorised as 'aretalogies'.[11] Morton Smith's citation of the inscriptional collections of cures by the gods Asklepios and Sarapis as further evidence for aretalogy failed to convince scholars because they are cures of gods as opposed to divine men, and the cures themselves were never assembled into any type of connected biography: instead, we are left with unconvincing scholarly chestnuts such as the figure of Heracles[12] and the biographies of so-called 'divine men' from the Second and Third Centuries AD. At best, these late biographies are anachronistic sources for the proposed genre resemblances to Luke-Acts and its presentation of the miraculous. Nor can we glean any evidence for the concept of a 'divine man' in Hellenistic Judaism. Certainly, Philo and Josephus exalt the figure of Moses, but they lay no stress on his performance of miracles: it was as 'lawgiver', not as a miracle worker, that Moses was a man of God (θεῖος ἀνήρ), Josephus informs us (A.J. 3.179–180). Both D. L. Tiede and C. Holladay have shown that the figures of Abraham, Joseph, Moses, and Solomon were never divinised, being modelled on the Hellenistic stereotype of the wise and virtuous man.[13] The case is just as clear-cut for pre-Christian Hellenistic miracle-workers. Barry L. Blackburn has demonstrated that there was little homogeneity amongst the figures attributed divinity, with even fewer features of their depiction parallelling the Gospels.[14] Notwithstanding, caution is apposite here. As Reimer observes,[15] the acclamation of the miracle-working Paul and Timothy in Lystra as Zeus and Hermes (Acts 14:8–18) and the Maltese categorisation of Paul as a 'god' due to his survival of snake-bite (28:6: ἔλεγον αὐτὸν εἶναι θεόν) reveal local cultural codes about miracle workers being considered 'divine'.

Despite this scholarly divide over the existence of the genre of 'aretalogy' (and, indeed, its dismissal as a category by many), the Lukan accounts of the miraculous deserve re-examination against the backdrop of the three later Hellenistic *bioi* ('lives'), with a view to elucidating the miraculous legitimation espoused (or mocked) in each work: namely, Philostratus' philosophical romance, *Apollonius of Tyana*, and Lucian's satirical works, *Alexander the False Prophet* and *The Passing of Peregrinus*. Apart from the problematic figure of Apollonius of Tyana, we face the difficulty of the paucity of Hellenistic and Roman miracle-workers from the First Century AD.[16] Thus, to offset the imbalance of our predominantly late literary evidence, the miraculous tales of Apollonius the paradoxographer (*Historiae Mirabiles*, 2nd Cent. BC) should also be considered

---

11 For the ancient sources cited as aretalogies, see Smith, 'Prolegomena to a Discussion of Aretalogies: Divine Men, the Gospels and Jesus', 174–81.

12 See Rose, 'Heracles and the Gospels' for a demolition of the idea that the Gospels were contaminated by Heracles' motifs.

13 See Bieler, *ΘΕΙΟΣ ΑΝΗΡ*; Tiede, *The Charismatic Figure as Miracle Worker*; Holladay, *Theios Aner in Hellenistic Judaism*. For critiques of the notion of aretalogy and divine men, see Kee, *Aretalogies, Hellenistic "Lives" and the Sources of Mark*; Kee, 'Aretalogy and the Gospel'; Kee, *Miracle in the Early Christian World*; Liefeld, 'The Hellenistic "Divine Man" and the Figure of Jesus in the Gospels'; Lane, 'Theios Aner Christology and the Gospel of Mark'; Blackburn, *Theios Aner and the Markan Miracle Traditions*.

14 See Blackburn, *Theios Aner and the Markan Miracle Traditions*.

15 Reimer, *Miracle and Magic*, 59.

16 In terms of first-century AD Graeco-Roman examples, there are (apart from Apollonius) a handful of legitimating cures attributed to the emperors: Vespasian (Suetonius, *Vesp.* 8.7; Dio Cassius, *Roman History* 65.8; Tacitus, *Hist.* 4.81), and Hadrian (*Life of Hadrian* [*Historia Augusta*], 25.1–4). Significantly, the first-century AD biographer Plutarch, who was alert to supernatural phenomena, mentions only one case of a charismatic healing (Pyrrhus, 3.4). See Mackay, 'Plutarch and the Miraculous'. On the 'astonishingly small' number of miracles recorded comparable to those of Jesus, see Harvey, *Jesus and the Constraints of History*, 103. Since we are concentrating on the Graeco-Roman context, the miraculous deeds of the two Jewish rabbis, Honi the Rain-maker and Hanina ben Dosa, are omitted. See Evans, 'Jesus and Jewish Miracle Stories', here respectively 228–30, 231–36.

in relation to religious legitimation,[17] along with the epigraphic evidence of the Fourth Century BC cures of the Greek healing god Asclepius, though the latter are an oneirology and site-based phenomenon, as opposed to the wonders of peripatetic miracle workers. Last, the Magical Papyri, although much later than the New Testament documents, provide helpful insight into how the Lukan tradition of the miraculous might have been perceived by the practitioners of magic.[18]

In sum, the diversity of Graeco-Roman 'miraculous' genres, the lateness of the evidence, and the scarcity of first-century peripatetic miracle workers available for study underscore the difficulty of achieving a nuanced and balanced comparison with the Lukan portrait of miracles. However, the historical and theological legitimation articulated through the realised eschatology of the Lukan Pentecost pneumatic 'signs' raises the wider issue of the variegated legitimation of the miraculous espoused in the literature and documents of the Graeco-Roman world. This perspective unveils a profitable point of comparison between both traditions, allowing us to observe similarities and differences.[19]

Finally, the corpora of the medical literature and the papyri generally will not be discussed in this essay due to the exhaustive studies of Annette Weissenrieder and Thomas E. Grafton.[20] Weissenrieder has discussed Luke's intensification of the indicators of illness in the Gospel of Luke against the constructs of illness found in the ancient medical texts (i.e. the Hippocratic Corpus, the writings of Galen and Soranus). By contrast, Grafton compares illnesses in Luke-Acts with the papyrological evidence touching on medical diagnoses and treatments, expanding upon their cultural understandings and the social relations revealed therein. While these groundbreaking works illuminate with great clarity Luke's understanding of the miraculous against the professional medical and popular understandings of illness, with their various social outcomes, they do not address—due to their vastly different focus—Luke's framing of the miraculous within the legitimising text of Joel's prophecy, including its eschatological and pneumatic outworking in the ministry of the historical Jesus and the ensuing apostolic mission from Jerusalem to Rome.

We turn first to the role of 'signs' in the Old Testament: what would the LXX-literate auditors in Luke's audience have garnered from Luke's rendering of σημεῖα ἐπὶ τῆς γῆς κάτω there?

1. Luke and the Jewish Perception of 'Signs'

Joel's prophecy in Acts 2:19 promises that God will show 'signs upon the earth beneath' (σημεῖα ἐπὶ τῆς γῆς κάτω) in the new age of the resurrected and exalted Messiah, the Lord and Outpourer of the promised Spirit (Acts 2:24–36). Luke clearly understands the phrase to refer to the miraculous, seen by the way he continually links σημεῖα and τέρατα to the occurrence of miracles in Acts.[21] The importance of the 'fulfilment' motif in Luke-Acts, witnessed to by the usage of πεπληροφορημένων in Luke's preface (Luke 1:1), emerges in full light at this stage. Moreover, the Lukan 'signs on

---

17 For a translation, see Tiede, *The Charismatic Figure as Miracle Worker*, 313–16. For translations of all the works of the paradoxographers, with Greek texts, see 'Paradoxography—SENTENTIAE ANTIQUAE', https://sententiaeantique.com › paradoxography, accessed 19/05/2025.

18 For recent challenges to assumptions regarding magic in New Testament scholarship, see Horsley, *Jesus and Magic*; Sanzo, 'Early Christianity'.

19 See Pitts, 'Genre and Method in Luke-Acts Research', 48, who argues that in Luke-Acts genre studies 'Structuralism is unable to calibrate the role of context sufficiently and family resemblance theory only targets genre similarities, *not genre differences*' (my emphasis).

20 Weissenrieder, *Images of Illness in the Gospel of Luke*; Grafton, *Health and Healing in the Documentary Papyri*. Additionally, see Pilch, *Healing in the New Testament*.

21 σημεῖα καὶ τέρατα: Acts 4:30; 5:12; 14:3; 15:12; τέρατα καὶ σημεῖα: 2:19, 22, 43; 6:8; 7:36; σημεον: 4:16, 22; 8:6, 13.

the earth' recall Israel's redemption from Egypt. But, more importantly, they point us to their eschatological fulfilment in the redemption accomplished through Jesus the Messiah-Prophet, the message of which is later proclaimed by his Spirit-inspired prophets in both word and deed. The Christological point is powerfully driven home by Daniel J. Baker who observes:

> Peter will introduce Jesus as 'Jesus of Nazareth, a man attested to you by God with mighty works and wonders and signs (δυνάμεσιν καὶ τέρασιν καὶ σημείοις) that God did through him' (2:22). Thus, any 'signs and wonders' in the early church are merely echoes of the greater works that 'Jesus of Nazareth' has done.[22]

In the Old Testament, 'signs and wonders' have a dual role.[23] In the case of Moses at the Exodus, they operated as accreditation for God's spokesmen.[24] However, by the time of Deuteronomy, they referred to God's saving acts for his people.[25] Luke reflects the same theological mentality. In Acts 'signs and wonders' have saving significance too: they manifest the Lordship of Jesus (Acts 4:30; 14:3) or point to the reality of the Spirit's eschatological outpouring (2:17–19 cf. Luke's addition of ἐν ταῖς ἐσχάταις ἡμέραις [v.17a]). Additionally, the prophetic credentials of Jesus and his apostles are attested by the 'signs and wonders' that they perform.[26] However, in Deuteronomy 13:2–3 Moses warns Israel of the danger of 'signs and wonders' being accomplished by false prophets. Significantly, Luke ignores Jesus' apocalyptic prediction of false Christs deceiving the elect through 'signs and wonders' (Mark 13:22, *et par.*). This could be due to Luke's consistently positive evaluation of 'signs and wonders', as O'Reilly suggests.[27] By contrast, Luke warns against similar groups of deceivers (Simon Magus; Elymas Bar Jesus) by employing some of the stock expressions of abuse in his culture (μάγος; ψευδοπροφήτης).[28]

To conclude with a speculation: could Luke's heightened emphasis on 'signs and wonders' be occasioned in part by the rise of sign prophets and eschatological imposters—so amply documented by Josephus—in the apostolic age?[29] On two occasions Luke refers to them in passing in the Acts narrative (5:36–37; 21:38). Was Luke seeking to demonstrate the superiority of the apostolic 'signs and wonders', through the risen and exalted Lord, in the face of those claimed by contemporary deceivers—both Jewish and Gentile?

2. Luke, Philostratus, and the Miraculous

The most celebrated example of a late 'aretalogy' is Philostratus' *Life of Apollonius of Tyana*, published shortly after AD 217 at the behest of Julia Domna.[30] Since its genre is difficult to

---

22 Baker, *Acts 2:17–21*, 56.
23 For discussion, see McCasland, 'Signs and Wonders'; Rengstorf, 'πνεμα'; O'Reilly, *Word and Sign in the Acts of the Apostles*; Baker, 'The Complete Theological Program of Acts 2:17–21'; Marx, '"Signs and Wonders"'.
24 Exod.7:8; 7:9; 11:9; 11:10.
25 Deut. 4:34; 6:22; 7:19; 13:2; 13:3; 26:8; 28:46; 29:3; 34:11.
26 Acts 2:22; 2:43; 5:12; 18:3; 14:13.
27 O'Reilly, *Word and Sign in the Acts of the Apostles*, 161 n.1.
28 On the standard expressions of abuse, see Liefeld, *The Wandering Preacher as a Social Figure in the Roman Empire*, 274–80. On the charges against miracle workers, see Reimer, *Miracle and Magic*, 212–25.
29 On this see, Barnett, 'The Jewish Sign Prophets'; Horsley with Hanson, *Bandits, Prophets, and Messiahs*, 88–189.
30 On Philostratus' *Life of Apollonius of Tyana*, see Koskenniemi, *Theios Sophistès: Essays on Flavius Philostratus' Vita Apollonii*; idem, 'Apollonius of Tyana: A Typical θεῖος ἀνήρ?'; Reimer, *Miracle and Magic*; Francis, 'Truthful Fiction'; Anderson, *Philostratus*; Bowie, 'Apollonius of Tyana'; Petzke, *Die Traditionen über Apollonius von Tyana und das Neue Testament*; Harris, 'Apollonius of Tyana: Fact and Fiction'; Meyer, 'Apollonios von Tyana und die Biographie des Philostratos'.

determine, we ought not base wide-ranging conclusions on the presumption that it is a typical example of Greek biography.[31] Notwithstanding, the work has been plundered for parallels with the New Testament, but the accuracy of its presentations of the wandering sage's life (c. AD 40–110) is suspect.[32] Moreover, it is possible, though not provable, that the work has been written as an early third-century AD 'pagan' counterblast to the portrait of Christ in the Gospels, congregating around the memories of the first-century Apollonius.[33]

In the face of slanders that Apollonius was a magician, Philostratus had the apologetic aim of rehabilitating his hero's reputation, by showing that Apollonius was a wise man who merited consideration as 'a supernatural and divine being' (σοφίας...δαιμόνιος...θεῖος, Vita 1.2). Nevertheless, there is reserve on Philostratus' part towards Apollonius' divinity. Apollonius, for example, repudiates the charge of his deification and Philostratus links Apollonius' divinity to his wisdom (Vita, 4.40,44; 8.27; cf. 2.39).[34] However, the major problem is the nature of our evidence concerning Apollonius. Although we have impressive posthumous fragments concerning Apollonius' reputation, there is no first-century attestation of his life until the hostile reference of Lucian.[35] This leaves us with Philostratus, whose sources are highly polemical and, in the case of Apollonius' travelling companion, Damis, could be a literary invention.[36] The work is perhaps best consigned to the genre of a historical romance, animated by Pythagorean philosophy, though not divorced from any historical connection to its first-century AD protagonist.[37]

Several fruitful areas of comparison exist between Philostratus and Luke. First, regarding birth and childhood stories, Apollonius' birth is heralded by dream, swan, and thunderbolt portents (Vita 1.5). Similarly, Luke mentions visions and angelic visitations to Zacharias, Mary, and the shepherds (Luke 1:11, 26–39; 2:8–14). However, differences outweigh the similarities. Philostratus wants to highlight Apollonius' divine transcendence (τὸ ἀρχοῦ θεῶν, Vita 1.5), whereas Luke is interested in Jesus' fulfilment of the Davidic Sonship (2 Sam. 7:14; Ps. 2:7). The boyhood of the

---

31   For the range of genres, see Aune, 'The Problem of the Genre of the Gospels', 51 n.19.
32   For discussion, see Bowie, 'Apollonius of Tyana: Tradition and Reality', 1655–57, 1686; MacMullen, *Enemies of the Roman Order*, 112–15.
33   See Harris, 'Apollonius of Tyana: Fact and Fiction'. Klutz, *The Exorcism Stories in Luke-Acts*, 124–25, writes: 'In view of the documents' respective dates of composition, ... and with Philostratus' claim to knowledge of written testimony transmitted by a witness (i.e. Damis) continuing to invite scholarly suspicion, any literary influence in this case in more likely to run from Luke (or related Synoptic traditions) to Philostratus than vice versa'.
34   Reimer, *Miracle and Magic*, 62, writes: 'The divine power and wisdom available in Apollonius in the earthly realm is made possible by the access he has had and continues to have to the heavenly realm. Hence one can correctly identify Apollonius as θεός or δαίμων, since he does mingle with the heavenly crowd, without implying that all his divine power and wisdom is self-originating'.
35   Lucian, *Alex.* 5. For evidence concerning Apollonius' reputation, see Philostratus, *Vita* 8.20 (Hadrian's collection of Apollonius' letters); *Vita* 31 (Caracalla's erection of a shrine at Tyana in Apollonius' honour); Lampridius *Vita, Alex. Sev.* 29 (Severus Alexander's worship of Apollonius).
36   Philostratus' main source was the memoirs of Damis, a work which came into Julia Domna's hands and from which Philostratus extracted incidents (*Vita* 1.3–4; 6.35). On Damis being a literary invention, see Bowie, 'Apollonius of Tyana', 1653–55, 1663. More cautiously, however, see Reimer, *Miracle and Magic*, 20 n.61. The polemical thrust of the *Vita* derives from Philostratus' desire to counter the view of Apollonius' pupil, Euphrates, who labelled his master a wizard (*Vita* 1.13; 2.26; 5.33, 37–39; 6.7, 28; 7.9; 8.3; 8.8; *Ep.* 14–18, 50–52). Lastly, there was Moeragenes' four volume *Life of Apollonius*, rejected by Philostratus as ignorant (Bowie, 'Apollonius of Tyana', 1673). Moeragenes (*Vita*, 1.3; 3.41) 'had negatively labelled Apollonius as a magician' (Reimer, *Miracle and Magic*, 18).
37   Anderson, *Philostratus*, 212–39, argues against the *Vita* being a fictitious historical romance, positing a continuity between the Third-century AD *bios* and the first-century AD historical traditions concerning Apollonius. See also Reimer, *Miracle and Magic*, 19–22. For Pythagorean views, *Vita* 4.16; 6.2; 8.7. For an excellent discussion of Apollonius' Pythagorean traits, see Liefeld, *The Wandering Preacher as a Social Figure in the Roman* Empire, 71–85. Stoic thought (*Vita* 2.24; 5.36; 6.29; 7.14–15) and Cynic influences (Apollonius' impoverished lifestyle) are also present in the work. For discussion of the teaching of Apollonius, see Petzke, *Die Traditionen über Apollonius von Tyana und das Neue Testament*, 161–229.

precocious Apollonius, schooled under philosophers, is reminiscent of the boy Jesus at the temple (*Vita* 1.7; Luke 2:47). However, Luke does not place emphasis on Jesus' wisdom so much as his filial relationship with the Father (Luke 2:49,52; *pace*, Luke 19:45–48).[38]

Second, whereas Apollonius can exorcise by means of (presumably) magical curses, Jesus uses only his authoritative word (*Vita* 3.38; Luke 4:36).[39] Parallels exist between Apollonius' exorcism of the youthful demoniac and the Lukan Gerasene episode (*Vita* 4.20; additionally, Luke 8:26–39).[40] Here Apollonius depends on sheer personal force.[41] In Jesus' case, traditional expectations of God's eschatological work of liberation are finding fulfilment in him (Luke 11.20). When Jesus exorcises by 'the finger of God', God's release of Israel from bondage is recalled (Exod. 3:6; 7:4–5; 8:19; 9:3) and we are pointed to a greater liberation now occurring through him. Moreover, in the case of Apollonius, the fear of repossession is real: the spirit is ordered to knock over a statue to show he has left the boy (*Vita* 4.20).[42] Jesus admits the possibility of re-possession in cases of exorcism by Pharisaic experts (Luke 11:19,24–26). But Jesus himself, as the Stronger Man, plunders Satan's kingdom (11:21–22; cf. 10:18), empowered by the Spirit (Luke 5:17; cf. 1:35; 3:22),[43] and continues the work of despoliation through his apostles (Luke 10:18–20; Acts 16:6–10).[44] A final point: Apollonius does not view the demonic as the work of a single agency but responds to each demon as a unique entity.[45] Jesus, in contrast, categorises the demonic under a single agency—Satan—in the image of the strong man ruling the house (Luke 12:21).

Third, Apollonius' miracles cover a range of techniques: magic, physical manipulation of limbs, natural therapy, or the plain bizarre (*Vita* 3.39; 6:43; 7:34,38). He operates by a keen sensitivity to the gods' spirits, coupled with wisdom and knowledge of the natural order (*Vita* 7:34; 8:7).[46] Jesus' understanding of the miraculous is different: it actualises God's reign (Luke 17:18–22; 11:20; 13:22). Importantly, the issue of magic surfaces in both authors. Magical overtones to Jesus' work—such as in the Markan and Johannine use of spittle[47]—are omitted by Luke to avoid any imputation of magical technique in the cures. Luke, like Philostratus, does not omit charges of sorcery against his subject (Luke 11:19–22). But he highlights Jesus' subsequent refutation of that charge and corrects popular superstitions that it was the hand's touch which secured healing (8:43–46; cf. 6:19). However, despite Philostratus' attempts to clear Apollonius of wizardry (*Vita* 1.2), evidence to the contrary remains (4:44). The closest Luke comes to magic is in Peter's shadow healings or the handkerchief and apron cures (Acts 5:15; 19:11).[48] Yet, given the strong anti-magical polemic in Acts (8:14–24; 13:6–12; 19:19) and the credit given to God in 19:11, it is highly unlikely

---

38 Fitzmeyer, *The Gospel According to Luke I-IX*, 436–37.
39 Loos, *The Miracles of Jesus*, 324. In discussing Jesus' raising of the widow's dead son in Nain (Luke 7:11–17) and its Old Testament echoes (1 Kgs 17:22; 2 Kgs 4:35), Dawson, *Healing, Weakness and Power*, 126–27, writes: 'Luke emphasises the great power of Jesus to heal, by raising the man by word only, compared with the efforts required by Elijah and Elisha'.
40 In addition to *Vita* 4.20, there are five other contests between evil spirits and Apollonius: 3.38; 4.10; 4.25; 6.27,43.
41 Twelftree, *Christ Triumphant*, 52. Additionally, see Twelftree, *Jesus the Exorcist*. On exorcism in Luke-Acts, see Twelftree, *In the Name of Jesus*, 129–55.
42 In Josephus, *A.J.* 8.48, the spirit is told to knock over a bowl of water.
43 Dawson, *Healing, Weakness and Power*, 107–109.
44 Dawson, *Healing, Weakness and Power*, 111, observes: 'Luke, more than Mark (3:27), emphasises the strength and power of God against demons, with words such as "armour", "armed", "castle", and "overpowered" (11:21–22)'.
45 A good example of Apollonius treating each case of demon possession as a unique entity is *Vita* 4.10.
46 Kee, *Medicine, Miracle and Magic in New Testament Times*, 86.
47 For a fine discussion of the options concerning the use of spittle in antiquity, see Yamauchi, 'Magic or Miracle? Diseases, Demons and Exorcisms', 137–40.
48 For discussions, see Kee, *Medicine, Miracle and Magic in New Testament Times*, 95–121; Hull, *Hellenistic Magic and the Synoptic Tradition*, 87–115.

Luke has strayed into magical belief. Rather these miracles are an extension of Jesus' healing presence through the apostles themselves and in what they touch—much as in the parallel cure by their Master in Luke 8:44.[49]

Fourth, the resurrections of the dead bride (*Vita* 4.45) and the widow's son at Nain (Luke 7:11–17) have interesting similarities.[50] Yet, whereas in Luke no doubt exists that the son had died, Philostratus is uncertain in the bride's case. Was it a mere resuscitation (with Apollonius detecting the presence of life) or a genuine magical restoration (effected by a whispered spell)? Observers of Apollonius simply did not know.

Fifth, post-mortem appearances figure in both Philostratus and Luke. In each case Apollonius and Christ are mistaken for a ghost by their disciples (*Vita* 8.12; Luke 24:36–39). Again, key differences emerge between the writers. Where 'Apollonius proves he has not been killed', to cite Barry Blackburn, 'Jesus proves his bodily life after death'.[51] Apollonius had vanished miraculously from Domitian's court at Rome before midday (*Vita* 8.5,8) and was translated to Dicaearchia by dusk (*Vita* 8.10). Philostratus had already prepared his audience for this through Apollonius' (magical?) ability to unfetter himself at will (*Vita* 7.38; cf. *PGM* I.42–195, l.102; *PGM* Xll.160–78; *PGM* Xll.270–350. ?? ll.279–80).[52] As for Luke, there is the case of the miraculous rapture of Jesus in his resurrection body (Luke 24:31,36): but this is clearly different from Apollonius who has not yet died. A closer parallel exists in Philip's miraculous rapture in Acts 8:39. Even here Luke accentuates the role of the Spirit, with the experience of Old Testament prophets probably being recalled.[53] Finally, the stories of Apollonius' assumption into heaven (*Vita* 8.30) could be viewed as having points of contact with the Lukan ascension accounts (Luke 24:50–53; Acts 1:6–11). A more balanced view of this episode is that Philostratus is presenting Pythagorean beliefs about the transmigration of souls, whereas Luke's emphasis is on the tangible nature of Jesus' resurrection body (Luke 24:34–43).

The last area of comparison between Luke-Acts and Philostratus' *Vita* is the role which dreams, prophetic discernment, and prediction play in both works. Philostratus' picture of Apollonius as a sage and miracle-worker has many prophetic features. Apollonius experiences dream warnings to visit Crete (*Vita* 4.34). He is trained in the Indian gift of prescience (*Vita* 3.16) and is skilled in divination (3.42). As a result, Philostratus' narrative is littered with prophecies from Apollonius. They range from predictions of plagues and earthquakes (*Vita* 4.4, 6) to the cutting of the Isthmian canal (4.24), the lengths of emperors' reigns (5.11–12), the sinking of ships (5.18) and, finally, the death of rulers (1.12; 6.32). According to Philostratus, these prophecies are 'uttered under divine impulse' (ἐπεθείαζε: *Vita* 4.6). Therefore, Apollonius' foreknowledge was not acquired via wizardry, but 'from what the gods revealed to him' (ἐξ ὧν θεοὶ ἔφαινον: *Vita* 5.12). Only a single case of second sight is attributed to Apollonius (*Vita* 4.30), but there are several instances of prophetic discernment of hearts (1.10; 5.24; cf. 5.42). Finally, Apollonius is said to have 'seen' Domitian's death in Rome, even though the sage was in Ephesus at the time (*Vita* 8.25–26).

In his Gospel, Luke includes several popular reactions to Jesus, which underline the prevalent notion that he was a prophet (Luke 7:16,39; 9:19; 24:19). Significantly, these popular appraisals of Jesus link a perceived prophetic role with his miraculous works (Luke 7:11–15, cf. v.15; προφήτης

---

49 Lane, 'Theios Aner Christology and the Gospel of Mark', 161. On shadow healings, see Horst, 'Peter's Shadow'.
50 See Harris, 'The Dead are Restored to Life', 301–303.
51 Blackburn, 'Miracle Working ΘΕΙΟΙ ΑΝΔΡΕΣ', 193.
52 The Acts accounts of unfettering are not magical but involve angelic intervention (Acts 12:6–7) or seismic phenomena (16:26). On similarities between Euripides' *Bacchae* and miraculous prison escapes in Acts, see John Weaver, *Plots of Epiphany*.
53 1 Kgs 18:12; cf. 2 Kgs 2:11–12, 16; Ezek. 8:3; see 11:1–2.

δυνατὸς ἐν ἔργῳ: Luke 24:19). Overall, the self-estimate of the Lukan Jesus matches the popular perception at several points. As the Spirit-empowered prophet, Jesus announces God's Jubilee Year of liberation, which is accomplished through cures, exorcisms and preaching to the poor (Luke 4:1,14, 18–19,24; cf. 7:21).[54] In Luke 13:32–33 Jesus understands his prophetic vocation to involve a ministry of driving out demons and healings. Aune is correct when he says that 'the wonders which (Jesus) performed provided a conceptual legitimation for the message he proclaimed'.[55] Yet Luke heightens the prophetic perception of Jesus, according him a status greater than the Old Testament prophets (Luke 11:52) and identifying him with the Mosaic eschatological prophet (Acts 3:22–23; 7:37; cf. Deut. 18:15–18).[56] But any triumphal picture of Jesus as a miracle-working prophet is downplayed by a strong emphasis on the violent fate which Jesus, like the Old Testament prophets, will experience (Luke 4:24; 13:31–33; Acts 7:52). Furthermore, the prophets sent out by Jesus will suffer the same fate as their Master (Luke 11:49–51).

Concerning prophetic activities, Jesus predicts the destruction of Jerusalem (Luke 13:34–35; 19:41–44; 23:28–31) and its temple (21:6; Acts 6:13–14). His own death and resurrection are foreshadowed (Luke 9:22,44; 18:31–32)—as is the fate of key disciples (22:21,31–34) and his return as Son of Man spotlighted (9:26; 11:30; 12:8–9; 17:26–30). Certain impenitent cities receive prophecies of eschatological judgement (Luke 10:13–15), while specific groups (the Pharisees, the rich) are also singled out in woe oracles (Luke 6:24–26; 11:45,52). Finally, if Luke 10:18 is correctly interpreted as visionary,[57] Jesus sees the final conquest of Satan by God.

How does the Lukan presentation of Jesus as a prophet differ from Philostratus' prophetic portrait of Apollonius? First, in contrast to Jesus, there is no intimate connection between Apollonius' miraculous acts and prophetic ability. They seem to be largely independent activities. Second, in the case of Jesus there is no hint of divinatory technique at all (cf. Luke 3:42). Third, there is no indication that Apollonius would establish a prophetic succession after his death. The closest Philostratus comes to the Lukan understanding of prophets endowed with the Spirit of Jesus is at *Vita* 8.31. There the ghost of Apollonius talks to a youth about the soul's immortality and, according to Philostratus, the sage's inspired argument was 'established like an oracular tripod' (τρίπους ἕστηκεν). Fourth, Apollonius is dependent upon the gods' revelation for his prophetic knowledge. By contrast, Luke strongly emphasises Jesus' personal authority in prophetic revelation. Nowhere does he use the traditional Old Testament introductory prophetic formulae (e.g. 'Thus says the Lord').[58] Even more surprisingly, he employs the 'divine I' of prophetic speech in Luke 13:34–35:[59]

> O Jerusalem, Jerusalem, killing the prophets and stoning those who are sent to you! How often would I have gathered your children together as a hen gathers her brood under her wings, and you would not! Behold your house is forsaken!

Indeed, although Luke presents Jesus as the receiver and bearer of the Spirit, there is no hint that Jesus is dependent upon the Spirit (unlike the apostles: Luke 11:49; cf. 12:11–12) for prophetic revelation.

In sum, unlike Apollonius, the focus of Jesus' prophecies is both christological and soteriological. The contours of the presentations of Luke and Philostratus are quite different. Each reveals a different panorama of the miraculous. But to obscure the uniqueness of Luke's view by

---

54 See Ringe, *Jesus, Liberation, and the Biblical Jubilee*.
55 Aune, *Prophecy in Early Christianity*, 171.
56 See Teeple, *The Mosaic Eschatological Prophet*; Eve, 'The Miracles of an Eschatological Prophet'.
57 Aune, *Prophecy in Early Christianity*, 163. Contra, see Ladd, *A Theology of the New Testament*, 67.
58 Aune, *Prophecy in Early Christianity*, 171.
59 Borg, *Jesus, A New Vision*, 162.

the hypothesis of aretalogy is to miss—echoing Luke's preface—what has been fulfilled among us (Luke 1:1: πεπληροφορημένων ἐν ἡμῖν).

However, the complexity of the comparison between Luke and Philostratus is also seen in their similarities as well. Todd Klutz has convincingly demonstrated ten impressive similarities between Luke's Gerasene demoniac pericope (8:26–39) and Apollonius' healing of the demon-possessed youth in *Vita* 4.20, discussed above.[60] But this is not an issue of direct literary dependence, Klutz argues, on the part of Luke or Philostratus.[61] Rather we are witnessing 'an area of overlap in Luke and Philostratus' cultural resources and assumptions', notwithstanding the ideological collision between the Pythagorean heritage of Apollonius and 'the Jewish-biblical tradition in which Luke firmly places Jesus'.[62] As Klutz concludes, 'the cultural universe of the Lucan story has just as much in common with the wider magico-religious conglomeration of the Imperial age as it does with Jewish Scripture in particular'.[63] Luke speaks in ways that were conceptually and rhetorically similar and culturally recognisable to his Graeco-Roman audience, but without thereby compromising the distinctiveness of Jesus.

3. Luke, Lucian, and the Miraculous

In this section we will discuss the role of the miraculous in two of Lucian's works and contrast them with Luke-Acts. The works to be examined are *Alexander the False Prophet* and *The Passing of Peregrinus*. Although Lucian in his *Life of Demonax* regards his protagonist as a divine man, we will leave aside discussion of this work since its emphasis is on the virtues of the true philosopher, as opposed to any presentation of supernatural origin or miraculous aretalogies.[64] Nor will we examine Lucian's parody of contemporary superstition in *The Lover of Lies*,[65] or explore his parody of the miracles and fables of Ctesias and Iambulus found in his *True History*.[66] Lucian's accounts of the

---

60 Klutz, *The Exorcism Stories in Luke-Acts*, 122–23. The similarities between the accounts of Philostratus and Luke are as follows: demonic indwelling, the severity of the demonic effects, the loud demonic utterances, the demon driving its victim, the demon acknowledging its inferiority before the exorcist, a verbal command as the healing method, the visible effects of the demon's expulsion on a physical object, the healing as a dramatic reversal, the changed dress of the healed victim, and the adoption of the healer's teaching and healing by the former demoniac. For a redactional comparison of Luke 8:26–39 with Mark 5:1–20, see Kirchschläger, *Jesu exorzistisches Wirken aus der Sicht des Lukas*, 96–130. On Luke's redaction of the miraculous in Mark generally, see Dawson, *Healing, Weakness and Power*, 118–24.
61 Note also the comment of Reimer, *Miracle and Magic*, 22 n 69: 'even if one denies direct dependence, it is worth noting Bowersock's contention ... that the New Testament stories were a key ingredient in the rise of marvellous fiction and its motifs, of which VA [= *Vita Apollonii*] is an excellent example, hence the uncanny similarities without any direct evidence of dependence'.
62 Klutz, *The Exorcism Stories in Luke-Acts*, 124.
63 Klutz, *The Exorcism Stories in Luke-Acts*, 125.
64 For discussion, see Tiede, *The Charismatic Figure as Miracle Worker*, 82–84.
65 In Lucian's *The Lover of Lies* various exotic supernatural phenomena appear: (a) the Chaldean spells range from resuscitations of corpses to a magical pestle (*Philops.* 13–14,35–36); (b) the holy man Pancrates rides crocodiles bareback and swims with untamed beasts (34); (c) a Hyperborean magician flies through the air, walks on water (or fire), revivifies corpses, summons supernatural beings, and produces love charms (13–15); (d) there are fantastic tales of magic statues and a snake-footed woman (19–20); (e) Aristognatis the Pythagorean used Egyptian imprecations in exorcisms of phantasmata (31); (f) the prophetic revelation of Apollo's oracular ring is also mentioned, as are visionary experiences of Hades (25–28,38).
66 In *True History* we find the same supernatural material as in *The Lover of Lies*. The snake-legged woman (*Philops.* 22) finds her counterpart in the Bullheaded Men, Ass-legged Women, and the Dragon forces (*Ver. hist.* 1.10–30; 2.44,46). The air travel of the Hyperborean magician, along with his water-walking (*Philops.* 13), reappears in different form in the *True History* (*Ver. Hist.* 2.10–30, 44). Visions of Hades are present in both works (*Philops.* 25–28; *Ver. Hist.* 2.23–26). Pancrates' wonders involving travel on beasts (*Philops.* 34) also reappear with some changes in the *True History* (*Ver. Hist.* 1.30–40).

miraculous in these works are anecdotal, as opposed to being sustained bioi of their protagonists. Both works, however, are perhaps much closer to the exotic religious beliefs and deep-seated fears animating the common populace at the time than Lucian's biting satire allows for.[67]

3.1 Alexander the False Prophet and Luke-Acts

In the satirical work *Alexander the False Prophet*,[68] the rhetorician Lucian of Samosata (c. AD 120–180) describes the establishment of a new Asclepius cult in Abonuteichos by Alexander, its prophet, during AD 150–170. Capitalising on the gullibility of the inhabitants of Abonuteichos and Paphlagonia generally,[69] Alexander stage-managed elaborate epiphanies of a reborn Asclepius.[70] The snake Glycon, the god's oracular mouthpiece, gave oracles which attracted brisk business, wellplaced clientele, and personal fame for Alexander through his missionary workers.[71] David L. Tiede describes the work as 'a parody of a semi-literary attempt to glorify the prophet', which focused on oracular and magicalmiraculous means.[72]

From Lucian's point of view, Alexander's motives are either base, mercenary, fraudulent, or self-aggrandising.[73] According to Walter Liefeld, in this attack Lucian uses the stock expressions of abuse employed by preachers to depreciate or discredit rivals.[74] Thus, despite the 'godlike' (θεοπρεπής) appearance of Alexander, the prophet's soul is seen as filled with falsehood and deceit.[75] Lucian brings this crescendo of invective to a climax in the following:

> … imagine please … a highly diversified soul-blend, made up of lying (ψεύδους), trickery (δόλων), perjury, and malice: facile, audacious, venturesome, diligent in the execution of its schemes, plausible, convincing, masking as good, and wearing an appearance absolutely opposite to its purpose.[76]

Such a jaundiced presentation is to be treated with care. We must remember that Lucian represents 'the critical epistemological tradition of the philosophical counterculture'.[77] Thus, Lucian's stinging critique of the new Asclepius and its deluded followers originates from Epicurean sympathies held by the author.[78] Also, granted the effect of Lucian's rhetorical flourishes, his reporting is carefully culled, often (one suspects) at the expense of more positive

---

67 Glover, *The Conflict of Religions in the Early Empire*, 209.
68 For discussion of Alexander, see Thonemann, *Lucian: Alexander or the False Prophet*; Remus, *Pagan-Christian Conflict Over Miracle in the Second Century*, 159–73; Robert, *À travers l'Asie*, 393–421; Tiede, *The Charismatic Figure as Miracle Worker*, 63–70; Nock, 'Alexander of Abonuteichos'.
69 On the oracular cult at Abonouteichos, see Thonemann, *Lucian: Alexander or the False Prophet*, 21–25, 28–34.
70 Lucian, *Alex.*, 8–19.
71 Lucian, *Alex.*, 23–24. For detailed discussion of the Glykon-cult, see Thonemann, *Lucian: Alexander or the False Prophet*, 15–21. On Alexander's well-placed clientele and social status (Lucian, *Alex.* 27, 30, 33, 35, 43), see Remus, *Pagan-Christian Conflict Over Miracle in the Second Century*, 170–71. On Lucian's attitude towards the clientele, Remus, 163–65.
72 Tiede, *The Charismatic Figure as Miracle Worker*, 163–64. Thonemann (*Lucian: Alexander or the False Prophet*, 6–9) argues for a composite of genres in *Alexander the False Prophet*. He concludes that the work is 'parodic anti-biography, invective, oracular critique, quasi-philosophical critique' (11).
73 Remus, *Pagan-Christian Conflict Over Miracle in the Second Century*, 172.
74 Liefeld, *The Wandering Preacher as a Social Figure in the Roman Empire*, 87; cf. 274–80. See also Reimer, *Miracle and Magic*, 163–73 on the motif of 'rejection' in the book of Acts and in Philostratus' *Vita*.
75 Lucian, *Alex.*, 3.
76 Lucian, *Alex.*, 4.
77 Remus, *Pagan-Christian Conflict Over Miracle in the Second Century*, 173.
78 For Lucian's Epicurean sympathies, see Lucian, *Alex.*, 25, 38, 46–47, 61. On Epicurean apologetic in the work, see Thonemann, *Lucian: Alexander or the False Prophet*, 8–9.

counterbalancing evidence.[79]

Lucian's portrait of Alexander is relevant to Luke-Acts and its presentation of the miraculous in several areas. First, healings are claimed for the cult of Alexander, but they are merely prescriptions of medical treatments or diets.[80] Rumours of resurrections from the dead were just that—rumours, propagated by his oracle mongers.[81] Here Alexander's role recalls Apollonius' reliance upon natural therapy or special insight. Undoubtedly, Walter Liefeld and A. D. Nock are correct in supposing that Lucian parodies developing aretalogical traditions to be adopted by Philostratus some decades later.[82]

Second, there is mention of Alexander's golden thigh gleaming, a phenomenon which Lucian rationalises.[83] Thonemann observes that 'The precise significance of this curious story escapes us, although the golden thigh was taken to indicate Pythagoras' divinity in some way'.[84] This finds a 'parallel' with the Lukan transfiguration of Jesus (Luke 9:28–36). But in such cases involving the golden thigh motif (Alexander, Pythagoras), there is no talk of a transformation, in contrast to the Lukan account.[85] Also, Lukan fulfilment motifs are present: Moses and Elijah speak with Jesus, the fulfilment of the Law and Prophets (Luke 24:25–28), about the 'new exodus' (9:31: τὴν ἔξοδον) he will accomplish at Jerusalem (9:30–31).

Third, Alexander feigned a divine frenzy (θεῖόν τι καὶ φοβερόν: *Alex.* 13; the nonsense-oracles at 51 and 53), in which he uttered meaningless words (glossolalia? oracles? incantations?) in Hebrew or Phoenician.[86] Significantly, the Lukan parallel in Pentecost presents an occurrence characterised by intelligible speech, universally distributed, with no ecstatic overtones.[87]

Fourth, Lucian devotes considerable attention to Alexander's lucrative trade in oracles (his shrine grossing 70,000–80,000 obols p.a.).[88] Several such oracles are cited, with Lucian's caustic editorial comments on their veracity.[89] Oraclemongers were sent out by Alexander into the Roman Empire, with warnings of plagues, conflagrations, and earthquakes.[90] These predictive oracles are reminiscent of Agabus' prophecy of famine throughout the Roman empire. In Agabus' case, they involve inspiration from the Spirit (Acts 11:27; cf. 2:17), whereas there is no suggestion of Alexander's inspiration. The prophecy of Agabus concerning Paul's fate at Jerusalem (Acts 21:10–11) is also Spiritinspired (cf. v.11) and involves a symbolic gesture reminiscent of Old Testament prophetic acts.[91]

Fifth, Luke shares common ground with Lucian in his distaste for the mercenary attitudes of the cults in exploiting the miraculous (Acts 8:18–23; 16:16–19; 19:23–27). Therefore, Luke

---

79   See Phillips, 'Religious Fraud in the Roman Empire: Alexander and Others', 333-35. Note Phillips' perceptive comment: 'Although Lucian himself furnishes the counter-evidence of the Glykon coinage, Marcus Aurelius, and two Roman consulars, this evidence palls beside his repeated emphases on the throngs of yokels following Alexander' (334).
80   Lucian, *Alex.*, 25.
81   Lucian, *Alex.*, 24. Alexander also employed magic, as his doorway amulet against plague demonstrates (p.36).
82   Liefeld, *The Wandering Preacher as a Social Figure in the Roman Empire*, 85-86; Nock, *Conversion*, 91.
83   Lucian, *Alex.*, 40.
84   Thonemann, *Lucian: Alexander or the False Prophet*, 123. For evidence pertaining to Pythagoras' golden thigh, see Iamblichus, *VP* 92, 135, 140; Apollonius, *Marvellous Tales* 6; Aelian, *VH* 2.6; 4:17; Diogenes Laertius, *Vitae* 8.11.1(9).
85   Blackburn, 'Miracle Working ΘΕΙΟΙ ΑΝΔΡΕΣ', 193.
86   Thonemann, *Lucian: Alexander or the False Prophet*, 93, writes: 'Hebrew prayer formulae and other religious terms are widely used in Greek magical texts of the Roman imperial period and Late Antiquity'.
87   Blackburn, 'Miracle Working ΘΕΙΟΙ ΑΝΔΡΕΣ', 44.
88   Lucian, *Alex.*, 8-9, 23.
89   Lucian, *Alex.*, 11, 22, 25-29.
90   Lucian, *Alex.*, 36.
91   For background, see Fraser, 'Symbolic Acts of the Prophets'.

presents Paul as working with his hands for his maintenance as an apostle (Acts 20:32–35). Luke, like Lucian, has no hesitation in employing stock expressions of abuse to disparage and discredit competitors in the field of the miraculous (μαγεύων: Acts 8:9; ταῖς μαγείαις: 8:11; μάγον ψευδοπροφήτην: 13:6; δόλου: 13:10).[92] In connection with Acts 20, Martin Dibelius has pinpointed the reason for Luke adopting such apologetic tactics:

> Paul's mission might easily have been confused by the public with the activities of wandering speakers, mendicant philosophers, pseudo-prophets and sorcerers. Therefore, the missionary's first concern had to be to dissociate himself from them by emphasising that his aims were not self-seeking.[93]

But the issue is wider than just the public perception of the Christian mission. According to G. W. H. Lampe, Acts 20:17–35 reflects a situation of 'counter-evangelism' by anti-Christian prophets.[94] These 'grievous wolves', whose credentials were supernatural acts of power (pagan 'signs and wonders'), caused apostasy within the church by their false teaching. Lampe's argument, in my view, is cogent. The success of Alexander's mission caused second-century Christians to protest over its trickery.[95] Indeed, within Acts itself, the μάγος and ψευδοπροφήτης, Elymas Bar-Jesus, endeavoured to turn Sergius Paulus from faith (Acts 13:6–12) and both Simon Magus (8:9–24) and the sons of Sceva (19:13–16) tried to mimic Christian miraculous acts of power. The earlier narrative of Acts, with its fraudulent prophets and itinerant exorcists, presaged the arrival of the type of figure later satirised by Lucian in *Alexander the False Prophet*.

3.2 The Passing of Peregrinus and Luke-Acts

Lucian's entertaining piece of Levantine gossip, *The Passing of Peregrinus*, attacks Peregrinus' pretensions to be a Cynic philosopher and a new Heracles.[96] Again, we must recognise the hostile agenda that underlies Lucian's polemic, especially in view of two favourable references to Peregrinus in Aulus Gellius.[97] Also, Athenagoras refers to a statue erected to Peregrinus at Parum (Peregrinus' birthplace), from which oracles were delivered.[98]

Peregrinus Proteus (c. AD 100–165) had fled to Palestine—reputedly due to parricide charges—where he converted to Christianity.[99] There Christians appointed him as prophet, cult leader, and head of the synagogue—a role entailing the interpretation of the sacred books and law.[100] Arrested and jailed, he amassed sizeable revenue from Christian gifts.[101] On his subsequent conversion to Cynicism in Egypt, he wandered as an itinerant philosopher to Italy and Greece, only to die at Olympus by self-immolation.[102] In sum, the satirical significance of Lucian's work remains disputed in modern scholarship. Dana Fields argues that the account of Peregrinus represents a satire on the culture of self-display to which both Lucian himself and Peregrinus were deeply

---

92 For useful background, see Barrett, 'Light on the Holy Spirit from Simon Magus (Acts 8:4–25)', 287–89.
93 Dibelius, *Studies in the Acts of the Apostles*, 156.
94 Lampe, 'Grievous Wolves (Acts 20:29)', 254.
95 Lucian, *Alex*, 38.
96 Bagnani, 'Peregrinus Proteus and the Christians', 107, styles the *Passing of Peregrinus* as Levantine gossip. On the new Heracles theme, see Lucian, *Peregr*, 4–5, 33.
97 Aulus Gellius, 8.3; 12.11.
98 Athenagoras, *Leg*, 11–12.
99 See Bremmer, 'Peregrinus' Christian Career'; Edwards, 'Satire and Verisimilitude: Christianity in Lucian's "Peregrinus"'.
100 Lucian, *Peregr*, 11–12.
101 Lucian, *Peregr*, 13.
102 Lucian, *Peregr*, 14–20.

committed.[103] By contrast, Kanavou Nikoletta views the work more conventionally as an extended satire of Christianity.[104]

Several points of contact exist between Lucian's account of Peregrinus and Luke Acts. Like the apostles in Acts (14:11–12; 28:1–6), Peregrinus was revered as a θεός, although for law-giving not miraculous acts.[105] Curiously though, this estimation of Peregrinus is attributed to Christians, in sharp contrast to the Lukan apostles who deny divine status to men (apart from Jesus). Theagenes the Cynic speaks of the apotheosis of Peregrinus by 'wings of fire': as a new Heracles, he would depart from among men to the gods (ἐξ ἀνθρώπου εἰς θεούς).[106] Lucian was an eyewitness of the event and predicted that post-mortem aretalogies would build around Peregrinus, vaunting his supposed miraculous powers:

> By Zeus, it would be nothing unnatural if, among all the dolts that there are, some were found to assert that they were relieved of quartan fevers by him…Then too those accursed disciples of his will make an oracular shrine, I suppose, with a holy of holies, at the site of the pyre, because the famous Proteus, son of Zeus, the progenitor of his name, was given to soothsaying.[107]

Even Lucian mischievously indulged himself in such aretalogies with 'the dullards, agog to listen', embroidering Peregrinus' death with portents—earthquakes and the obligatory vulture.[108] Luke, however, would not countenance any posthumous accreditation of miraculous aretalogies to Jesus. It was conspicuously the historical Jesus who was accredited by 'signs and wonders' prior to his ascension (Acts 1:1–2; 2:22–24; 10:38–41). Certainly 'signs and wonders' continued after the ascension: but they are carried out by Jesus' Spiritendowed heirs and effected by faith in the name of the risen Christ (Acts 3:1–16, esp. v.16; 4:8–10).

Interestingly, we see the establishment of a Peregrine mission on its founder's apotheosis by fire. Missionaries were sent to famous cities, along with ambassadors, who were styled 'messengers from the dead' and 'underworld couriers'.[109] These Cynic missionaries, armed with Peregrine aretalogies, were to set up statues in his honour.[110] They reflect that emerging rivalry we see in Acts, between the Christian mission and their opponents, all with competing claims of the supernatural (oracular revelation, miraculous acts, apotheosis, or resurrection).

A final point. Aune has shown that the wanderings of the prophet Peregrinus are different from the Lukan instances of prophetic itinerancy (Acts 11:27–30; 15:22–35; 21:8–11; cf. Luke 9:1–6; 10:1–20). They are undertaken for specific purposes, involving the edification of believers through their prophetic charismata.[111] Paul Bowers has expressed the contrast between Hellenistic wandering preachers (such as Peregrinus) and the apostles and prophets (such as Paul): 'They wandered; Paul progressed'.[112]

---

103 Fields, 'The Reflections of Satire: Lucian and Peregrinus'.
104 Nikoletta, 'Satirizing Christianity in Lucian's Peregrinus'.
105 Lucian, *Peregr.*, 11.
106 Lucian, *Peregr.*, 6.
107 Lucian, *Peregr.*, 28.
108 Lucian, *Peregr.*, 39. On the portentous significance of earthquakes and vultures respectively, see Krauss, *An Interpretation of the Omens, Portents and Prodigies Recorded by Livy, Tacitus, and Suetonius*, 49–53, 101–103.
109 Lucian, *Peregr.*, 28, 41.
110 We see expressions of these Peregrine aretalogies in Theagenes' speech, Lucian, *Peregr.*, 5–6. Also, note the claim: 'some…assert, that they were relieved of quartan fevers by him' (28).
111 Aune, *Prophecy in Early Christianity*, 212.
112 Bowers, 'Paul and Religious Propaganda in the First Century', 319. See Reimer, *Miracle and Magic*, 70–82, on travelling intermediaries in Acts and Apollonius' maintenance of his fringe status by constant travel.

4. Luke, the Paradoxographers, and the Miraculous

Apollonius the paradoxographer was the second-century BC author of the *Marvellous Tales* (*Historiae Mirabiles*).[113] The *Tales* belonged to a tradition fascinated by the out-of-the-ordinary, abstruse, or marvellous. Apollonius employs several sources, including Bolus, a third-century writer, whose *Marvels* (θαυμάσια) was a pioneering example of the paradoxographic genre (*Marvellous Tales I*: 'According to Bolus'). Theopompus, the fourth-century historian, also wrote a world history, 'Philippica', which contained extensive digressions, some of which acquired separate titles (*Marvellous Tales I*: 'as Theopompus reports'). Another source was Aristotle's Περὶ τῆς Πυθαγορείων, known to us by literary references to the work and of which only fragments remain,[114] which described various of Pythagoras' marvels (*Marvellous Tales VI*: 'as Aristotle reports', 2x). Despite Apollonius' disclaimer that he was not a 'copyist' (μεταγραφέων: *Marvellous Tales VI*), it is likely that he adopted this exact methodology for his sources (ἱστορεῖται: *Marvellous Tales V*). He also added any exotic myths he found relevant (μυθολογεῖται: *Marvellous Tales III*). This means that Apollonius does not display the insight of Lucian's biting satire. His narratives are not as heavily pruned of positive counterbalancing evidence as are those of Lucian. Finally, in terms of Apollonius' selection of evidence, he seems to have had an interest in figures associated with the god Apollo (Aristeas, Abaris, Pythagoras).

Traditions differ concerning the dating of Epimenides' career as a Cretan wonderworker and propagandist for the Cretan Zeus. Plato believed Epimenides prophesied and performed religious rites at Athens around 500 BC (*Leg.* 1.642d). Other writers associate him with Athens' purification after the massacre of Cylon's associates in 600 BC (Aristotle, *Ath. Pol.* 1). Legends disagree over his age (Apollonius, *Marvellous Tales I*: 157 years; other writers, Diels, *Vorsokr* 5.1.28: 299 years).[115] According to Apollonius, Epimenides had been sent out to the country by his father and brothers to bring back a sheep. Straying from his path, he went to sleep for fifty-seven years, only to return to a totally different city (*Marvellous Tales I*). The closest Luke comes to such a miracle story—and the resemblances are minimal—is the account of Eutychus in Acts 20:7–12. There, upon falling asleep during Paul's preaching, Eutychus fell out of a third-floor window and was found dead in the street below. The Lukan miracle of Eutychus' restoration to life (Acts 20:10) involves resurrection, modelled on Old Testament prophetic acts (1 Kgs 17:21; 2 Kgs 4:34). No adequate parallel to Apollonius' wonder exists in early Christian literature.

In the case of the servant of Apollo, Aristeas of Proconnesus, Apollonius reports a post-mortem appearance of Aristeas in Sicily precisely at the moment of his death in Proconnesus (*Marvellous Tales II*). Whether Apollonius understood this as a case of ecstasis (literal separation of soul from body, as in Herodotus, *Hist.* 4.13), or a ghost appearance (as with Apollonius of Tyana: Philostratus, *Vita* 8.31) is difficult to say. Certainly, if it is a case of ecstasis, Apollonius' account of Aristeas' feat in this regard is much more cryptic than the full-blown account given of the soul wanderings of Hermotimus (*Marvellous Tales III*). The only Lukan approximations

---

113 On the paradoxographers, see Yu, 'Paradoxography'; Lightfoot, *Wonder and the Marvellous from Homer to the Hellenistic World*; Greene, 'A Most Amazing Conversation'; Geus and King, 'Paradoxography'. For English translations of the *Marvellous Tales* of Apollonius with accompanying Greek text, see https:// sententiaeantiquae.com › paradoxography, accessed 3/11/2025; Tiede, *The Charismatic Figure as Miracle Worker*, 313–16.

114 See Philip, 'Aristotle's Monograph on the Pythagoreans', 191: 'the theme of *mirabilia* was a favorite theme in the third century and thereafter; and Aristotle's monograph apparently provided ample material for the writers in the biographical tradition. They excerpted accounts of miracles, prophecies, divine signs; proofs of divine status; tales of encounters with the Hyperborean Abaris. The fragments give us no biographical information'.

115 Diels, *Fragmente der Vorsokrater*, 1.28.

of these phenomena are the resurrection appearances of Jesus (Luke 24:31,36; Acts 1:3) and the Spirit-rapture of Philip (Acts 8:39). In neither case is there any mention of a body-soul separation. Instead, the emphasis is on the corporeality of the resurrected Jesus: 'handle me (ψηλαφήσατέ με) and see, because a spirit (πνεῦμα) has not flesh (σάρκα) and bones (ὀστέα) as you see I have' (Lule 24:39). In Philip's case, parallels to the Old Testament Spirit-raptures (1 Kgs 18:12; 2 Kgs 2:11–12,16) differentiate Luke's narrative from Apollonius' understanding.

In *Marvellous Tales III–VI* Apollonius devotes considerable attention to the meteorological and seismic phenomena predicted by his wonderworkers: in particular, rains and droughts (Hermotimus), and earthquakes (Hermotimus, Abaris, Pherecydes). The prophecies are not just limited to natural phenomena. Plagues feature in several places (Hermotimus, Abaris, Pherecydes) and there is mention in a prophecy of Pythagoras of future divisions among the Pythagoreans (*Marvellous Tales VI*). Further, Pherecydes' prediction that a particular ship would not enter the harbour is fulfilled when the ship is raptured from sight in a cloud (*Marvellous Tales VI*; Porphyry, *Life of Pythagoras*, 27–29).[116] Significantly, in these accounts there is no mention of inspiration on the part of the prophet—apart from Pherecydes' drinking water (*Marvellous Tales V*).[117] Therefore, whilst the fulfilment of these predictions happens 'by the favour of heaven' (κατ'οὐρανόν: *Marvellous Tales IV*), the techniques of those wonder-working manteis are decidedly divinatory.[118] Moreover, the considerable space Apollonius devotes to their mantic abilities points to the fact that he considered prediction the most common form of miraculous power.[119]

Undeniably, in this area, Luke shares common motifs with Apollonius. In Luke 21:19, Jesus predicts earthquakes, pestilences, and famine (as does Agabus, Acts 11:28). Paul also predicts division in the Ephesian church (Acts 20:29–30) and receives an angelic oracle of assurance from God, outlining safety for Paul and his ship (27:23–24). But the Lukan understanding of prophecy differs markedly from Apollonius. As argued above, Luke highlights Jesus' personal authority in prophetic revelation, allowing no suggestion of divinatory technique. Jesus' prophetic heirs (Paul, Agabus) are dependent on the outpoured Spirit of prophecy, the personal agent of revelation to his church. As a result, Lukan prophecy embraces a wider spectrum of inspired speech than the predictive oracles of Apollonius' wonderworkers. The latter belong to that disreputable class which Plutarch describes as follows:

> the tribe of wandering soothsayers and rogues that practised their charlatanry, about the shrines of the Great Mother and of Serapis, making up oracles, some using their own ingenuity, others taking by lot from certain treatises oracles for the benefit of servants and womenfolk, who are most enticed by verse and a poetic vocabulary.[120]

---

116 There is a narrative discrepancy between the account of Apollonius, *Marvellous Tales VI*, where a dead body is at the ship's helm, in comparison to the account of Porphyry, *Life of Pythagoras*, 27–29, where a dead body is on board the ship. I am indebted to Associate Professor Paul McKechnie for drawing my attention to this fascinating variation between both accounts of the same event.
117 On the drinking of water for prophetic inspiration, see Halliday, *Greek Divination*, 124-28.
118 This is confirmed by the fact that Abaris, a chresmologue, recorded oracles (*Marvellous Tales IV*). On chresmologues generally, see Fontenrose, *The Delphic Oracle*, 158–65. On an oracle book of Abaris, see Fontenrose, *The Delphic Oracle*, 162–63: for one of the (supposed) Apolline oracles of Abaris, see Q79: Fontenrose, *The Delphic Oracle*, 294. The practice of chresmologues was divinatory, as opposed to being inspiration-based. On this, see Forbes, *Prophecy and Inspired Speech*, 231–32.
119 Blackburn, 'Miracle Working ΘΕΙΟΙ ΑΝΔΡΕΣ', 190.
120 Plutarch, *Pyth. orac.*, 407C; see also Plato, *Resp.* 2.364b-c.

Further, as Blackburn observes, 'divination, the most prevalent power (among Graeco-Roman wonderworkers), plays a comparatively minor role in the miracle traditions associated with Jesus in the Gospels'.[121] The same is true of Acts where predictive oracles are scarce.

Finally, there are four miracles of the mathematician Pythagoras. We have already discussed the golden thigh motif (*Marvellous Tales VI*) and the miraculous appearances in two places at once (*Marvellous Tales VI*: in this case, Croton and Metapontium). In the case of survival from snake bite (*Marvellous Tales VI*), there is the account of Paul's miraculous preservation from the viper's bite on Malta (Acts 28:3–6). But the comic over-estimation of Paul as a god by the islanders is used by Luke to underline his real point. In Luke's view, Paul was the 'heaven-protected man', whose safety had been indicated by divine oracle (Acts 27:23–26) and subsequently by two acts of divine intervention (27:39–44; 28:6).[122] Last, the divine acclamation of Pythagoras ('Hail Pythagoras!': *Marvellous Tales VI*), has its counterpart at Jesus' baptism: 'You are my beloved Son; with you I am well pleased' (Luke 3:22; cf. 9:35), with each acclamation occurring in a river (respectively, near Kosa, and at the Jordan). But again, Lukan fulfilment motifs cluster around the affirmation of Jesus' Sonship: he is simultaneously the Davidic king and the Spiritfilled Servant (Ps. 2:7; Isa. 42:1).

5. Luke, Asclepius, and the Miraculous

In the last decade, three studies have appeared on the relationship between the Asclepian epigraphic healings (iamata) and the miraculous acts of Jesus in the Gospels,[123] though the New Testament miracles are designated by different terminology (dynamis, ergon, semeion).[124] It is a curiosity of scholarship that the Religionsgeschichtliche Schule of a previous generation devoted so little attention to this important strand of Graeco-Roman religious evidence in antiquity.[125] Furthermore, this unexpected momentum in New Testament scholarship on the Asclepius cult and the miracles in the Gospels has only recently occurred and is given even greater impetus when the new seminal work of Christopher D. Stanley on Asclepius, Paul, and the apostolic mission in Acts, is taken into account.[126] The focus of the aforementioned gospel studies is upon Johannine and Markan pericopes (John 5:1–11; Mark 2:1–10), though Robin Thompson occasionally mentions the Gospel of Luke in her article. Consequently, the evidence of Luke-Acts is bypassed.

It is beyond the scope of this essay to conduct the detailed documentary and exegetical study required to address properly the intersection of the Asclepian epigraphy with the Lukan portrayal of the miraculous. However, before we look at several intersections of the Asclepius epigraphic corpus (i.e. at Epidauros, Athens, Lebena, Pergamum, and Rome) with Luke-Acts, it is worth summarising the main conclusions emanating from the gospel studies above. Several observations are particularly apposite, mainly underscoring the differences of presentation of the miraculous in the Asclepian and gospels corpora:

---

121 Blackburn, 'Miracle Working ΘΕΙΟΙ ΑΝΔΡΕΣ', 190.
122 Longenecker, 'Acts', 564.
123 Wojciechowski, 'The Differences Between the Healing Stories'; Thompson, 'Healing at the Pool of Bethesda: A Challenge to Asclepius?'; Giambrone, 'Jesus and the Paralytics', 389–404. On the Epidaurian *iamata*, see Prêtre, 'The Epidaurian Iamata: The First "Court of Miracles"?', 17–30.
124 Wojciechowski, 'The Differences Between the Healing Stories', 159.
125 Wojciechowski, 'The Differences Between the Healing Stories', 158.
126 Stanley, *Paul and Asklepios*.

- The miracle stories of Asclepius and the Gospels are generically analogous in their use of 'small literary forms';[127] but they are fundamentally different in their schematic ordering and focus, adopting in the Epidauros texts the viewpoint of the sick, as opposed to the healer-centric approach of the Gospels.
- In the Gospels the humanity of Jesus as a healer is emphasised in contrast to the apotheosised Asclepius.[128]
- The Gospels do not link miracles with the incubation practices and sanctuary concerns of Epidauros (i.e. purity, cult, and oracles),[129] or with its priestly personnel (LiDonnici, B3 [23]), the surgical procedures of its physicians (LiDonnici, A13; C5 [48]), its curative springs and drug applications, and its use of Hippocratic medical knowledge.[130]
- The substratum of the Gospel tradition 'stems from the biblical world', as opposed to Fate communicating at Epidauros 'through the natural forces, or through visions, omens and dreams'.[131]
- Jesus' 'ostentatious neglect of the health-bringing waters at Bethesda' (John 5:1–11)—a feature of the sanctuary that is reminiscent of the Asclepian springs at Epidauros—is heavily accented in John's Gospel. Jesus cures the lame man by his word alone, 'making him appear … as the true life-giving spring' (cf. John 4:13–15; 7:37–39).[132]
- A question remains whether the pool of Bethesda was an Asclepieion or not, provoking the original auditors to ponder the identity of Jesus in the wider Graeco-Roman context.[133]

What picture emerges from a comparison of the Asclepian epigraphy at several sites with the evidence of Luke-Acts? The most extensive collection of the iamata ('healings', 'treatments', 'remedies'), seventy in total, has been found in the sanctuary of Asclepius at Epidauros, carved in four stelae, and erected there by the sanctuary authorities in the Fourth Century BC.[134] Notably, Pausanias (AD 115–180) observes that he saw six stelae when he visited the sanctuary and posits

---

127 Wojciechowski, 'The Differences Between the Healing Stories', 159
128 Wojciechowski, 'The Differences Between the Healing Stories', 159–60
129 Wojciechowski, 'The Differences Between the Healing Stories', 161. For discussion of the sacrifices, fees-payment, purity regulations, and ritual bathing at the Epidauros Asclepieion, see Dillon, 'The Didactic Nature of the Epidaurian Iamata', 244–46. Oracles are scarce in the Epidauros corpus (LiDonnici, *The Epidaurian Miracle Inscriptions* B13 [33]), as is the interpretation of enigmatic prophecy by a seer (LiDonnici, *The Epidaurian Miracle Inscriptions* C3 [46]).
130 Panagiotidou writes regarding the fourth-century BC Epidauros sanctuary: 'It was the time when Hippocratic medicine made its first steps. People had begun to familiarize themselves with Hippocratic doctors, but the perception of health and disease as being dependent on divine will still prevailed. In this conceptual context, Asclepius was presented as the healing god who had supernatural powers to perform miraculous treatments. An early inscription from Epidaurus, however, indicates that patients started to expect from Asclepius the use of mundane medical practices … So, it was not the dream of the god per se, but the god's actions as a doctor which brought about the desired recovery'. See Panagiotidou, 'Religious Healing and the Asclepius Cult', 85; additionally, 82–83. For the inscription mentioned above ('After saying this, (the god) cut the diseased eyeball and poured in some drug'), see LiDonnici, *The Epidaurian Miracle Inscriptions* §A.4. Note, too, the detailed prescription articulated by Asclepius for the chronic cough of Poplius Granius Rufus at the Asclepieion of Lebena. See Edelstein, *Asclepius, Volume 1*, §439. For a discussion of Rufus' miraculous healing (1st cent. BC–1st cent. AD), necessitated by the inability of the 'new' Hippocratic medicine to handle the condition of Rufus, see Rivoli, '*Sanatio* di Publius Granius Rufus da Lebena', 191. The therapy prescribed at Lebena in this case was quite elaborate: the consumption of herbs, spicy wine, a bread bun, sacred ash, an egg, resins, a vegetable decoction and figs. For further discussion of Asclepian comparanda with contemporary medical science, see Ehrenheim, 'Causal Explanation of Disease in the Iamata of Epidauros'.
131 Wojciechowski, 'The Differences Between the Healing Stories', 162.
132 Giambrone, 'Jesus and the Paralytics', 398. Note the similarity of the testimony of Damosthenes—who was paralysed in the legs and had to be carried into the sanctuary of Asclepius on a couch (LiDonnici, *The Epidaurian Miracle Inscriptions* §C 21 [64])—to the Bethesda episode of John 5:5–8 (cf. Mark 2:4).
133 Thompson, 'Healing at the Pool of Bethesda', 79–80, 83.
134 For a translation, see LiDonnici, *The Epidaurian Miracle Inscriptions*, 85–131. See also Edelstein, *Asclepius: Volume 1*, 221–37, §423.

that there were more there in earlier times (*Geogr.* 2.27.3). LiDonnici has argued that the fourth-century BC inscriptions (c. 350 BC) have been edited and inscribed from smaller inscriptions at the site dating at the earliest to the Fifth Century BC (c. 450 BC).[135]

The vast majority of Asclepian healing narratives involve dreams: in the case of the two largest Epidaurian stelae (IG 4.1.121-22 [= SIG3 1168]), an oneiric experience precedes twenty-six out of the forty-three healings recounted.[136] When the four inscriptions are taken into account, there are thirty-six dreams or visions out of a total of seventy testimonies of cures and miracles. But, as noted above, there is no direct connection between the Lukan Pentecost outpouring of oneiric revelation (Acts 2:17) and the miraculous performance of 'signs on the earth below' (2:19b) other than that the outpoured Spirit of the risen, ascended, and exalted Jesus is the common revelatory source and the agent of miraculous empowerment.

In the four stelae at Epidauros,[137] there are miracles and healings which deal with ailments loosely equivalent to the medical conditions we find in the Gospels: paralysis in the fingers (LiDonnici, A3); paralysis of the body (A15; B17 [37]; B18 [38]; C14 [57]) or of the legs (C21 [64]); blindness in one eye/both eyes (A5, 9, 11, 18, 20; B1 [21] or a damaged eye (C19 [62]); B12 [32]; B20 [40]); dropsy (B1 [21]; C6 [49]); the miraculous birth of a son/two sons/five children (B11 [31]; B14 [34]; B19 [39]; B22 [42]); lameness (B15 [35]); fever (B21 [41]); and, finally, muteness (C1 [44]; C8 [51]).

However, there are healings without any correspondence in the New Testament: namely, five- and three-year (hysterical?) pregnancies (LiDonnici, A1, A2); the removal of tattoos (A6, 7), suffering from a (kidney?) stone (A8) or a stone in the penis (A14); the removal of leeches (A13); the ulceration of a toe (A17); baldness (A19); the presence of a worm/creatures/a festering sore in the belly (B3 [23], B6 [26], B7 [27]); body lice (B8 [28]); a headache (B9 [29]); pus in the lung due to an arrow (B10 [30]) or general bodily pus (C5 [48]); consumption (B13 [33]); gout (B23 [43]); a tumour (C2 [45]); a spear wound (C15 [58]); and, last, a cancerous sore inside the mouth (C32 [66]). There is also the healing of Thersandros for an unspecified sickness by one of the sanctuary's snakes (B13 [33]).

There are also other rare miracles that are not cures of ailments: the miraculous repair of pieces of a broken cup (A10); the finding of the lost son, Aristokritos, by his father (B4 [24]); the discovery of buried treasure (C3 [46]). It is fascinating how few of these non-medical miracles are cited in the Epidauros corpus: Asclepius is pre-eminently the all-powerful healer god.

Other Asclepian sanctuaries reveal epigraphic cures of further ailments. Diophantus of Sphettus prays eloquently to Asclepius for the cure of his gout at Athens (Edelstein, *Asclepius*, §428): 'For no mortal man may give release from such sufferings. Only you, blessed one, have

---

135 LiDonnici, *The Epidaurian Miracle Inscriptions*, 78–82.
136 I disagree with Paraskevi Martzavou's totalling of the dream numbers ('Dream, Narrative, and the Construction of Hope in the "Healing Miracles" of Epidauros', 182) in IG 4.1.121–22 ("30 out of 45 acts of healing involving dreams"), rendering instead my own count of the dreams and visions above. Other details are worthy of comment. Three cures are mentioned where it is explicitly asserted that no dream or vision had taken place (LiDonnici, *The Epidaurian Miracle Inscriptions* A20; B5 [25]; B13 [33]). In other cases where there is no oneiric revelation mentioned, the god comes to the suppliant in what appears to be an epiphanic visitation and effects the cure (e.g. A4, A8, A12, A19; C5 [48], C18 [61], C22 [65]). On several occasions there is mention of suppliants sleeping in the sanctuary and being cured (or restored to health after demonstrating ingratitude), but no dream or vision is indicated in these instances (e.g. A1, A11, A15; B2 [22]). Sometimes animals (dogs) or reptiles (snakes) from the sanctuary perform the cure (A17, A20; B6 [26], B13 [33], B22 [42]; C1 [44], C2 [45]), as well as, quite unexpectedly, a goose on one occasion (B23 [43]). Sometimes prayer to the god brings about the cure (A11; B16 [36]; C4 [47]). Note, too, that human doctors are also depicted as waiting to cauterise pus emissions in a suppliant (C5 [48]), but the god intervenes to accomplish the cure. In sum, there is a great variety in the curative rituals and operations of the sanctuary of Asclepius at Epidauros.
137 On the archaeology of the Epidauros sanctuary, see LiDonnici, *The Epidaurian Miracle Inscriptions*, 1–14.

the power. For the gods who are eminent above all gave you to mortal man as a great gift, the compassionate one, the deliverance from sufferings'. In sum, the divinely-appointed saviour for humankind, Asclepius, who is providentially a gift from the pantheon of gods above, is the only one with the power to deliver his mortal suppliants from physical suffering. We gain here a precious insight into (what would be) a rival Graeco-Roman alternative to the Christian gospel, though, apparently, in sharp contrast to the ascended and reigning Christ, its divine deliverer had no ability to deliver his dependants from death by resurrection (by contrast: Luke 7:11–17; 8:40–56; Acts 9:36–42; 20:7–12).[138] In the case of Lebena, we hear of cures from sciatica and a miraculous birth of a child (Edelstein, *Asclepius*, §426), as well as a cough cure (§439) and a prescription for a painful shoulder (§440).[139] Finally, at Pergamum, quartan fever is assigned as a 'substitute' cure to epilepsy (§425), whereas at Rome cures of blindness, pleurisy, and the spitting up of blood are mentioned (§438).

Apart from the healing of common maladies, the differences between the Asclepian and Luke-Acts traditions are clear enough: there is no hint of site-based incubation in Luke's writings, nor is there any direct link between oneirology and miraculous cures, and 'signs on the earth' are performed by Spirit-guided peripatetic missionaries as opposed to a local apotheosised healer. Nevertheless, there are some interesting intersections of the Epidauros corpus with Luke-Acts. Five examples will suffice.

First, a punitive and restorative miracle is employed against Kaphisias who mocked Asclepius (LiDonnici, B16 [13]):

> Kaphisias [...] he laughed against the treatments of Asclepios [...] he paid no heed, saying that if he had the power, [...] he suffered punishment for this outrage, [...] while sitting on the back of his bull-headed horse it trampled him underfoot and wounded him in the foot immediately and was in an even worse condition before. Much later, after he had earnestly prayed to the god (?) he became well.[140]

Second, a miracle uncovered the deception of the fishmonger Amphimnastos, who had promised a tenth of his profit from his catch of fish to Asclepius, only to renege on his promise and have his ruse exposed by the god (LiDonnici, C4 [47]). Another blind suppliant does not make an offering after his cure, is punitively blinded by the god once more, but after sleeping at the sanctuary again he is divinely restored to health (B2 [22]).

In the cases above, one is reminded of the deception of Ananias and Sapphira in secretly keeping back some of the funds from the sale of their property for the common purse, resulting in their prophetic exposure and subsequent punitive deaths (Acts 5:1–11). Furthermore, the opposition to Paul's gospel of the Jewish prophet and sorcerer, Elymas Bar-Jesus, at Paphos in

---

138 Dillon, 'The Didactic Nature of the Epidaurian Iamata', 257, writes: 'In myth, Asklepios could resurrect the dead before he was punished by Zeus for doing so'.
139 LiDonnici, *The Epidaurian Miracle Inscriptions*, 48, comments: 'The great difference between the Iamata and the Lebena tales lies in the manner of cure or treatment. The Lebena group shows an element which is not used in Epidauros, namely the employment of specific plants or other items from the pharmacopoeia ... used by the secular medicine of the day'. On the sanctuary of Asclepius at Lebena, see Melfi, *Il santuario di Asclepio a Lebena*, not seen by me.
140 Angelos Chaniotis, 'Illness and Cures in the Greek Propitiatory Inscriptions', 326, observes: 'We find here the same pattern as in the propitiatory inscriptions: sin, sickness, repentance, and cure'. On the propitiatory inscriptions and the epistle to the Romans, see Harrison, 'Paul's Legacy in Romans and the Confession Inscriptions of Asia Minor'. Note, too, the mockery of a blind man by outsiders at the sanctuary at Epidauros: 'Some people in the sanctuary were laughing at his simple-mindedness in thinking that he could be made to see, having absolutely nothing, but only the socket' (LiDonnici, *The Epidaurian Miracle Inscriptions*, A9).

Cyprus is characterised as deceit, trickery, and a perversion of the right ways of the Lord (Acts 14:6–12), resulting in the punitive miracle of temporary blindness being inflicted upon him by the apostle Paul. In Graeco-Roman and Jewish-Christian cultures, therefore, any hard-hearted impunity and impenitence towards the priorities, demands, and reciprocity system undergirding the divine world is met with punitive miraculous judgement.

Third, a man with paralysed fingers was disparaging regarding the epigraphic cures on the plaques which he had viewed in the sanctuary at Epidauros (LiDonnici, A3). He was confronted by the god concerning his unbelief thus: 'Therefore, since you doubted them before, though they were not unbelievable, from now on your name shall be "unbeliever" (Ἄπιστος)'. Notwithstanding, the man was cured by Asclepius.

In the Gospel of Luke Jesus upbraids the disciples regarding their lack of faith displayed in the boat despite Jesus' miraculous calming of the storm on the lake of Galilee (8:25; cf. 18:8). However, in another case, Luke removes the Markan confession of a lack of faith on the part the father when he is confronted with his son's overpowering demon-possession (Mark 9:14–29; Luke 9:14–29). Instead, Luke emphasises Jesus' superior exorcistic power in the face of his disciples' failure as 'faithless' exorcists (Luke 9:37–41). Furthermore, the formula 'Your faith has saved you' is a frequent refrain in Luke (7:50; 8:48; 17:19; 18:42), as are faith-evoking events in Acts (2:7,12,41; 3:9–12; 8:8–13; 9:35,42; 10:45; 12:16; 13:12; 14:11; 28:6).[141] A concern for proper faith responses belongs to the Epidaurian and Luke-Acts traditions.

Fourth, because the Epidaurian miracles are sanctuary-based, it is interesting that in Acts 3:1–10 Peter heals a crippled beggar who was conveyed by helpers each day to the Beautiful Gate of the Jerusalem temple to secure alms from visitors to the precincts. The purity status of a person with a disability being so close to the temple precincts is worthy of consideration. In first-century AD sectarian Judaism, the blind and lame were excluded from the Dead Sea Scrolls community (1QSa II.3-9; cf. 4QMMT 51-57; 11Q19 XLV.13,14), whereas, according to the Old Testament Levitical holiness codes, people with disabilities were prohibited from the inner temple courts and the sanctuary (Lev. 21:16–23; 2 Sam. 5:6–8; Hagigah 1.1; *pace*, 2 Sam. 9:3,7 9; Isa. 35:5–6).[142] It seems, therefore, that the Beautiful Gate was the furthest that the blind, crippled, or lame could go.[143] We are confronted here by an intriguing collision between the Asclepian and Lukan social worlds. Purity concerns are paramount for each tradition, though here they are diametrically opposed in their social expression. Those with leg paralysis could only be cured within the purity protocols of the Asclepian Abaton ('dream chamber') at Epidauros (LiDonnici, C21 [64]),[144] whereas in a Jewish context all those with disability were excluded by the purity boundaries of the temple precincts (Acts 3:1–10).

Peter's healing of the crippled beggar (Acts 3:3–8) obviates the dilemma posed above by his responding to the need of the person alone, as opposed to undertaking serious prior reflection regarding locale and purity considerations before proceeding to the healing. As a sidelight, even more remarkably (and indeed shockingly) in a Jewish context, Matthew 21:14 presents blind and lame people coming to Jesus in the temple amidst the chaos of his staged cleansing of the Court

---

141 For discussion, see Seglenieks, 'Faith and Faithfulness in Luke'.
142 Comprehensively, see Bengtsson, 'On the Borderline—Representations of Disability in the Old Testament'.
143 Razafiarivony, 'Exclusion of the Blind and Lame from the Temple', 15.
144 LiDonnici, *The Epidaurian Miracle Inscriptions* C21 [64]: Damosthenes, paralysed in the legs and carried into the sanctuary of Asclepius on a couch, saw a vision. As the testimony concludes, 'It seemed to him the god ordered him to remain in the sanctuary for four months, because in that time he would become well. After this, in the last days within the fourth month, he went into the Abaton with two canes, [but] he left well'.

of the Gentiles (21:12). Having violated the purity boundary marker of the 'Beautiful Gate' entry to the temple (Acts 3:2,10), these unclean suppliants were healed onsite by Jesus, who, in so doing, overturned the Levitical holiness codes of access to and purity in the temple[145] and thereby earned the indignation of the chief priests and scribes (Matt. 21:15c). A collision of enormous consequence over purity protocols and classification, whether location-based or imposed upon groups as social categorisations, had been unveiled.

Fifth, the failure of the 'new' Hippocratic medicines to heal the form of pulmonary tuberculosis afflicting Publius Granius Rufus, necessitating his need for an Asclepieion cure at Lebena (Edelstein, *Asclepius*, §439: n.130 supra), is reminiscent of Luke 8:43–48. There the woman with a haemorrhage had squandered all her money on doctors with no result until she encountered Jesus as her healer.[146]

6. Luke, the Magical Papyri, and the Miraculous

Another fruitful area of investigation of the miraculous is to compare Luke-Acts with the Magical Papyri for their respective methods of treatment of the same ailments, even though the Magical Papyri significantly postdate the New Testament documents, mostly emanating from the Third Century AD onwards.[147] The Magical Papyri reveal a variety of exorcistic techniques, ranging from spells to phylacteries, charms, prescriptions, rings, and amulets.[148] Epilepsy, too, is linked with demonic attack and is to be treated with magical remedies and amulets.[149] Prophetic foreknowledge is achieved through spells or (most commonly) charms.[150] Eye disease and discharges are treated with varying techniques: amulets, spells, or figura magica.[151] Of the nineteen references to fever cures, most centre on amulets, phylacteries, and spells.[152] One fever amulet is particularly interesting for its citation of the LXX (Ps. 90:1–2) and the Lord's prayer (Matt. 6:9–11),

---

145 For the wider theological implications of Jesus' actions, see Razafiarivony, 'Exclusion of the Blind and Lame from the Temple', 16–20.

146 Many Greek manuscripts have an alternative reading for Luke 8:43: 'Now there was a woman who had been suffering from haemorrhages for twelve years; and though *she had spent all she had on physicians*, no one could cure her'. For textual support of this reading, see Borland, 'The High Cost of Physicians: The Textual Criticism of Luke 8:43'.

147 For methodological cautions in using the Magical Papyri for discussions of the New Testament evidence, see Harrison, 'Prophecy, Divination, and Oneirology in the Greek Magical Papyri', 100–102. The edition of Betz, (ed.), *The Greek Magical Papyri in Translation, Including the Demotic Spells*, is used here. The new collection of Farone and Tovar, *Greek and Egyptian Magical Formularies: Volume 1* has also been consulted, but no new additions to Betz's edition were observed.

148 PGM.IV.86–87; IV.1227–1264; IV.3007–3086; LXXXV.1–6; LXXXIX.1–27; XCIV.17–21; CXIV.1–14. For the Lukan evidence regarding exorcism: Luke 4:33–27; 7:21; 8:26–39; 9:1; Acts 8:7; 16:16–18.

149 PGM.XCV.14–18; CXIV.1–14. For the Lukan evidence regarding 'epilepsy', Luke 9:37–43 (*pace, infra*).

150 PGM III.263–275; III.282–409; III.424–466; III.479–483; III.483–488; III.488–494. For the Lukan references regarding false prophecy, see the magician and Jewish false prophet, Elymas Bar-Jesus (Acts 13:6: μάγον ψευδοπροφήτην Ἰουδαῖον) at Cyprus, as well as the Python-possessed slave girl prophesying at Philippi (Acts 16:16). Note, too, Peter's prophetic ability to discern hidden thoughts (Acts 8:20–23), the prophecies of Agabus (Acts 11:28; 21:11), the three prophetess daughters of Philip (Acts 21:9), and the presence of prophets at pivotal decisions of the early church (Acts 13:1; Acts 15:31).

151 PGM VII.197–198; XIV.115; XIV.116; PDM XIV.1097–1103; PGM XCIV.22–26; XCVII.1–6. For the Lukan evidence regarding blindness: Luke 4:18b; 7:21; 18:35–43; Acts 9:17.

152 PGM VIII.211–212; VII.213–214; VII.218–222; XVIIIb.1–7; XXXIII.1–21; XLIII.1–27; XLV.1–18; XLVII.1–17; LXXXIII.1–20; LXXXVII.1–11; LXXVIII.1–19; XC.14–18; XCI.1–14; XCIV.10–16; CIV.1–8; CVI.1–10; CXIXb.4–5; CXXVIII.1–12; CXXX.1–13. For the Lukan evidence regarding fever and dysentery: Luke 4:38–39; Acts 28:8–9.

a case of Jewish-Christian syncretism in a magical context. Surprisingly, given Acts' shadow healing, there is only one reference to shadows in the Magical Papyri: a spell for gaining control of one's shadow.[153] There are also two prescriptions to restrict menstrual bleeding.[154] One significant omission in the Magical Papyri prescriptions, but which is found in Luke and Acts (Luke 13:10–17; Acts 3:1–10; 14:8–10), is any mention of the cure of the lame and crippled: prescriptions for the lesser ailments of gout and stiff feet are the only podiatry-related issues.[155] Seemingly the cure of debilitating limb ailments is beyond the ability or concern of the magical formularies.

In contrast to the elaborate apparatus and incantational techniques prescribed for cures in the Magical Papyri, the cures of the Lukan Jesus are marked by their simple technique. Jesus' authoritative word is paramount. As we have seen, Luke repudiates any suggestion of magical or demonic influence technique in the cures of both Jesus and his apostles (the use of spittle or hand's touch, the shadow and handkerchief cures), even if Luke's unbelieving characters made such imputations or drew wrong conclusions about the origins of the pneumatic power of Jesus and the apostles (e.g. Luke 11:14–22; Acts 8:18–24; 13:6–11; 16:16–18). Also, as noted, Luke explains Jesus' prophetic ability solely in terms of his personal authority and, in the apostles' case, the role of the Spirit is determinative, not magical revelation.

Moreover, Luke does not link epilepsy with demon possession in Luke 9:37–43. Walter L. Liefeld has pinpointed the issue well: 'Since Luke was a physician, it is interesting he does not identify the boy's condition as epilepsy, as Matthew 17:15 does'.[156] The boy's affliction is understood solely in terms of the demonic. Elsewhere, Luke differentiates demon possession from disease (Luke 4.40–41; 13.32; Acts 8.7), but, significantly, on occasion he does link demonic influences with ailments (inability to speak: Luke 11:14; lameness: Luke 13:11). But even in cases of fever where demonic activity is suspected (ἐπετίμησεν: Luke 4:39; cf. Luke 4:35,41), the emphasis is on Jesus' authoritative command, not the intricate rituals prescribed for fevers in the Magical Papyri.

Nor does Luke, in contrast to the Magical Papyri and Pliny (*Nat.* 28.23.86), show any interest in the so-called magical properties—beneficial or punitive[157]—of menstrual fluid. If, as is probably the case, the woman in Luke 8:43–48 suffers from a uterine haemorrhage, then Luke's focus of interest is instructive. Jesus, oblivious to the purity demands of Levitical Law (Lev. 15:19–30) and the distractions of the pressing crowd, responds to the smallest act of faith with his healing power (Luke 8:48).[158]

Last, Howard Kee observes that the powers invoked in the Magical Papyri are 'negative and prophylactic: they are uttered as protection against demons, enemies and disease'.[159] Jesus, by contrast, speaks of the establishment of God's eschatological kingdom. This brought liberation, as part of God's Jubilee Year of release (Luke 4:18–19; esp. v.18: κηρύξαι αἰχμαλώτοις ἄφεσιν ... ἀποστεῖλαι τεθραυσμένους ἐν ἀφέσει; cf. Lev. 25:10–11,13,28,39–42),[160] to those held by the strong man, Satan (Luke 11:20–22). Importantly, there exists one case in the Magical Papyri (PGM IV.3007–3086) where the Old Testament salvation motifs of 'signs and wonders' are linked to

---

153 PGM. III.612–632. For the Lukan evidence regarding shadow healing: Acts 5:12–15.
154 PDM XIV.953–955; XIV.961–965. For the Lukan evidence regarding menstrual bleeding: Luke 8:43–44.
155 PDM XIV.985–92, 992–1002, 1021–23.
156 Liefeld, 'Luke', 930.
157 See Aubert, 'Threatened Wombs: Aspects of Ancient Uterine Magic'. Note also the nuancing from a Roman perspective in Chavarria, 'Menstrual Blood: Uses, Values, and Controls in Ancient Rome'.
158 For an incisive 'disability' reading of the Lukan parallel pericope (Mark 5:25–34), see Gosbell, *'The Poor, the Crippled, the Blind, and the Lame'*, 229–77.
159 Kee, *Medicine, Miracle and Magic in New Testament Times*, 107.
160 See Ringe, *Jesus, Liberation, and the Biblical Jubilee*.

an exorcism. It is a charm of the Egyptian magician Pibechis, which invokes 'Jesus, god of the Hebrews' (l. 3020), Sabaoth ('great god', ll. 3053–54) and the Old Testament demons to liberate the possessed. The magician would have at his disposal all the powers of the exodus (the plagues and the Red Sea/Jordan crossings, ll. 3036–38, 3055), provided he did not eat pork (l. 3080)! The charm is inverted testimony to Jesus' reputation as an exorcist, and whose power recalled that of the 'finger of God' in the exodus (Luke 11:20; cf. Exod. 7:4–5; 8:19; 9:3).

7. Conclusion

We turn briefly to the issue of the 'legitimation' of the miraculous, bringing our discussion of σημεῖα ἐπὶ τῆς γῆς κάτω (Acts 2:19b) in their Graeco-Roman context to a conclusion. The book of Acts appeals to Joel's prophecy (LXX 2:28–32: Acts 2:16–21) as textual legitimation for the diverse genres of the 'miraculous' (prophecy, dreams, visions, portents, miracles) that undergirded the development and expansion of early Christian mission. The citation of this Old Testament text, with its Exodus echoes of 'signs and wonders' (σημεῖα καὶ τέρατα) and the Lukan addition of 'eschatological arrival' to the LXX text (Acts 2:17a: ἐν ταῖς ἐσχάταις ἡμέραις), fits the 'prophecy and fulfilment' paradigm that characterises the pneumatic outpouring of the risen, ascended, and exalted Jesus to his waiting church. These pneumatic gifts of the exalted Jesus, the Lord of the Spirit, are woven seamlessly into the narrative of Acts, including, as we have seen, σημεῖα ἐπὶ τῆς γῆς κάτω. As such, Joel's LXX prophecy not only points forward to the establishment of the church and its empire-wide mission in Acts but also refers its auditors backwards to its foundation in the earthly ministry of the Spirit-filled and resurrection-vindicated Messiah in the Gospel of Luke. For his church, Jesus of Nazareth will always remain a man attested by God with mighty works and wonders and signs (δυνάμεσιν καὶ τέρασιν καὶ σημείοις) that God did through him (Acts 2:22), as much as he is now the eternally reigning Messiah-King and Lord of all (2:24–27).

The closest analogy to this textual form of legitimation of the 'miraculous' amongst our Graeco-Roman miraculous genres is found in the Asclepius inscriptions of Epidauros. We have seen reference to the epigraphic cures on the plaques which one could view in the sanctuary at Epidauros (LiDonnici, A3). These original records of miracles, recorded originally on plaques, were edited epigraphically by (presumably) the priestly personnel of the sanctuary into the narratives of each cure that we now possess. Undoubtedly, the initial miraculous experience, no matter how it was experienced and subsequently conceived by the suppliant, would have been enhanced in its retelling and ultimate oral transition to text (i.e. from plaque to inscription), both by the suppliant and the priestly overseers of the sanctuary. Moreover, pilgrims who came to the sanctuary would have themselves responded to the texts as 'introductions' to what they could expect in terms of the 'miraculous', which they recounted orally to all and sundry as they moved, cured from their ailment, from the sanctuary back to their cities and villages in their homelands. In so doing, they proclaimed and exemplified the arete ('virtue') of Asclepius the healer to anyone who would listen. Anxiety was replaced by hope in the face of such personal testimony, the pilgrims operating in a didactic manner to reinforce 'the primacy of Epidauros, and to assert Epidauros' position as the home of Asklepios'.[161] As such, the Epidaurian pilgrims functioned as missionaries of Asclepius in the same way as did the Cynic missionaries of the apotheosised Peregrinus, discussed above.

---

161 Dillon, 'The Didactic Nature of the Epidaurian Iamata', 242.

Finally, we have consistently seen the distinctiveness of Jesus and his missionaries in Luke-Acts in the performance of the miraculous in ways too numerous to recount here fully, which reflected their Jewish heritage, the eschatological intervention of God in the ministry of Jesus, the advent of the Spirit's indwelling the church, and the rich Christology that emerged from Jesus' own self-understanding revealed in his miracles and in the apostles' preaching. Suffice it to say, to cite just one example, Luke's emphasis on the healing word of Jesus alone obviated the need for magical amulets and healing spells, stripped the Asclepian sanctuaries of any importance or status in the diagnosis and performance of miraculous cures, severed the link between incubation and oneirology in the healing process, and totally outperformed the Hippocratic profession in their area of meticulous expertise. Notwithstanding, we have also observed intriguing intersections between the Lukan traditions and our five strands of Graeco-Roman evidence of the miraculous: they indicate Luke's great sensitivity to local traditions in his portrait of the first-century eastern Mediterranean world. Luke has captured accurately and perceptively in Acts the emerging rivalry between the Christian mission and their opponents, all with competing claims to the 'supernatural' and its legitimation. Twenty centuries later we stand in debt to Luke for his riveting portrait of the theocentric, Christocentric, and pneumatic signs performed on the earth below by the early disciples and their Master.

James R. Harrison
Australian University College of Divinity

Bibliography

Achtemeier, Paul J. — 'The Lucan Perspective on the Miracles of Jesus: A Preliminary Sketch', *Journal of Biblical Literature* 94 (1975), 547–62.

Anderson, Graham — *Philostratus: Biography and Belles Lettres in the Third Century* AD (London: Croom Helm, 1986).

Aubert, J. — 'Threatened Wombs: Aspects of Ancient Uterine Magic', *Greek, Roman, and Byzantine Studies* 30.3 (1989), 421–49.

Aune, David E. — 'The Problem of the Genre of the Gospels: A Critique of C. H. Talbert's "What is a Gospel?"' in R. T. France and David Wenham (eds.), *Gospel Perspectives, Volume 2: Studies of History and Tradition in the Four Gospels* (Sheffield, JSOT Press, 1981), 9–60.

Aune, David E. — *Prophecy in Early Christianity and the Ancient Mediterranean World* (Grand Rapids: Eerdmans, 1983).

Bagnani, Gilbert — 'Peregrinus Proteus and the Christians', *Historia* 4 (1955), 107–112.

Baker, Daniel J. — 'Acts 2:17–21: A Programmatic Text in Luke-Acts and in the New Testament' (ThM Diss., Southeastern Baptist Theological Seminary, 2018).

Baker, Daniel J. — 'The Complete Theological Program of Acts 2:17–21', *Pneuma* 42.1 (2020), 50–67.

Barnett, P. W. — 'The Jewish Sign Prophets—AD 40–70: Their Intentions and Origins', *New Testament Studies* 27 (1981), 679–97.

Barrett, C. K. — 'Light on the Holy Spirit from Simon Magus (Acts 8:4–25)', in J. Kremer (ed.), *Les Actes des Apôtres,* (BETL 48; Leuven: Leuven University, 1979), 281–95.

Bengtsson, Staffan — 'On the Borderline—Representations of Disability in the Old Testament', *Scandinavian Journal of Disability Research*, 16.3 (2014), 280–92.

Betz, Hans Dieter — 'Jesus as Divine Man', in F. Thomas Trotter (ed.), *Jesus and the Historian: Written in Honor of Ernest Cadman Colwell* (Philadelphia: Westminster, 1968), 114–33.

Betz, Hans Dieter (ed.) — *The Greek Magical Papyri in Translation, Including the Demotic Spells* (Chicago and London: The University of Chicago Press, 1986).

Bieler, Ludwig — ΘΕΙΟΣ ΑΝΗΡ: *Das Bild des 'Göttlichen Menschen' in Spätantike und Frühchristentum* (Darmstadt: Wissenschaftliche Buchgesellschaft, 1967).

Blackburn, Barry L. — 'Miracle Working ΘΕΙΟΙ ΑΝΔΡΕΣ in Hellenism (and Hellenistic Judaism)', in David Wenham and Craig Blomberg (eds.), *Gospel Perspectives. Volume 6: The Miracles of Jesus* (Sheffield: JSOT Press, 1986), 185–218.

Blackburn, Barry L. — *Theios Aner and the Markan Miracle Traditions: A Critique of the Theios Aner Concept as an Interpretative Background of the Miracle Traditions Used by Mark* (WUNT 2.40; Tübingen: Mohr Siebeck, 1991).

Borg, Marcus J.	*Jesus, A New Vision: Spirit, Culture, and the Life of Discipleship* (San Francisco: Harper and Row, 1987).
Borland, James A.	'The High Cost of Physicians: The Textual Criticism of Luke 8:43' (2013). *SOR Faculty Publications and Presentations* 190. https://digitalcommons.liberty.edu/sor_fac_pubs/190, accessed 02/07/2025.
Bowers, Paul	'Paul and Religious Propaganda in the First Century', *Novum Testamentum* 22.4 (1980), 316–23.
Bowie, Ewen L.	'Apollonius of Tyana: Tradition and Reality', in H. Temporini and W. Haase (eds.), *Aufstieg und Niedergang der römischen Welt* (2.16.2; Berlin and New York: Walter de Gruyter, 1978), 1652–99.
Bremmer, Jan N.	'Peregrinus' Christian Career', in J. J. Collins (ed.), *Flores Florentino: Dead Sea Scrolls and Other Early Jewish Studies in Honour of Florentino García Martínez* (JSJSup 122; Leiden/Boston: Brill, 2007), 729–47.
Bultmann, Rudolf	'The Gospels (Form)', in Jaroslav Pelikan (ed.), *Twentieth Century Theology in the Making, Volume 1* (London: Harper and Row, 1969), 86–92.
Chaniotis, Angelos	'Illness and Cures in the Greek Propitiatory Inscriptions and Dedications of Lydia and Phrygia,' in H. F. K Horstmanshoff, Philip J. van der Eijk, and P. H. Schrijvers (eds.), *Ancient Medicine in its Socio-Cultural Context. Papers Read at the Congress Held at Leiden University, 13–15 April 1992, Volume II* (Clio Medica, Volume 28; Amsterdam-Atlanta: Brill Rodopi, 1995), 323–44.
Chavarria, Sophie	'Menstrual Blood: Uses, Values, and Controls in Ancient Rome', *Cahiers Mondes anciens* 16 (2022), 1–16.
Dawson, Audrey	*Healing, Weakness and Power: Perspectives on Healing in the Writings of Mark, Luke and Paul* (Paternoster Biblical Monographs; Milton Keynes: Paternoster, 2008).
Dibelius, Martin	*Studies in the Acts of the Apostles* (London: SCM, 1956).
Dibelius, Martin	'The Structure and Literary Character of the Gospels', *Harvard Theological Review* 20 (1927), 151–70.
Diels, H.	*Fragmente der Vorsokrater* (Berlin: Weidmannsche Buchhandlung 1906; 6th ed. Diels-Kranz, 1952).
Dillon, M. P. J.	'The Didactic Nature of the Epidaurian Iamata', *Zeitschrift für Papyrologie und Epigraphik* 101 (1994), 239–60.
Edelstein, Emma J., and Ludwig Edelstein	*Asclepius: A Collection and Interpretation of the Testimonies, Volume 1* (2 vols., Baltimore: John Hopkins, 1945).
Edwards, M. J.	'Satire and Verisimilitude: Christianity in Lucian's "Peregrinus"', *Historia* 31.8 (1989), 89–98.
Ehrenheim, Hedvig von	'Causal Explanation of Disease in the Iamata of Epidauros', *Kernos* 32 (2019), 101–18.

Evans, Craig A.   'Jesus and Jewish Miracle Stories', in Craig A. Evans, *Jesus and His Contemporaries: Comparative Studies* (Leiden: E. J. Brill, 1995), 213–43.

Eve, E.   'The Miracles of an Eschatological Prophet', *Journal for the Study of the Historical Jesus* 13.2–3 (2015), 131–45.

Faraone, Christopher A., and Sofia T. Tovar   *Greek and Egyptian Magical Formularies: Text and Translation, Volume 1* (Berkeley: California Classical Studies, 2022).

Fenton, John   'The Order of the Miracles performed by Peter and Paul in Acts', *Expository Times* 77 (1966), 381–83.

Fields, Dana   'The Reflections of Satire: Lucian and Peregrinus', *Transactions of the American Philological Association* 143.1 (2023), 213–45.

Fitzmeyer, Joseph A.   *The Gospel According to Luke I–IX: Introduction, Translation, and Notes* (Anchor Bible 28; New York: Doubleday, 1981), 436–37.

Fontenrose, Joseph   *The Delphic Oracle: Its Responses and Operations* (Berkeley: University of California Press, 1978).

Forbes, Christopher   *Prophecy and Inspired Speech in Early Christianity and Its Hellenistic Environment* (WUNT 2.75; Tübingen: Mohr Siebeck, 1995).

Francis, James   'Truthful Fiction: New Questions to Old Answers on Philostratus' "Life of Apollonius"', *American Journal of Philology* 119.3 (1998), 419–41.

Fraser, Elouise Renich   'Symbolic Acts of the Prophets', *Studia Biblica et Theologica* 55.2 (1974), 45–53.

Garrett, Susan R.   *The Demise of the Devil: Magic and the Demonic in Luke's Writings* (Minneapolis: Fortress, 1989).

Georgi, Dieter   *The Opponents of Paul in Second Corinthians* (Edinburgh: Fortress, 1987).

Gerolemou (ed.), Maria   *Recognizing Miracles in Antiquity and Beyond* (Trends in Classics: Supplementary Volumes, 53; Berlin/Boston: De Gruyter, 2018).

Geus, Klaus, and Colin King   'Paradoxography', in Paul Keyser and John Scarborough (eds.), *Oxford Handbook of Science and Medicine in the Classical World* (Oxford: Oxford University Press, 2018), 431–44.

Giambrone, Anthony   'Jesus and the Paralytics: Memorializing Miracles in the Greco-Roman World of the Gospels', *The Biblical Annals* 10.3 (2020), 389–404.

Glover, T. R.   *The Conflict of Religions in the Early Empire* (London: Methuen, 1909).

Gosbell, Louise A.   *'The Poor, the Crippled, the Blind, and the Lame': Physical and Sensory Disability in the Gospels of the New Testament* (WUNT 2.469; Tübingen: Mohr Siebeck, 2018).

Grafton, Thomas E.   'Health and Healing in the Documentary Papyri: A Comparison with the Healing Texts in Luke-Acts' (PhD Diss, Asbury Theological Seminary, 2017).

Greene, Robin	'A Most Amazing Conversation: The Social Contexts of Wonder-Telling and the Development of Paradoxography', *New England Classical Journal* 46.2 (2019), 28–45.
Hadas, Moses, and Morton Smith	*Heroes and Gods: Spiritual Biographies in Antiquity* (New York: Arno, 1965).
Halliday, W. R.	*Greek Divination: A Study of Its Methods and Principles* (London: MacMillan, 1913).
Hamblin, Robert Lee	'Miracles in the Book of Acts', *Scottish Journal of Theology* 17 (1974), 19–34.
Hamm, Dennis	'Acts 3:1–10: The Healing of the Temple Beggar as Lucan Theology', *Biblica* 67 (1986), 305–19.
Hamm, Dennis	'The Freeing of the Bent Woman and the Restoration of Israel: Luke 13.10–17 as Narrative Theology', *Journal for the Study of the New Testament* 31 (1987), 23–44.
Harris, B. F.	'Apollonius of Tyana: Fact and Fiction', *Journal of Religious History* (1969), 189–99.
Harris, Murray	'The Dead are Restored to Life: Miracles of Revivification in the Gospels', in David Wenham and Craig Blomberg (eds.), *Gospel Perspectives. Volume 6: The Miracles of Jesus* (Sheffield: JSOT Press, 1986), 295–326.
Harrison, James R.	'Paul's Legacy in Romans and the Confession Inscriptions of Asia Minor', in Peter G. Bolt and James R. Harrison (eds.), *Romans and the Legacy of St Paul: Historical, Theological, and Social Perspectives* (Macquarie Park: SCD Press, 2019), 337–88.
Harrison, James R.	'Prophecy, Divination, and Oneirology in the Greek Magical Papyri: Situating Joel's Prophecy (Acts 2:16–21) in Its Graeco-Roman Revelatory Context', in Christine M. Kreinecker, John S. Kloppenborg, and James R. Harrison (eds.), *Everyday Life in Graeco-Roman Times: Documentary Papyri and the New Testament. Essays in Honour of Peter Arzt-Grabner*, (SCCB 16; Leiden: Brill/Schöningh, 2024), 99–124.
Hartsock, Chad	*Sight and Blindness in Luke-Acts: The Use of Physical Features in Characterization* (Leiden: Brill, 2008).
Harvey, A. E.	*Jesus and the Constraints of History: The Bampton Lectures, 1980* (London: Duckworth, 1982).
Hemer, Colin J.	*The Book of Acts in the Setting of Hellenistic History*, (WUNT 49; Tübingen: Mohr Siebeck, 1989).
Holladay, C. L.	*Theios Aner in Hellenistic Judaism* (Missoula: Scholars Press, 1977).
Horsley, Richard A.	*Jesus and Magic: Freeing the Gospel Stories from Modern Misconceptions* (Eugene: Cascade, 2014).

Horsley, Richard A., with John S. Hanson   *Bandits, Prophets, and Messiahs: Popular Movements in the Time of Jesus* (San Francisco: Trinity Press International, 1985).

Horst, P. W. van der   'Peter's Shadow: The Religio-Historical Background of Acts v. 15', *New Testament Studies* 23 (1977), 204–12.

Hull, John M.   *Hellenistic Magic and the Synoptic Tradition* (London: SCM-Canterbury Press, 1974).

Kee, Howard C.   *Aretalogies, Hellenistic "Lives" and the Sources of Mark* (PCCHSHMC 12; Berkeley: The Center for Hermeneutical Studies in Hellenistic and Modern Culture, 1975), 1–21.

Kee, Howard C.   'Aretalogy and Gospel', *Journal of Biblical Literature* 92.3 (1973), 402–22.

Kee, Howard C.   *Medicine, Miracle and Magic in New Testament Times* (Cambridge: Cambridge University Press, 1986).

Kee, Howard C.   *Miracle in the Early Christian World: A Study in Sociohistoric Method* (New Haven: Yale University Press, 1983).

Keener, Craig S.   *The Spirit in the Gospels and Acts: Divine Purity and* Power (Peabody: Hendrickson, 1997).

Kirchschläger, Walter   *Jesu exorzistisches Wirken aus der Sicht des Lukas: Ein Beitrag zur Lukanischen Redaktion* (Österreichische biblische Studien 3; Klosterneuburg: Österreichisches Katholisches Bibelwerk, 1981).

Klauk, Hans-Josef   *Magic and Paganism in Early Christianity: The World of the Acts of the Apostles* (Edinburgh: T&T Clark, 2000).

Klutz, Todd   *The Exorcism Stories in Luke-Acts: A Sociostylistic Reading* (SNTSMS 129; Cambridge: Cambridge University Press, 2004).

Koester, Helmut   'One Jesus and Four Primitive Gospels', *Harvard Theological Review* 61 (1968), 203–47.

Koskenniemi, Erkki   'Apollonius of Tyana: A Typical θεῖος ἀνήρ?' *Journal of Biblical Literature* 177.3 (1998), 455–67.

Koskenniemi, Erkki   *Theios Sophistès: Essays on Flavius Philostratus' Vita Apollonii* (Mnemosyne Supplements 305; Leiden/Boston: Brill, 2009).

Krauss, Brunell   *An Interpretation of the Omens, Portents and Prodigies Recorded by Livy, Tacitus, and Suetonius* (Philadelphia: University of Pennsylvania, 1930).

Ladd, George Eldon *A Theology of the New Testament* (London: Lutterworth, 1974).

Lampe, G. W. H.   'Grievous Wolves (Acts 20:29)', in Barnabas Lindars and Stephen S. Smalley (eds.), *Christ and Spirit in the New Testament: Studies in Honour of Charles Francis Digby Moule* (Cambridge: Cambridge University Press, 1973), 159–200.

Lampe, G. W. H.	'Miracles in the Acts of the Apostles', in C. F. D. Moule (ed.), *Miracles: Cambridge Studies in Their Philosophy and History* (London: Mowbray, 1965), 165–78.
Lane, W. L.	'Theios Aner Christology and the Gospel of Mark', in R. N. Longenecker and M. C. Tenney (eds.), *New Dimensions io New Testament Study* (Grand Rapids: Eerdmans, 1974), 146–61.
LiDonnici, Lyn R.	*The Epidaurian Miracle Inscriptions: Text, Translation and Commentary* (Atlanta: Scholars Press, 1995).
Liefeld, Walter L	'The Hellenistic "Divine Man" and the Figure of Jesus in the Gospels', *Journal of the Evangelical Theological Society* 16 (1973), 195–205.
Liefeld, Walter L.	'Luke', in Frank E. Gaebelein (ed.), *The Expositor's Bible Commentary*, Volume 8 (Grand Rapids: Eerdmans, 1984), 821–1059.
Liefeld, Walter L.	'The Wandering Preacher as a Social Figure in the Roman Empire' (PhD Diss., Columbia University, 1967).
Lightfoot, Jessica	*Wonder and the Marvellous from Homer to the Hellenistic World* (Cambridge: Cambridge University Press, 2021).
Longenecker, Richard N.	'Acts', in Frank E. Gaebelein (ed.), *The Expositor's Bible Commentary*, Volume 9 (Grand Rapids: Eerdmans, 1981), 207–573.
Loos, Hendrick van der	*The Miracles of Jesus* (NovTSup 9; Leiden: E. J. Brill, 1968).
Mackay, B. S.	'Plutarch and the Miraculous', in C. F. D. Moule (ed.), *Miracles: Cambridge Studies in Their Philosophy and History* (London: Mowbray, 1965), 95–111.
MacMullen, Ramsay	*Enemies of the Roman Order: Treason, Unrest, and Alienation in the Empire* (Cambridge, MA: Harvard University Press, 1996).
Martzavou, Paraskevi	'Dream, Narrative, and the Construction of Hope in the "Healing Miracles" of Epidauros', in Angelos Chaniotis (ed.), *Unveiling Emotions: Sources and Methods for the Study of Emotions in the Greek World* (Stuttgart: Franz Steiner Verlag, 2012), 177–204.
Marx, Benjamin	'"Signs and Wonders" in Acts: The Use and Function of Σημεῖα καὶ Τέρατα', *Journal of Pentecostal Theology* 32 (2023), 2014–30.
McCasland, S. Vernon	'Signs and Wonders', *Journal of Biblical Literature* 76 (1957), 149–52.
Melfi, M.	*Il santuario di Asclepio a Lebena* (Monografie della Scuola archeologica di Atene e delle missioni italiane, in Oriente 19; Athens: Scuola Archaeologica Italiana di Atene, 2007).
Meyer, Eduard	'Apollonios von Tyana und die Biographie des Philostratos', *Hermes* 52 (1917), 371–424.
Neirynck, Frans	'The Miracle Stories in the Acts of the Apostles', in J. Kremer (ed.), *Les Actes des Apôtres: traditions, rédaction, théologie* (Leuven: Leuven University Press, 1979), 169–213.

Nikoletta, Kanavou	'Satirizing Christianity in Lucian's Peregrinus and Achilles Tatius' Leucippe and Clitophon', *Novum Testamentum* 67.1 (2025), 99–123.
Nock, A. D.	'Alexander of Abonuteichos', *Classical Quarterly* 22 (1928), 160–62.
Nock, A. D.	*Conversion: The Old and the New in Religion from Alexander the Great to Augustine of Hippo* (Oxford: Oxford University Press, 1933).
Nolland, John	'Classical and Rabbinic Parallels to "Physician, Heal Yourself" (Lk. IV 23)', *Novum Testamentum* 21 (1979), 193–209.
O'Reilly, Leo	*Word and Sign in the Acts of the Apostles: A Study in Lucan Theology* (Rome: Gregorian and Biblical Press, 1987).
Panagiotidou, Olympia	'Religious Healing and the Asclepius Cult: A Case of Placebo Effects', *Open Theology* 2 (2016), 79–81.
Prêtre, C.	'The Epidaurian Iamata: The First "Court of Miracles"?' in Maria Gerolemou (ed.), *Recognizing Miracles in Antiquity and Beyond* (Trends in Classics: Supplementary Volumes, 53; Berlin/Boston: De Gruyter, 2018), 17–30.
Petzke, G.	*Die Traditionen über Apollonius von Tyana und das Neue Testament* (Leiden: E. J. Brill, 1970).
Philip, J. A.	'Aristotle's Monograph on the Pythagoreans', *Transactions and Proceedings of the American Philological Association* 94 (1963), 185–98.
Pilch, John J.	*Healing in the New Testament: Insights from Medical and Mediterranean Anthropology* (Minneapolis: Fortress, 2000).
Pilch, John J.	'Sickness and Healing in Luke-Acts', in Jerome Neyrey (ed.), *The Social World of Luke-Acts: Models for Interpretation* (Peabody: Hendrickson, 1991), 181–209.
Pitts, Andrew W.	'Genre and Method in Luke-Acts Research', in Andrew W. Pitts, *History, Biography, and the Genre of Luke-Acts: An Exploration of Literary Divergence in Greek Narrative Discourse* (Biblical Interpretation Series 177; Leiden: Brill, 2019), 1–48.
Phillips, Charles Robert	'Religious Fraud in the Roman Empire: Alexander and Others', in Kent Harold Richards (ed.), *SBL 1983 Seminar Papers* (Chico: Scholars Press, 1983), 333–36.
Porter, Stanley E.	'Magic in the Book of Acts', in Michael Labahn and Bert J. Lietaert Peerbolte (eds.), *A Kind of Magic: Understanding Magic in the New Testament and Its Religious Environment* (LNTS 306; London/New York: T&T Clark 2007), 107–21.
Razafiarivony, Davidson	'Exclusion of the Blind and Lame from the Temple and the Indignation of the Religious Leaders in Matt 21:12–15', *The American Journal of Biblical Theology* 19.34 (2018), 1–21.

Reimer, Andy	*Miracle and Magic: A Study in the Acts of the Apostles and the Life of Apollonius of Tyana* (JSNTSup 235; London: Sheffield Academic Press, 2002).
Remus, Harold	*Pagan-Christian Conflict Over Miracle in the Second Century* (Patristic Monograph Series 10; Cambridge, MA: The Philadelphia Patristic Foundation, 1983).
Rengstorf, Karl H.	'πνεῦμα', *Theological Dictionary of the New Testament* 7 (1971), 201–69.
Ringe, Sharon H.	*Jesus, Liberation, and the Biblical Jubilee: Images for Ethics and Christology* (Overtures to Biblical Theology 19; Philadelphia: Fortress, 1989).
Rivoli, Matteo	'Sanatio di Publius Granius Rufus da Lebena', *Axon* 3.1 (2019), 192–98.
Robert, Louis	*À travers l'Asie Mineure: Poetes et Prosateurs, Monnaies Grecques, Voyageurs et Geographie* (Athens/Paris: Bibliothèque des Écoles françises d'Athènes et de Rome 1980).
Roberts, Ronald D.	'Conflicts of ΜΑΓΕΙΑ and Miracles in the Acts of the Apostles: Social Discourse on Legitimate and Deviant Use of Spiritual Power' (PhD Diss, Brite Divinity School, 2013).
Rose, H. J.	'Heracles and the Gospels', *Harvard Theological Review* 31 (1938), 113–42.
Sanzo, Joseph E.	'Early Christianity', in David Frankfurter (ed.), *Guide to the Study of Ancient Magic* (Religions in the Graeco-Roman World 185; Leiden: Brill, 2019), 198–239.
Seglenieks, Christopher	'Faith and Faithfulness in Luke', *Australian Biblical Review* 70 (2022), 48–60.
Smith, J. Z.	'Good News Is No New News: Aretalogy and Gospel', in Jacob Neusner (ed.), *Christianity, Judaism and Other Graeco-Roman Cults, Pt. I* (Leiden: Brill, 1975), 21–28.
Smith, Morton	'Prolegomena to a Discussion of Aretalogies: Divine Men, the Gospels and Jesus', *Journal of Biblical Literature* 90 (1971), 174–99.
Stanley, Christopher D.	*Paul and Asklepios: The Greco-Roman Quest for Healing and the Apostolic Mission* (LNTS 639; London: T&T Clark, 2023).
Teeple, Howard M.	*The Mosaic Eschatological Prophet* (JBLMS 10; Society of Biblical Literature, Philadelphia, 1957).
Thompson, Robin	'Healing at the Pool of Bethesda: A Challenge to Asclepius?', *Bulletin of Biblical Research* 27.1 (2017), 65–84.
Thonemann, Peter	*Lucian: Alexander or the False Prophet* (Clarendon Ancient History Series; Oxford/New York: Oxford University Press, 2021).
Tiede, D. L.	*The Charismatic Figure as Miracle Worker* (Missoula: Scholars Press, 1973).
Twelftree, Graham H.	*Christ Triumphant: Exorcism Then and Now* (London: Hodder and Stoughton, 1985).

Twelftree, Graham H.   *In the Name of Jesus: Exorcism among Early Christians* (Grand Rapids: Baker Academic, 2007).

Twelftree, Graham H.   *Jesus the Exorcist: A Contribution to the Study of the Historical Jesus* (Peabody: Hendrickson, 1993).

Votaw, Clyde Weber   *The Gospel and Contemporary Biographies in the GraecoRoman World* (Philadelphia, Fortress, 1970).

Wasiac, Grafton Wojciech   'Miracle Stories and Praise: Two Neglected Topics in Luke', *New Testament Studies* 70.4 (2022), 452–69.

Weaver, John B.   *Plots of Epiphany: Prison Escape in the Acts of the Apostles* (BZNW 19; Berlin/New York: De Gruyter, 2004).

Weissenrieder, Annette   *Images of Illness in the Gospel of Luke: Insights of Ancient Medical Texts* (WUNT 2.164; Tübingen: Mohr Siebeck, 2003).

Wojciechowski, Michal   'The Differences Between the Healing Stories from Epidaurus and From the Gospels', *Biblica et Patristica Thoruniensia* 9 (2016), 153–64.

Yamauchi, Edwin   'Magic or Miracle? Diseases, Demons and Exorcisms', in David Wenham and Craig Blomberg (eds.), *Gospel Perspectives. Volume 6: The Miracles of Jesus* (Sheffield: JSOT Press, 1986), 89–183.

Yu, Kenneth W.   'Paradoxography', *Oxford Classical Dictionary*, 2022, 1–6, https://doi.org/10.1093/acrefore/9780199381135.013.4728, accessed 22/05/2025.

Book reviews

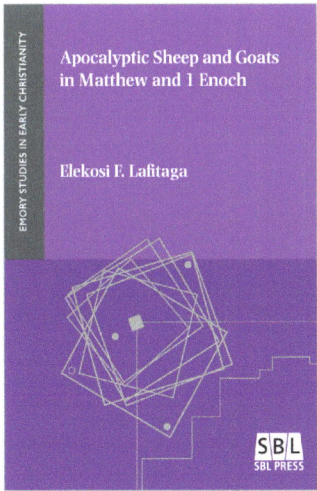

Elekosi F. Lafitaga. *Apocalyptic Sheep and Goats in Matthew and 1 Enoch.* ESEC 24. Atlanta, GA: SBL Press, 2022. 335pp. ISBN 978-1628373073. €49.00. $58.00.

Lafitaga's work examines the apocalyptic discourse of Matthew 25:31–46. The volume is divided into five chapters. In the first, he provides a historical overview of how scholars have understood the relationship between 'apocalypse' and 'apocalyptic'. Lafitaga then suggests a slight modification of the definition offered by John Collins in the 1976 *Semeia* 14 volume and excludes Collins's emphasis on eschatology. Moreover, he defines apocalyptic as 'the adjective that describes the literary communication of esoteric knowledge through heavenly revelation and symbols, which may take the form of dreams, visions, or angelic pronouncements' (pp.12–13). Lafitaga then provides a survey of studies on apocalyptic eschatology and apocalypticism in Matthew. He observes that an emphasis on eschatology has dominated the discussion. Alternatively, Lafitaga demonstrates that while eschatology plays a part in Matthew's apocalyptic discourses, the primary function of such material is to exhort the present audience. In particular, his thesis is that Matthew 25:31–46 functions as 'paraenesis for Israel to teach the will of the Father [...] as did the Son, to the world of gentiles despite expecting [...] the end of the age to take place' (p.40).

In chapter two, Lafitaga first defines apocalyptic discourse as the use of various apocalyptic imagery (or topics) in early Jewish and Christian works (p.42), then introduces the method of his study in two parts. He first discusses modern metaphor theory which provides a conceptual framework for the interpreter to analyse metaphors which may or may not have more than one meaning. He expands on these concepts in his two appendices. Because apocalyptic discourse frequently utilises polyvalent metaphors, Lafitaga also utilises the analytical framework of sociorhetorical interpretation (SRI). In this way he is able to use traditional literary, cultural, and historical-critical tools in order to analyse the rhetorical features of an apocalyptic discourse.

In chapter three, Lafitaga examines the Book of Dreams (*1 En.* 83–90) in order to identify a 'possible cultural precedent and significant intertexture' for the reference to sheep in Matthew 25:31–46 (p.79). After a brief introduction to *1 Enoch*, he begins his two-part analysis. First, he examines the allegory as a literary work. In the second part of his analysis, he argues that the Animal Apocalypse does not omit references to torah or the Sinai covenant but interprets the statements that the sheep open their eyes and follow the path as indicative of their obedience to torah. In addition, he interprets *1 Enoch* 90:30, 33 as describing a

> **apocalyptic discourse [is] the use of various apocalyptic imagery**

positive relationship in which the sheep (i.e. Israel) instruct the rest of the animals (i.e. humanity) in torah. He concludes his chapter by addressing the concept of scripture as it relates to the Apocalypse and suggests that the Gospel of Matthew would have considered the Book of Dreams as one of its 'canonised interpretations of the torah' (p.171).

In chapter four, Lafitaga begins his analysis of Matthew 25:31–46. He argues that Matthew's purpose is not to emphasise the immanence of Jesus's return, but rather to emphasise that when Jesus does return, he will return as the glorious Son of Man. He then proceeds to analyse two other apocalyptic discourses in Matthew (3:11–17; 13:24–30, 36–43) to better frame the apocalyptic discourse in Matthew 25. He suggests that 3:11–17 emphasises Jesus's role as the Son of God who baptises by the Holy Spirit and by fire through his teaching and healing ministry. For 13:24–30, 36–43, he argues that the parable and its interpretation link the status of the Son of Man with the role of the Son of God as teacher and thus elevates the authority of Jesus's instruction. Both roles coalesce again in Matthew 25:31–46. Lafitaga observes that while the judgement scene introduces all humanity as the subject of judgement, the judgement of the sheep and the goats refers to a subsection of humanity. He argues that the sheep and the goats represent elect Israel who are being judged in terms of their treatment of gentiles who have responded positively to Jesus's message.

In chapter 5, Lafitaga reiterates that the function of Matthew 25:31–46 is not to merely educate readers on future events but to exhort readers on how they are to acquire salvation in the present. According to his analysis of the Animal Apocalypse, he identifies a significant similarity between the Apocalypse and Matthew of the elect's responsibility to the non-elect in the proper instruction of the will of God. As stated, Lafitaga argues that this similarity is a result of the Apocalypse being a possible part of Matthew's scriptures and as such should help elucidate the metaphorical use of sheep in Matthew 25.

Lafitaga's work demonstrates the usefulness of a strong theoretical framework for interpreting the rich language typically found in apocalypses and other apocalyptic discourses. While the work focuses particularly on Matthew, his work is a helpful contribution to the study of Enoch's Book of Dreams. The work could have possibly benefited from additional discussion on a few points significant for his study. First, for *1 Enoch* 90:30, Lafitaga offers a positive portrayal of the other animals' obedience to the sheep yet does not seem to address alternative interpretations that suggest that the obedience implies complete subjugation or inferiority of the gentiles. Additionally, for *1 Enoch* 90:33 he argues that the sheep along with all the other animals are gathered together in the new house. Yet, Nickelsburg, in his commentary on Enoch, emends the texts in such a way that suggests that only the sheep are gathered into the house. Lafitaga himself cites this translation (p.233), but does not address its significance. However, in favour of Lafitaga's point all the manuscripts attest to the reading that supports his conclusions.

Eric Espinoza
Gateway Seminary
Ontario, CA

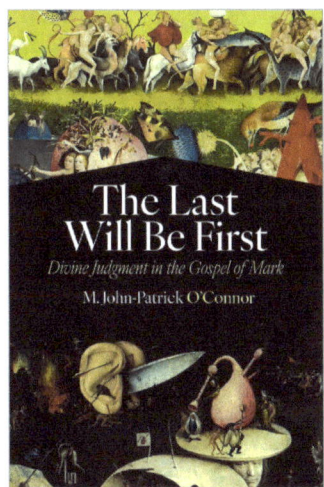

M. John-Patrick O'Connor. *The Last Will Be First: Divine Judgment in the Gospel of Mark.* Waco, TX: Baylor University Press, 2024. xvi + 240 pp. ISBN 9781481319997 (hardcover). $US70.00.

M. John-Patrick O'Connor is Associate Professor of New Testament at Northwest University in Kirkland, Washington, and the author of *The Moral Life according to Mark* (T&T Clark, 2022). With this new book O'Connor not only extends his investigations into moral dimensions of Mark's Gospel but also continues his advocacy of the moral value of this Gospel, which is often overlooked. In his preface O'Connor traces the impetus for his second book to a remark by Ernst Käsemann challenging the supposition of a zone of neutrality between the gospel and idolatry. Regarding both the rationale and purpose of this volume, he writes: 'This book examines a single topic—judgment—that at its core interacts with nonneutrality. Judgment tells us that we must choose a side… This book explores the nature and rhetoric of judgment in the Bible and Second Temple Judaism leading up to its expression in the Gospel of Mark for the purpose of moving beyond simple accounts of neutrality to determine the nature of the Christian's moral responsibility in the public sector' (pp.ix–x). In short, *The Last Will Be First* is a call to commitment.

O'Connor devotes his introductory chapter to exploring the use and abuse of the notion of divine judgment in various contexts, from sermons to social critique. Acknowledging that the theme of judgment features prominently from Genesis to Revelation, he first surveys ways in which divine judgment has been variously 'weaponized', especially (but not only) by preachers in certain ecclesial traditions. Within this section O'Connor makes the sobering, albeit unqualified, observation 'that theological agendas sensitive to God's justice have been historically violent and punitive in nature' (p.6). After considering various contexts in which divine judgment tends to be marshalled, he discerns these central questions: 'If God is indeed a God of judgment, then whom does God judge? And for whom does God judge?' (p.10). The answers to these questions found within Mark's Gospel constitute the focus of this book. As discerned by O'Connor, Mark's construal of divine judgment is neither arbitrary nor opaque; rather, divine judgment reflects God's concern and care for the vulnerable.

The topic of chapter 1 is divine judgment in the Old Testament. In relatively brief compass, O'Connor first surveys key terms and images for judgment and then homes in on judgment by fire, as in the archetypal destruction of Sodom and Gomorrah, judgment associated with the 'day of the Lord', and judgment scenes in the book of Daniel. Worth noting, however, is that O'Connor's exploration of divine judgment in the Old Testament is neither comprehensive nor disinterested: 'I am interested in key places in which divine judgment is leveraged against more powerful groups in defense of vulnerable ones' (p.37). One wonders whether this selectivity reflects a personal bias, perhaps influenced by Mark's construal of divine judgment.

On the likely supposition that both early traditions about Jesus and Mark's Gospel are indebted to apocalyptic thought and literary features, chapter 2 selectively explores judgment imagery in various parts of 1 Enoch and the Dead Sea Scrolls (specifically the War Scroll, 1QM), with occasional comparative comments on the book of Jubilees. 'Once more', O'Connor writes, 'I am interested in the locations [within apocalyptic texts] in which divine judgment operates as a form of accountability against forces of domination and in defense of the socially vulnerable' (p. 42). Despite diverse depictions of judgment within the various texts that comprise 1 Enoch, O'Connor observes that 'a binding theme throughout the entire work is that God intends to right every wrong' (p. 46). As for texts of eschatological vengeance in the War Scroll, O'Connor perceives a potential twofold function of such texts: first, to offer hope of liberation from oppressors as part of a reversal of power dynamics; and second, to strengthen in-group solidarity and loyalty.

Chapter 3, 'Divine Judgment in the Early Roman Empire', is a continuation of chapter 2, albeit focused on texts written within the context of Roman imperialism. Although O'Connor briefly discusses the Psalms of Solomon and the Apocalypse of Abraham, much of this chapter examines the theme of divine judgment in the letters of Paul, the Gospel according to Matthew, and the Revelation to John. 'In Paul', according to O'Connor, 'divine judgment fosters community building and, sometimes, protection for those on the margins. While God's judgment certainly operates to keep boundary markers in place in Paul, it is refinement, the use of judgment language to provoke change, that is more frequent' (pp.83–84). Matthew's Gospel is shown to be the most judgment-oriented of the canonical Gospels, and in Revelation O'Connor detects a threefold rationale for divine judgment—proportional punishment of wrongdoers, protection from destruction, and refinement of character. Perceptive is this remark regarding Revelation: 'John utilizes the judgment of God, and of God's proxy, the Lamb (Rev 6:1–11; 19:11), throughout the book as a means of rectification' (p.90). Puzzling, however, is this comment about the moral basis for divine judgment in the same book: 'The degree to which John enforces this ethical standard is recalcitrant…' (p.94). Especially with respect to Revelation, O'Connor wrestles with the violence apparently associated with divine judgment.

The final two chapters in the body of this book address the theme of judgment in Mark's Gospel. According to O'Connor, 'this book argues that the neglect of judgment material in Mark has led to misleading claims about Markan theology' (p.106). Wisely, in chapter 4 O'Connor casts his net wider than specific judgment sayings of Jesus; instead, he examines judgment motifs associated with Mark's characterization of God, Jesus, John the Baptist, and the Sanhedrin. Even so, it is surprising that within this chapter 'Mark's most extensive discourse on judgment' in Mark 9:42–50 is discussed in a single paragraph (pp. 112–13), although O'Connor does return to this pericope in chapter 5 (pp.138–39).

There is much to appreciate about chapter 4 regarding the Markan construct of judgment, particularly Mark's presentation of God as the principal agent of judgment, with Jesus also judging as a divine delegate, especially in his role as the Son of Man. If 'God is the silent engine that powers all other motifs in Mark' (p.109), however, one wonders why God's appraisal explicitly expressed on the two occasions when the divine voice intrudes into Mark's narrative is not discussed, despite being noted (p.109). Mark 1:11 and 9:7 imply that, for Mark, the primary focus of divine judgment is positive approval and authorization of Jesus and his way, thereby signalling that the way of Jesus reflects the will of God. Jesus is not merely God's proxy in judgment but first and foremost the 'moral shape' of God's judgment, also implied by the announcement in Mark 16:6 of the raising to life (by God) of the crucified Jesus of Nazareth.

Of chapter 5 O'Connor writes: 'My case in the present chapter is that the neglect of judgment contributes to the underutilization of Mark for issues pertaining to the justice of God' (p.133). His case is built, in part, by deftly relating judgment tropes to the paradoxical Markan theme of insiders and outsiders. Yes, 'the rhetorical effect of judgment against "outsiders" produces justice for "insiders"' (p. 147), but Mark destabilizes this insider-outsider binary such that O'Connor can conclude that 'the rhetoric of divine judgment in Mark plays on the cosmic reversal of insiders and outsiders' (p.169). O'Connor is a perspicacious interpreter of Mark's Gospel, and his discussions of Markan passages are invariably illuminating.

In his conclusion to this volume, O'Connor proposes 'a constructive theology of judgment from the Gospel of Mark that operates in defense of the least of these…' (p.172), in part by means of engagement with various expressions of liberation theology. From his Markan source, O'Connor constructs a theological conception of judgment in line with the biblical depiction of divine justice on behalf of the lowly and downtrodden. The reality of evil and human complicity in evil must be acknowledged and addressed. Divine judgment is an expression of divine justice—against oppressors and in favour of the vulnerable. Since divine judgment is an expression of God's determination to right wrong and reverse inequity, 'judgment also offers salvation in unexpected places' (p.185), provided it provokes repentance. In view of the human propensity to distort divine judgment to serve our own ends, however, O'Connor ends by advising: 'The interpretive process must begin by asking: For whom is God's judgment? For what purpose does God judge? My case here is that readers of Mark must pay careful attention to the *mikra* [little ones] within their own communities' (pp.191–92).

This book, beautifully produced by Baylor University Press, is a welcome contribution both to Markan studies and to New Testament theology and ethics. If much of O'Connor's prior research has focused on retrieving Mark's Gospel for moral reflection and theological ethics, this book composes an exercise in retrieving the Markan perspective on divine judgment for making better sense of God's justice. *The Last Will Be First* may not compose the final word on divine judgment in Mark's Gospel, but it will repay careful study of this relatively neglected theme.

David Neville
St Mark's National Theological Centre
Charles Sturt University, Canberra

Jens-Arne Edelmann. *Das Römische Imperium im Lukanischen Doppelwerk.*
WUNT II.547. Tübingen: Mohr Siebeck, 2021.
Xv + 289 pp., sewn paperback.
ISBN 978-3-16-160111-8. 99 Euro

Studies on the New Testament's relation to the Roman Empire in all their variety and different approaches have often focused on the letters of Paul. Luke-Acts has also received a fair share of attention as both volumes have a lot to offer. For instance, there are the various encounters of Jesus with the representatives of Roman power and the many occurrences in Acts. In the present volume, Edelmann observes that Luke-Acts presents both a positive and negative view of the Empire as it seeks to provide guidance for its readers with regard to the Empire and its representatives.

In view of the succinct survey of research (pp.1–9), Edelmann pleads a comprehensive approach which seeks to include all references in both volumes (pp.9–10). His focus is on the readers of Luke-Acts and their situation and interaction with the texts (their reception of the potential of the text, 'the impact of the text on the recipients as I have reconstructed their identity and situation', p.11), not on the narrated events themselves. Other approaches to Luke-Acts and this particular theme are not sufficiently accounted for.

Edelmann sets out with considerations of the original readers of Luke-Acts in the last quarter of the first century AD (pp.13–42). For the reconstruction of their identity, he refers to the eschatological discourse of Jesus as a pointer to the readers' situation, the uncertainty they face because of the threat of trials before Roman officials (a reconstruction influenced by the late date!), their social situation and public reputation at the time and their lack of normal contact with the representatives of the Empire in their daily living (lack of experience of dealing with them). Edelmann argues that in view of this reconstruction, the readers were insecure about the Empire. The reconstruction is based on the assumption that the themes and the selection of material in Luke-Acts reflects the situation of the readers at the time of writing, not necessarily the situation at the time of the reported events. There is no interaction with persuasive proposals that Luke writes as an historian, primarily concerned about the past.

The main bulk of the monograph consists of a detailed analysis of the 19 more or less direct occurrences of the Roman Empire in Luke's Gospel (pp.43–100) and the 22 occurrences in the Acts of the Apostles (pp.100–187). This is followed by a systematic presentation of the portrayal of the Empire in Luke-Acts (pp.187–201). Discussion includes the Roman Empire as a given reality that is not questioned *per se*, the Empire as space of protection and administration of justice, and the Empire as a cultural realm. Luke-Acts also notes the various failures of individual representatives of Rome (the protagonists end up in threatening circumstances because these representatives fail to follow proper legal procedure, which should actually have protected Jesus, Paul or the Christ-followers). The Empire is also characterized as the realm of the activities of the devil. Although not a dominant theme, Luke-Acts also provides clues with regard to the relationship of the servants of God to the Empire. Edelmann also examines the interplay between the power of the Empire and the power of God in Jesus (the Empire is clearly subordinate) and Christian behaviour in the shadow of the Empire (the Empire is the backdrop or even appears in contrast to the concrete shape of Christian living as advocated by the author). Edelmann summarises as follows:

> Lukas erkennt die Realität des Imperiums an. Er schätzt Rom wert als Schutzmacht und Rechtsinstanz. Er weiß um das Imperium als Kulturraum. Er benennt auch negative Züge einzelner Repräsentanten. Er weiß um die macht des Teufels in imperialen Strukturen, aber auch um Gottes Wirken in der Geschichte. Er verkündigt die Macht Gottes, die sich durch den erhöhten Jesus und im Heiligen Geist manifestiert und die Christen zu christlichem Verhalten ermächtigt (pp.200–201).

Through this characterisation of the Empire in Luke-Acts, the readers receive assistance in dealing with the Roman Empire (pp.203–217). They are to believe in God's power displayed in Jesus in view of the power of the Empire (while powerful, the Empire does not hold absolute power). Luke-Acts seeks to encourage its readers to a Christian behaviour in view of the Empire. Insecure readers are to receive certainty in what to make of the Empire and instructions on how to behave accordingly.

The short study does not interact with the various post-colonial readings of Luke-Acts and does not draw on narrative approaches to the characterization of the Empire or of Jesus and the Christian protagonists in their interactions with the Empire (the Empire as a character of its own in Luke-Acts). The functions of the occurrences of Empire for the characterisation of Jesus and of Paul are not discussed. It is not sufficiently in view that in ancient historiography (there is no discussion of the genre of Acts and its implications for interpretation), the behaviour of Jesus and the Christian protagonists serves as an *exemplum* for the readers. Despite these observations, Edelmann offers a helpful survey and analyses of all occurrences of the Roman Empire in Luke-Acts and relates this portrayal to the purpose of Acts.

Christoph W. Stenschke
Biblisch-Theologische Akademie Wiedenest and Department of Biblical and Ancient Studies

BOOK REVIEWS

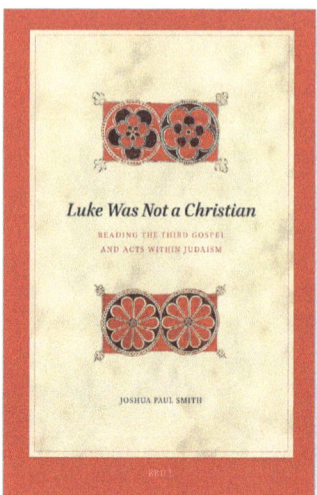

Joshua Paul Smith. *Luke Was Not a Christian: Reading the Third Gospel and Acts within Judaism.* BINS 218 (Leiden, Boston: Brill, 2024). Xii +344 pp., hardbound. ISBN 978-90-04-68471-3. 127 Euro.

The past ten years have seen an upsurge of studies of Paul 'within Judaism'. What precisely is meant by this designation is becoming increasingly vague. Only relatively recently have scholars taken this approach to Luke-Acts. In this monograph, Smith takes up this quest and argues that the author of Luke-Acts must have been Jewish, raised and encultured within a Jewish setting. As such, he describes 'the things that have come to fulfilment among us' (Luke 1:1) from a Jewish perspective. However, the scope of the volume is broader.

After a brief introduction (pp.1–20, including some reflection on methodology, 'biographical-critical – that is, centered primarily on the biographical background on the author', p.10, requiring 'a touch of disciplinary variety'), Smith sets out with a survey of the early reception history of Luke-Acts, in particular, consideration of the author (pp.21–74; the early reception of Lukan authorship, Luke in the New Testament – see his interpretation of Col 4:10–17 on pp.24–31 –, Luke the evangelist in the Patristic imagination, discussion of the reasons why Luke was remembered in different ways). Smith shows that there is little evidence to support the claim that Luke was a non-Jew.

Next Smith attempts to 'resurrect the author' (pp.74–104, theoretical discussions concerning the figure of the author, questioning claims with regard to the 'death of the author', authorship and Luke-Acts, the significance of the cultural context and of social and cognitive linguistics). Despite the doubts in the theoretical discussion regarding the possibility to determine authors and their identity, Smith concludes that it is possible and a worthwhile quest to look for clues of the author's identity in the extant text. This conclusion sets the course for the remainder of the study. Smith rightly notes that 'the author-function of Luke the Evangelist has served various ends and various points throughout the life and reception of Luke-Acts' (p.105).

Chapter three surveys Luke's distinctly Jewish interpretation of the Scriptures of Israel (pp.106–155; the way Luke refers to the Scriptures, Jewish interpretation vs. Christian interpretation, analysis of the interpretation of Scripture). Luke is keen to show 'that understanding Jesus to be Israel's Messiah requires a shift in the way one reads the scriptures, without suggesting that those scriptures should be superseded or abandoned altogether. [...] the role of scriptural interpretation once held by Jesus is now handed on to his disciples' (p.143). According to Smith, it is hardly conceivable that a proselyte or a God-fearer could have developed a technical knowledge of Israel's scriptures to the degree demonstrated by the author of Luke-Acts (p.152).

Then Smith examines Luke's key thematic concern with Mosaic law (pp.156–190). This includes Torah practice and *Halakah* in Luke and Acts, the Apostolic Decree and the demand for moral impurity and Jewish festival observance in Luke-Acts. Smith identifies the fulfillment and preservation of Jewish law as one of the dominant narrative themes. Luke suggests that Jews, including Jewish Christ-followers, must remain Torah-observant. The division in Israel (a theme taken over from J. Jervell) is between those Jews who are obedient to a way of life directed by the Torah and those who are not. In view of this emphasis, the crucial role of faith in the Messiah and obeying Him recedes to the background. According to Acts 3:18–23, continued membership to God's people depends on listening and believing in the prophet like Moses, not on observance of the law.

In closing, Smith takes a socio-cognitive perspective on the clues provided by Luke's use of insider/outsider language (pp.191–231; 'the nations' in Luke-Acts understood through an idealized cognitive model; detailed analysis of the terms Gentiles, strangers, foreskins, devout Greeks and the people of God). The 'nations' is an emic Jewish term for non-Jews. 'Luke's encyclopedic knowledge of Jews and gentiles closely adheres to that of a first-century Jewish cultural model' (p.224). When the contiguity and coherence of Luke's characterisation of non-Jews is taken seriously, it becomes clear that Luke conceptualized non-Jews from a Jewish cultural perspective. Smith notes that Luke's treatment of non-Jews in Acts is surprisingly ambivalent.

Smith argues and provides compelling arguments that Luke was raised and encultured within a Jewish setting (p.232). Luke understands the mission to non-Jews not as a supersession of Jewish law and tradition, but rather as a fulfilment and expansion of Israel's own salvation history (Luke 24:44–47). Smith shows the genuinely Jewish perspective of Luke-Acts that has also been noted by other recent studies. The question remains of why this Jewish emphasis was necessary in the endeavour to provide certainty to the readers (Luke 1:4). Who would have to be assured that this Messiah and the growing movement of his Jewish and non-Jewish followers had not abandoned its Jewish roots but continued to cherish them? Smith's title is little helpful in that there is consensus in scholarship that 'Christian' is anachronistic for the situation in the first century. One also wonders whether the focus on the author is helpful: rather than arguing for a Jewish author, would it be better to simply focus in the canonical text and its Jewish emphases and biases? The volume would have benefitted from chapters on the thoroughly Jewish characterisation of the disciples and of Paul (he is portrayed as an emissary to diaspora Judaism and rarely the missionary to non-Jews) in Acts.

Christoph W. Stenschke
Biblisch-Theologische Akademie Wiedenest and Department of Biblical and Ancient Studies

BOOK REVIEWS

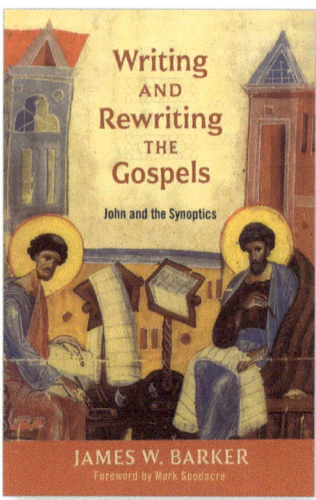

James W. Barker. *Writing and Rewriting the Gospels: John and the Synoptics.* Grand Rapids, MI: Eerdmans, 2025. xvi + 188 pp. ISBN 9780802874528 (paper). $US22.99.

James Barker is Associate Professor of New Testament at Western Kentucky University and the author of two previous monographs, *John's Use of Matthew* (Fortress, 2015) and *Tatian's Diatessaron: Composition, Redaction, Recension, and Reception* (OUP, 2021). With this new book Barker returns to the topic of his first book by setting out his case for the successive literary dependence of the four canonical Gospels in the following order: Mark, Matthew, Luke, John. In short, he defends but also extends the Farrer hypothesis on the interrelations of the Gospels without recourse to hypothetical sources or proto-Gospels, aiming to show how Matthew made use of Mark, Luke made use of both Mark and Matthew, and John made use of all three Synoptic Gospels. 'To explain the phenomenon of gospel proliferation', Barker writes, 'I focus on the material production of the Gospels, and I plot simple, snowballing trajectories from Mark to Matthew to Luke to John' (p.2).

Barker's introduction helpfully reviews the history of Gospel research without overburdening readers with excessive detail. His survey covers key contributors to the discussion of both the origins of and interrelations between the first three 'synoptic' Gospels and the relation of the Fourth Gospel to the other three, no mean feat in such a compressed presentation. The way in which these two related discussions crisscross over time is fascinating and absorbingly narrated by Barker. Concluding his historical survey, Barker acknowledges that the two-source hypothesis remains the regnant source theory for explaining the relations between the first three Gospels, but he positions his own preferred Farrer hypothesis as its main current rival. While explaining paths not taken in his book, Barker advises that he does not speculate on the source of material not evidently borrowed and adapted from one or more predecessor Gospels. In other words, he does not seek to explain all the material in Matthew's Gospel that could not have derived from Mark, nor all the material in Luke that could not have derived from Mark and Matthew's Gospel, nor all the material in the Fourth Gospel that could not have derived from any of the Synoptic Gospels. 'As a general rule', he notes, 'I work with the extant gospels and dispense with hypothetical sources' (p.15). One also learns that Barker holds that all four canonical evangelists were familiar with some of Paul's letters. Within this introductory chapter, Barker also demonstrates how the compositional processes that he attributes to Matthew, Luke, and John conform to conventional 'scribal practices of imitation and rewriting' (p.20) that were commonplace in both Jewish and Graeco-Roman contexts in antiquity.

Chapter 1, entitled 'How to Write a Gospel', goes back to basics by describing how books were produced and used at the time when the Gospels were composed. Barker discusses scribal habits, the use of sources in the process of composition, and materials used in the production of books. Although he acknowledges the role of oral tradition, he is sceptical of 'oral composition' as a model for gospel origins. 'I view the Gospels as compositions that were drafted and extensively revised before publication', he advises (p. 31). Barker allows for recourse to memory, but more along the lines of close familiarity with sources than of extensive memorization. He envisages that the respective Gospels were probably first drafted on waxed tablets, then revised during the process of transcription onto a scroll or bookroll, probably more than once. He allows for the possibility that one or more of the Gospels may have been published in codex form, but he considers it more likely that they were initially published as bookrolls. Especially important is the section of this chapter in which Barker seeks to refute the commonly held notion that authors roughly contemporaneous with the Gospel writers tended to rely on one source at a time. Appealing to Graeco-Roman scholars of Homer's epic poems, known recensions of Greek translations of Jewish biblical texts, Josephus' use of the books of Samuel, Kings, and Chronicles in writing his *Antiquities of the Jews*, and the harmonizing work of Tatian in the late second century CE, Barker provides ample evidence for his view that 'collation, conflation, harmonization, and scrolling to and fro with multiple scrolls would have been relatively simple processes for a competent first-century author' (p. 50). For the benefit of readers, he provides a figure (p. 47) to illustrate collation, annotation, and composition in the drafting of Luke 5:17–26 from Mark 2:1–12 and Matt 9:1–8. Readers also learn that, in seeking to comprehend compositional conventions that likely informed the Gospel writers, Barker constructed his own triptych (a four-surface wax tablet comprised of three bound boards), a bookroll of the Gospel according to John using the Greek text of Codex Vaticanus, and several single-quire codices, including 'full-scale models of the Gospels of Luke and John' (p. 41).

Barker begins chapter 2, 'Synoptic Trajectories', by advising that 'my purpose in this chapter is to defend the Farrer hypothesis' (p. 56), a purpose accomplished by drawing attention to selected examples of parallel passages in which Luke's version may plausibly be explained as edited versions of Markan or Matthean parallels or both. Cautioning against the notion that Mark's Gospel should be considered an unfinished draft text or incomplete notes, Barker revisits the topic of notebook use in antiquity. He then provides a big-picture overview of the Farrer hypothesis, describing the progressive development of the synoptic tradition as a form of 'snowballing', according to which 'Matthew augmented Mark's account, and Luke augmented Matthew's' (p. 63). Thereafter Barker focuses on phenomena and parallel passages that illustrate Lukan dependence on Mark and Matthew. Literary phenomena considered include conflation, doublets, minor agreements, evidence of apparent redaction, and editorial fatigue, whereas texts discussed to illustrate the kind of 'snowballing' envisaged on the Farrer hypothesis include the Beelzebul challenge and related sayings, woes against scribes and Pharisees, the forgiving and restoration of a paralysed man, the feeding of no fewer than 5,000 people, the parable(s) of the talents or minas, and various parallel pericopes relating to Jesus' final days in Jerusalem. Although illustrative rather than comprehensive or conclusive, this chapter aims 'to bolster the Farrer hypothesis, which may ultimately overturn the waning hegemony of the two-source hypothesis' (p. 81).

> He aims 'to bolster the Farrer hypothesis, which may ultimately overturn the waning hegemony of the two-source hypothesis'

The second half of the body of Barker's book is concerned with the Fourth Gospel. The burden of chapter 3, 'Johannine Trajectories', is to demonstrate that the 'snowballing' evident from Mark to Matthew and then also to Luke extends to the Fourth Gospel. Acknowledging that the question of the relation of the Fourth Gospel to the Synoptic Gospels is impossible to resolve definitively within a single chapter, Barker proceeds by discussing a series of Johannine passages susceptible to an explanation along the lines of creative rewriting of all three prior Gospels. Especially important for his case that the author of the Fourth Gospel rewrote sayings, events, and parallel episodes drawn from one or more of the Synoptic Gospels is the notion of *oppositio in imitando*, 'a modern term to describe an ancient technique of imitating a classic story while turning many elements inside out' (p.82). This storytelling technique features especially in Barker's discussion of the sign stories in John 5 and 11. Within this chapter Barker also comments on the Johannine rewriting of the duration of Jesus' public mission, the temple incident, the relation between Jesus and John the Baptist, the saying in Matt 18:3 (similar to John 3:3), the mission to Samaritans, the feeding of five thousand, several features of the passion story, and the rituals of baptism and the Eucharist, about which he writes: 'I read the flesh and blood portion of the Bread of Life Discourse as intentionally sacramental' (p.110). Taken in isolation, few single instances of alleged Johannine rewriting are likely to compel assent, but considered cumulatively they construct a compositional pattern deserving of deliberation.

> Each subsequent evangelist knew the work of his predecessor(s)

In chapter 4, 'Johannine Christology in Context', Barker ranges from Pauline Christology to christological and trinitarian developments in the fourth century. Few books concerned with the origins of and interrelations between the Gospels venture into patristic Christology and trinitarian theology, but Barker's reason for doing so is to trace broad Christological developments that broadly align with his proposed genealogical progression of the Gospels. 'At the risk of oversimplification', he comments (p.128), 'I contend that there is some degree of correlation between chronology and Christology... [S]uccessive gospels correlate with relative Christologies, beginning with Mark and proceeding in order to Matthew to Luke and to John. Each subsequent evangelist knew the work of his predecessor(s), so the Gospels' increasingly higher Christologies reveal intentional pieces of supplementation.' Indeed, Barker discerns within the Fourth Gospel the essential constituents of the economic Trinity that eventually came to be accepted as church doctrine.

In his conclusion to this volume, Barker recapitulates key features of his overarching argument. The priority of Mark's Gospel is avidly endorsed, with Barker even going so far as to assert: 'There is so much evidence for Markan priority that the Augustinian and Griesbach hypotheses should be ruled out' (p.145). He also sees Mark's Gospel as written from a Pauline perspective, Matthew as anti-Pauline, Luke as mediating between the contrasting perspectives of his predecessors, and the Fourth Gospel as strongly supersessionistic.

Many of the felicitous features of Barker's book are noted in the foreword by Mark Goodacre, whose own case for the Fourth Gospel's knowledge and use of all three Synoptic Gospels will also be published by Eerdmans in 2025. Barker's book is learned and lucid, deserving of careful consideration. With respect to content that the canonical Gospels share, his synoptic and Johannine trajectories are illuminating and meaningful. Pondered alongside the work of Goodacre, Eric Eve, and others, Barker's research and writing entitles him to claim: 'Today the Farrer hypothesis has rightfully gained a foothold as a viable alternative to the two-source hypothesis, which held the consensus for a century, dating to the publication of B. H. Streeter's *The Four Gospels* [1924]' (pp.145–46). His book also adds a distinctive voice to the swelling chorus of conviction regarding the Fourth Gospel's familiarity with and rewriting of the Synoptic Gospels.

David Neville
St Mark's National Theological Centre
Charles Sturt University, Canberra

BOOK REVIEWS

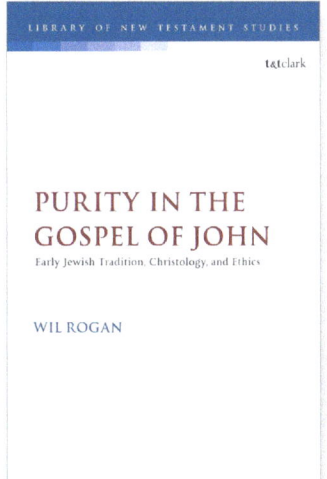

Wil Rogan. *Purity in the Gospel of John: Early Jewish Tradition, Christology, and Ethics.* LNTS 679. T&T Clark, London, 2023. 185pp. ISBN 9780567708663

Wil Rogan joins a growing number of scholars that are reading the NT texts 'within Judaism', and more specifically reading them without a presupposition of an opposition to Jewish purity practices and ideas. In this work, he addresses the theme of purity in the Gospel of John, seeking to set it within the diverse early Jewish discourse on purity. In this, he notes the different approach to purity in John as opposed to the Synoptics, but without endeavouring to provide an explanation for that difference. He states his main argument as 'the Fourth Gospel employs biblical traditions of purity associated with the revelation of God and the restoration of Israel in order to narrate how God's people are prepared for the coming of Jesus and enabled by him to have life before God characterised by love' (5). The key elements of the argument are that in John, John the Baptist is presented as providing ritual purification as preparation for Jesus, while Jesus provides the moral purification necessary for participation in God's life.

An important aim for Rogan is to argue against the popular idea that in John, purity is replaced by faith. This idea is traced back to the work of William Robertson Smith and evolutionary models of religion. Instead, Rogan argues that John makes use of early Jewish ideas around purity as a hermeneutical tool towards his theological aims. Rogan builds the picture of purity drawing substantially on the work of Mary Douglas and Jonathan Klawans. This includes the distinction between ritual and moral purity, arguing that the scholarly framework is useful in approaching a narrative such as John that does not make the purity system explicit. In this, he argues that the Fourth Gospel is traditional in its approach to purity, although it is innovative in applying it to Jesus.

Building on the framework of purity, Rogan has three substantial chapters that address elements of the use of purity in John. The first focuses primarily on John the Baptist and ritual purity. He relies primarily on the Sinai account to present purity as about preparing to perceive divine revelation. He notes that this is a marginal idea in subsequent discourse, although pointing to some elements in Philo, Sirach and the DSS. Turning to John, Rogan argues the presentation of John the Baptist, especially when contrasted with the Synoptic accounts, focuses on ritual purity and not moral purity. The purpose of his baptism is also set in terms of revelation. One significant implication is drawn from the fact that none of the contextual evidence links purity with receiving a mortal being, thus the Johannine presentation implies that Jesus is divine. The link between purification and receiving revelation is also seen subsequently in John 2 with the disciples who see Jesus' glory, as well as in John 9 with the man who washes in order to see Jesus.

The next chapter addresses Jesus and the provision of moral purification. Here

Rogan draws on the Major Prophets and their connection of moral purification to the restoration of Israel, including with associated images of marriage and birth. In these texts, Rogan argues, moral purification enables participation in restoration. He begins with John 1 to say that Jesus as the pure lamb has come to purify, while the washing with the Spirit is what takes sin away. John 3 is the primary focus for the chapter, as Nicodemus is taken as raising the question of Israel's election in response to Jesus' call for new birth. Thus, the statement about birth by water and Spirit in 3:5 is indicating that God provides what is needed for Israel's restoration. The second half of John 3 is taken as paralleling the first, where the issue is about who can administer a ritual washing, in the context of the idea of God as the one purifying Israel from sin. John 9—10 is then seen as depicting the fulfilment or outworking of this moral purification in Jesus' ministry.

God provides what is needed for Israel's restoration

The final main chapter then addresses the connection between moral purity and action. Purity in the Major Prophets is linked with sins that rupture the relationship between God and Israel, where purity is needed for worship. Rogan also identifies other early Jewish texts that give an ethical dimension to moral purity. Turning to John, Rogan does not read the footwashing of John 13 as effecting the disciples' ritual or moral purity, but as stating that Jesus' ministry has already made them morally pure. This moral purity is not the goal so much as the necessary condition for the disciples to be able to enact love. Rogan then brings out parallels with other Jewish texts that see moral purification as transformation and connects these with the vine image in John.

Overall, Rogan presents a compelling reading of purity in John that aligns with both early Jewish ideas around purity, but then also serves John's theological agenda. He does well in showing not only that the ideas of purity are compatibly Jewish, but in making a clear argument as to how the Gospel makes use of those ideas to support its theological purposes.

Where it has weaknesses, it might be at the more detailed level. For example, as Rogan notes, some of the configurations of purity are not well attested in wider Jewish literature (e.g. p.35,110). This doesn't necessarily negate the arguments, but it does mean some of the connections may be more conjectural. Or, perhaps it might be better framed that John may be more unusual within its Jewish context than Rogan suggests, which he already notes is at times 'highly peculiar' (p.144). This leaves open the door for further debate over the extent to which John can be read 'within Judaism'.

There are a few points where there is scope for development of some of the ideas. One point would be to further probe the connection between ideas of purification by the Spirit (in chapter 3) and that of purification by Jesus' word (in chapter 4). Another question left unresolved was that if birth in water and Spirit (John 3:5) refers to both John the Baptist's and Jesus' ablutions, then what is the ongoing significance of John's baptism, or more broadly the place of ritual purity in the view of the author writing to their audience from their post-resurrection perspective.

These critiques should not diminish what is overall a compelling case regarding the background and use of ideas of purity in John's Gospel. This should be essential reading for any Johannine scholar or those teaching the Gospel, as well as for those who are interested in purity and how the NT intersects with Jewish ideas of purity. It may even provide something of a model for further scholarly work thinking about how the NT authors engage with and use Jewish concepts.

Christopher Seglenieks
Bible College of South Australia

BOOK REVIEWS

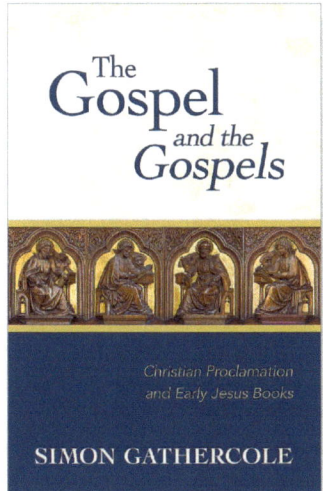

Simon Gathercole. *The Gospel and the Gospels: Christian Proclamation and Early Jesus Books.* Grand Rapids: Eerdmans, 2022. ISBN 9780802877759. xxiv + 576pp. $55.99 USD.

Simon Gathercole is Professor of New Testament and Early Christianity at Cambridge University. In respect of the subject of this review, he has previously published commentaries on the *Gospel of Judas* (OUP, 2007), and on the *Gospel of Thomas* (Brill 2013), and a translation of *The Apocryphal Gospels* (Penguin, 2021), while his earlier major publication on the canonical Gospels was *The Pre-existent Son: Recovering the Christologies of Matthew, Mark and Luke* (Eerdmans, 2006). *The Gospel and the Gospels* thus presents as a culmination of two significant strands of Gathercole's scholarship to date.

The essential thesis of the book is that 'the four New Testament Gospels share key elements of theological content that mark them out from most of the noncanonical Gospels' (p.12), which is because they 'follow a preexisting apostolic creed or preached gospel' (p.12). This is significant for Gathercole because it grounds the unity of the New Testament Gospels in their consistency with apostolic preaching and not in third- to fourth-century doctrinal controversies.

The thesis is set out in the introductory chapter (pp.1–16) where Gathercole reviews previous discussions of differentiation between canonical and non-canonical Gospels. He finds that, 'For the majority of scholars now, canonical and noncanonical Gospels alike are all in the same anonymous, unapostolic boat' (p.3). He reviews previous attempts to argue for essential difference in terms of circumstances of composition, attestation in early Christian literature, literary form and aesthetics, but finds them to be unsatisfactory. Instead, he considers theological content to be the criterion that successfully distinguishes canonical from non-canonical Gospels. While scholars of an earlier generation (F. F. Bruce, Robert M. Grant) argued for a similar criterion, Gathercole aims to avoid the kind of value judgements evident in those arguments and which would be unacceptable in today's guild (pp.11–12). That said, Gathercole is well aware that this criterion is 'very much out of vogue in today's scholarship' and that for many scholars, 'there is no real theological distinction between canonical and noncanonical Gospels' (p.11). In particular, the conclusions of scholars such as Francis Watson, Gregory Riley, and Ismo Dunderberg, that the Gospel of John and *Thomas* have more in common with each other than GJohn does with the Synoptics, present as a key point of contention for Gathercole (pp.11–12). Further, Gathercole seeks to argue against scholars such as Bart Ehrman and Elaine Pagels, that such theological differentiation among Gospels makes sense not just retrospectively, from the perspective of the proto-orthodox in the third- or fourth-century, but that the canonical Gospels already reflected a shared canonical kerygma from 'when they were first composed,' in distinction from non-canonical Gospels

> **theological content [is] the criterion that successfully distinguishes canonical from noncanonical Gospels**

which were written to reflect other theological concerns (p.14).

Gathercole makes his argument with meticulous care, laying out his methodology clearly in the next part of the book. His comparanda are selected by criteria of date (within the first two centuries CE), the title 'Gospel,' family resemblance, subject matter, and preservation; with the result that he will discuss, in addition to the canonical Gospels, *The Gospel of Peter, Marcion's Gospel, The Gospel of Thomas, The Gospel of Truth, The Coptic Gospel of Philip, The Gospel of Judas,* and *The Coptic Gospel of the Egyptians* (pp.20–33). His comparator is the kerygma of 1 Cor 15:3–4 in which he identifies four components: Jesus as messiah; Jesus' vicarious death; resurrection on the third day; and fulfilment of scriptures (pp.32–44). To justify this choice of comparator, Gathercole argues that the same 'elements of the apostolic kerygma in 1 Cor 15 are also reflected' in Hebrews, 1 Peter, and Revelation (pp.57–70). Thus, this kerygma predates Paul's letters, as he received it from others, and is evident in a wide range of other early Christian literature (p.59).

The next and largest part of the book is descriptive exegesis of each Gospel, each receiving a chapter in turn, where Gathercole assesses the presence or lack of each component of the kerygma. These assessments are carried out in considerable detail and with impressive engagement with recent scholarship as well as seminal older works. While Gathercole always keeps his wider thesis in view, the exegetical studies in each chapter are worth consulting whether or not one is concerned with the theological differentiation between canonical and noncanonical Gospels. For example, the discussion of the Markan ransom saying (Mk 10:45) draws on the wide spectrum of scholarship on this verse to advance the author's own nuanced reading of the passage (pp.98–105). Or, for another example, Gathercole's rebuttal of Deane Galbraith's "Whence the Giant Jesus and his Talking Cross? The Resurrection in Gospel of Peter 10.39–42 as Prophetic Fulfilment of LXX Psalm 18" (NTS 63.3 (2017): 473–491) presents the first critique of which I am aware.

The level of detailed engagement is both the strength of this book, as a work of reference, and a weakness, in terms of the readability of the basic thesis. Gathercole goes to great lengths to cover possible objections and nuance his argument. With so much exegetical discussion there are many possible points of disagreement, and not every analysis seems equally pertinent to the main argument. With eleven chapters going through the same four criteria (plus the odd excursus) for each Gospel in turn, the book requires some perseverance.

The final part has two chapters. Chapter 15 briefly consolidates the exegetical findings in regard to Gathercole's criteria and concludes that while some non-canonical Gospels contain some elements of the kerygma, none contain them all. In distinction, the canonical Gospels each contain all four. Chapter 16 makes the argument that the reason for these differences is because the canonical Gospels 'follow the theological position of the apostolic kerygma' while the noncanonical Gospels emerged from theological contexts where one or more elements of the kerygma were either transformed, contradicted or ignored (p.502). For Gathercole, this serves to demonstrate that the canonical Gospels alone preserve apostolic preaching as it would have been understood when the Gospels were composed (p501). The book is completed by a bibliography and author, subject, and ancient source indices.

This is a well written and carefully argued work of scholarship. With regard to the first half of its thesis, Gathercole effectively shows that the four kerygmatic criteria he applies reveal a theological distinction between canonical and non-canonical Gospels. Of course, if he had chosen Rom 1:2–4 or Phil 2:5–11 as a comparator instead of 1 Cor 15:3–4 he may have produced different results. But Gathercole's choice of 1 Cor 15:3–4 is hardly arbitrary and is well justified by the formula, 'what I received I handed on to you' (1 Cor 11:23; 15:3; pp.49–54). Notwithstanding, the work of comparison requires such judgements to be made, one cannot compare everything. Perhaps more critically, there is a danger of circularity in demonstrating the apostolic credentials of a set of books based on the evidence of the other books from the same canonical collection. We are faced here with the difficulty of the incompleteness of our data. We don't know what we are missing, either from the literary record or from early Christian faith and proclamation that was not written down. This is something that Gathercole shows sensitivity to, especially in his assessments of the *Gospel of Peter*.

I suspect Gathercole's argument will not easily convince those he argues against, such as Watson and Ehrman. But Gathercole does not argue that there are no similarities or theological overlaps outside of canonical boundaries or for monotonous unity within, only that in regard to these key kerygmatic criteria the NT Gospels are both unified and distinct. I think his methodical demonstration of this is of genuine significance: there is a common kerygmatic root to the NT Gospels from which most noncanonical Gospels show themselves largely disconnected. Put differently, the NT Gospels represent apostolic teaching in a way that the noncanonical Gospels do not. In my view, the burden of proof now lies with those who would argue otherwise.

Jonathan Robinson
Carey Baptist College
Auckland, New Zealand

Centre for Gospels and Acts Research Volumes

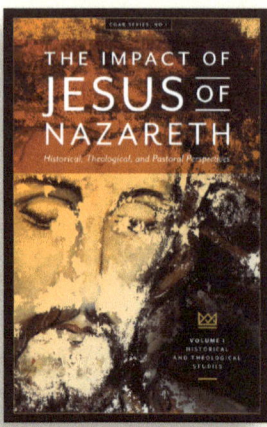 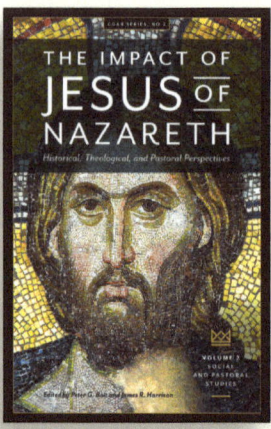 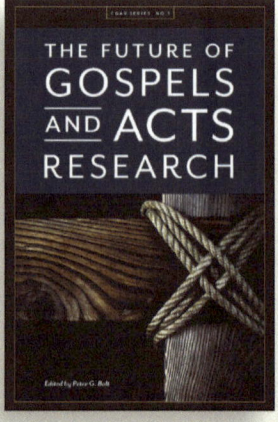 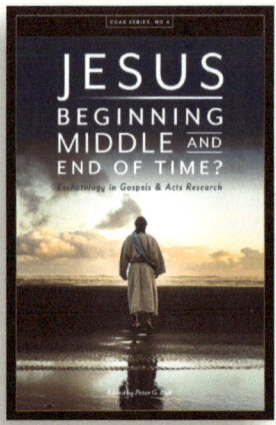

The Impact of Jesus of Nazareth: Historical, Theological, and Pastoral Perspectives
CGAR Series, No 1

Despite his relatively short life and his tragic death, Jesus of Nazareth made a profound impact upon the first-century Graeco-Roman world. Wherever his heritage is celebrated and remembered, Jesus of Nazareth continues to make an impact. The greatness of Jesus of Nazareth was supremely displayed in his moment of greatest weakness on the cross. Those who felt his immediate impact either chafed under his teaching, or embraced it, but rarely did anyone remain untouched by him. The mystery of his salvific death inspires; the power of his resurrection hope sustains; and his impact continues to work its way outwards in manifold implications as his gospel finds a hearing, wherever and whenever that might be.

The Impact of Jesus of Nazareth: Historical, Theological, and Pastoral Perspectives
CGAR Series, No 2

Writing from a variety of perspectives, the essays in these two volumes, explore the impact of Jesus of Nazareth on his own and subsequent times. After Volume 1 collects historical and theological essays, volume 2 moves from the historical and theological, towards the wider impact of Jesus on pastoral practice in our contemporary world.

The Future of Gospels and Acts Research
CGAR Series, No 3

This volume of essays represents a selection of eleven of the papers from the Centre for Gospels and Acts Research 2019 conference, 'Discerning the Trends'. This collection provides a sounding of current Gospels and Acts research. Each essay builds on current research and opens up new questions charting a direction for research in the future.

Jesus: Beginning, Middle, & End of Time? Eschatology in Gospels & Acts Research
CGAR Series, No 4

The Gospels and Acts not only use time, but they also seem to be about time. And back behind those who narrate his story, Jesus not only happened in time, he also thought he was happening to time. *Jesus: Beginning, Middle, and End of Time?* offers seventeen essays, each addressing in their own way, Eschatology in Gospels and Acts Research.

Centre for Gospels and Acts Research Volume 5

God Beyond Ideology
Rediscovering Theology Through Narrative
(CGAR Series, No 5; Norwest, NSW: AUCD Press, 2025)

Table of Contents

1. Peter G. Bolt, Introduction
2. Greg W. Forbes, Narratival Theology Identified: A Hermeneutical Grid
3. Mary J. Marshall, Revisiting the 'Cup Saying' Debate from a Narrative Perspective
4. Jonathan Thambyrajah, What do Herod and Peter have in Common? Oath-Breaking in Matthew's Discourse and Narrative
5. Timothy P. Bradford, Restoring and Revealing the Human Condition: Matthew's Servant and the Establishment of מִשְׁפָּט / ΚΡΙΣΙΣ on the Earth
6. Peter G. Bolt, Killing the Living while Appeasing the Dead? Herod's Day in Mark 6:21
7. Andrew Stewart, The Shame of the Son of Man. Honour and Shame in Mark 8:38 And Luke 9:26
8. Jonathan Rivett Robinson, 'All Things Are Possible'. The Narrative Conditioning of Omnipotence in the Gospel of Mark
9. Denise Powell, How Narrative Transforms (part 1): What the Gospel of Luke *Does* to Theophilus
10. Denise Powell, How Narrative Transforms (part 2): What the Gospel of Luke *Does* to Us
11. Danielle Terceiro and Louise A. Gosbell, Feasting with Good Humour? Retelling the Parable of the Great Banquet (Luke 14:15–24) for Children and the Risks of a Comedic Approach
12. James R. Harrison, The Threat of Caesar's Friendship Withdrawn (John 19:12b). The Collision of History, Narrative, and Theology in the Gospel of John
13. Stefano Salemi, Reinterpreting John's Passion Imagery. Contemporary Perceptions of God through 'Christian' and 'Midrashic' Hermeneutics
14. Christoph Stenschke, 'Sovereign Lord, who made the heaven and the earth and the sea and everything in them' (Acts 4:24). God as the Creator in the Acts of the Apostles and its Implications
15. Karen Nivala, Narrative Criticism And Narrative Therapy. Foundations Of A Dialogue